Uncombed

Unforeseen

Unconstrained

Ziba Ardalan

Uncombed, Unforeseen, Unconstrained
Edited by Ziba Ardalan

Exhibiting Artists

Foreword

Ziba Ardalan

Founder/Artistic and Executive Director of Parasol unit, London

The exhibition *Uncombed, Unforeseen, Unconstrained* is happening in 2022 as a collateral event of the 59th Biennale Arte di Venezia, but from the genesis of this project it has developed from many years of deep and constant observation of the state of the world, the fluctuations of which, unsurprisingly, reflect much that is inherent to human nature.

Homo sapiens have had a formidable evolution and a remarkable history. It would be daunting for anyone to reckon with all of humanity's innovative ideas and the vertiginous scale of their implementation, yet elements of their activity have also been disturbing and destructive. What does it mean to reign supreme in a world with a quasi-infinity of richness and resources? What does it mean to have seldom faced any truly insurmountable challenge? Sure, there have been periods of setback or stagnation throughout history, but within our own experience of the recent past, the ascendance of humanity since the Second World War has been radical, thanks to our dizzying technological progress, even though much of that has been achieved without sufficient consciousness of the cost to others of our species and to planet Earth itself.

In 2022, after two years of the Covid pandemic and repeated lockdowns, the powerful world of *Homo sapiens* is waking up to its greatest challenge yet, that of making proper plans to ensure that humanity acts responsibly to safeguard our planet for future generations. It is in this environment that critical voices are finally being heard, particularly when such important truths are manifested on one of the most prestigious stages in our world, the Biennale Arte di Venezia.

Due to my education and career, first in science then in art, I have been able to observe the world from several angles across many years. The countless conversations I have had the good fortune to have with scientists and artists have certainly helped me to coalesce many of the thoughts I have strived to express in this timely group exhibition and publication. I realise that my preoccupation with the multiple issues and challenges with which our world has been plagued had influenced much of the exhibition programme at Parasol unit foundation for contemporary art, which I founded in 2004 and ran for sixteen years in London. This also explains why several of the artists represented in the *Uncombed, Unforeseen, Unconstrained* exhibition have previously had exhibitions at Parasol unit.

By no means do the artists showing in this exhibition, nor I the curator, wish to spread negative vibes. Rather, and interestingly in keeping within the aesthetics of art, we unanimously strive to express the urgency of paying attention. We humans, like everything in this universe, are set with a distinct and specific resonance which enables us to live harmoniously, and any dramatic deviation from that thrusts us into a state of undesired imbalance leading to disorder and chaos. It is time for us to realise that phenomena, such as global warming, excessive consumption, waste, rootless greed, racist and colonial entitlement, all accelerate and contribute to what in scientific terms is considered entropy, which could potentially propel us, the inhabitants of this planet, towards irreversible destruction.

The thoughtful works by the eleven visual artists in this exhibition – Darren Almond, Oliver Beer, Rana Begum with Hyetal, Julian Charrière, David Claerbout, Bharti Kher, Arghavan Khosravi, Teresa Margolles, Si On, Martin Puryear, Rayyane Tabet – each make it uniquely clear that we must take greater care of our world and urgently need to bring dramatic corrections to the way we live in it.

For their inspiring works and enthusiastic reaction to this exhibition, I give my heartfelt thanks to all the artists exhibiting in *Uncombed, Unforeseen, Unconstrained*. I am hugely grateful for the motivation with which they approached their participation and respective installations. Some of the works on view were specifically created for this exhibition, which was not easy during the challenging times of the past two years. I am confident that such thought-provoking works, which have stemmed from considerable reflection, will leave no visitor unmoved.

I remain indebted to Julien Bismuth and Tom Morton, the two guest-writers for this publication. Over several years now, I have had the privilege of working with each of them and know well that their inspiring words will be greatly appreciated by their readers.

The lenders to the exhibition, both institutions and individuals, were vital to its realisation and it is a privilege for me to offer them my sincerest thanks. An exhibition of the scale of *Uncombed, Unforeseen, Unconstrained* could not have been realised without immense financial support. I am indebted to all the artists, who have made artworks or editions in support of the exhibition, and to the institutions, organisations, foundations, individuals, and several commercial galleries, who have so generously agreed to help this meaningful project. Pro Helvetia, Bareva Foundation, G+B Schwyzer Foundation, Akris, Atelier d'architectes Charrière-Partenaires, Richard and Claire Bruce, Laura Colnaghi Calissoni, Central Street Foundation, Christian and Kristine de Juniac, Key Capital, Conor and Mary Killeen, Bernard and Genevieve Mensah, Lukas and Dorothea Mühlemann, Benjamin Nieto, Iman and Jacques de Saussure, Marwan and Tania Shakarchi, Claudia and Christian Norgren Steinfels, Trinity Street Asset Management, Berna and Tolga Tuglular, Ruth Whaley, Yvonne and Pierre Winkler, Almine Rech, Esther Schipper, Galerie Peter Kilchmann, Hauser & Wirth, Perrotin, Sean Kelly Gallery, and White Cube, all have my deepest gratitude.

An enthusiastic word of thanks goes to Luca Berta and Francesca Jubilei at The Venice Art Factory, who for the second time, and after the successful collateral exhibition *The Spark Is You*, 2019, have again offered us their professional advice and guidance throughout the preparation and realisation of this exhibition. It has been a wonderfully rewarding professional relationship and friendship.

It has been an extraordinary and stimulating experience for us at Parasol unit to hold a second exhibition in the gracious ambience of the Conservatorio di Musica Benedetto Marcello di Venezia. To work with people of such warmth and generosity is a very special privilege, for which I thank them wholeheartedly.

Jonathan Kelly's team together with the We Exhibit team have carried through great and precise work to realise this complex installation during some challenging times. They all have my most thankful appreciation, as has Sam Forster, who built some of the complex plinths for this exhibition.

As always, I offer my grateful thanks to our esteemed copy editor, Helen Wire. It is simply wonderful to rely on her skills and astute mind. Working with the Mousse Publishing team is admirably dynamic and fluid, and I am pleased to thank them for all their flexibility and creative ideas.

Without the intelligent and strategic work of Karl Schenker, the exhibition preparation would never have followed such a smooth path. I will always be hugely grateful for his astute mind and great spirit. It has been a huge pleasure to have worked with him. Here, too, I would like to offer my appreciation to Anita Giansante, Sophie Moiroux and Kirsteen Cairns, who have all contributed variously to the preparation and realisation of this project under the challenging conditions of the last two years.

Finally, my appreciation goes to everyone who has contributed to the making of this timely exhibition, because any project realised by a non-profit institution is essentially a labour of love.

Sensing Time

Ziba Ardalan

Exhibition Curator

Whenever I stop and reflect on time elapsed in my life, two things tend to come readily to mind. First is the distant past when I was young, which considering my stage of life ought to seem somewhat hazy, but in this alignment of different phases of my existence it seems almost as vividly present as ever it was. Then, with this parallel sense of the past, I try to see as a child, as a teenager, or as a young woman how I pictured the future. With each train of thought, I recall thinking that the future seemed almost infinitely far off. I wonder why and ask myself many questions, but none of the reasons or theories I come up with ever wholly satisfy me. Did the future seem far off because it was unknown or was it because in the days of my youth, time seemed to pass more slowly? Clearly, in today's world, because we are all so much busier, our sense and experience of time has dramatically shifted, which in turn influences our observations and judgements.

I incline towards the latter explanation and realise, indeed, how each day I strive to achieve far more than I used to. Nowadays, a day signifies a certain number of hours which I attempt to optimally fill with countless tasks and activity, often wishing by the end of it that I had another 24 hours. Looking back on the past, I do not recall my parents or my grandparents seeing the concept of time in that way. Perhaps it is nostalgic to speak of the past but, if I may summarise my thoughts, I should say that in the past we enjoyed having time and took pleasure in considering how to use it. Whereas, today, we increasingly think of time as if it were a finite entity we must fill with tasks and duties. I could be wrong, but if that is true, it may also mean that within today's sense of time we leave too little of it free for our thoughts to wander, for playfulness, and even for mystery. By so intensively filling time, could humanity inadvertently risk losing its capacity for imagination and invention?

By nature, human beings thrive on being active and taking responsibility, and actions, once engaged, can cause all kinds of predictable and unpredictable outcomes, productive or destructive, chaotic or orderly, violent or peaceful, and so on. In scientific terms, such commotion could be described as entropy.[1] Defined as the second law of thermodynamics, entropy is a measure of disorder, but the connotation of disorder should not alarm us. Entropy is a fascinating phenomenon and, in many ways, alludes to the energy we need for life, as long as it comes in a reasonable amount and can be controlled.

The works by the eleven visual artists presented in the exhibition *Uncombed, Unforeseen, Unconstrained* are executed in different media and comment variously on the effect of entropy in some diverse areas of our life and surroundings. I strive, therefore, to discuss them in this essay whenever such conversations seem relevant. For example, the installation by Rana Begum, *No. 694 Hyetal*, 2016, [pp. 60–63] an interdisciplinary collaboration between herself and the artist-musician Hyetal, is a poignant and sophisticated piece within Begum's artistic body of work and is, coincidentally, an example of measured entropy. In her artistic practice, she deals with light, colour and space, creating works that are often also interactive. Working with such phenomena requires deep thought to invent and refine them in all their variations. It is almost as if the artist thinks, what if the deviation of the trajectory departs from its usual path and how far can it go? In this particular audio-visual piece, lasting about ten minutes, 46 small and enticingly colourful rectangles, fixed on to the wall and lit by the projection of light, respond with a rhythmic dance of shadows that vary in direction and dimension. The effect of the performance is enhanced by the music specifically composed for it by Hyetal. This visually harmonious work enlivens its viewers, stimulates their mind and soul, and often nurtures further innovative ideas. The dimension and direction of the shadows change, but always return to their initial position, providing a visual confirmation that change is part of any process and positive as long as it can happen in a measured way and be controlled.

We are aware that life in the twenty-first century, especially in large urban areas, is far from calm, settled or harmonious, and produces countless forms of entropy. We are also tremendously addicted to the effects of entropy, in that if there is not enough of it, we are likely to go about creating it. The *disruptive innovation* theory, familiar to many of us, is surely a form of entropy that is supposed to inject energy, innovation and heightened productivity into an organisation or business. The phenomenon of entropy is intertwined with all human life, activity, and society. Naturally like much else in life, there is some danger connected to increased entropy when we must face it in huge and uncontrolled amounts. Entropy can increase considerably under various external conditions, such as the rise in temperature and information overload, and if such situations prevail over a long period of time the danger could be imminent. In such circumstances and at a molecular level, particles within any system have the potential of becoming sufficiently animated to act both freely and unpredictably, and thereby cause chaos and irreversible impairment to the system.

Planet Earth can, of course, be considered in various ways. From the point of the distribution of energy, Earth is an open system because it constantly receives solar energy which ultimately escapes as thermal energy. This delicate balance of energy maintains Earth's surface temperature at a level essential to support its existing life forms. However, any deviation from it, even one degree centigrade, can have devastating consequences. From the point of view of matter, planet Earth is a closed system, which means all solids, liquids and gases produced on Earth do not escape beyond its atmosphere, but rather remain as if it were all inside a sealed box.

When it comes to creatively alerting us to the looming danger to planet Earth, seldom has an artist done so as forcefully as Julian Charrière. From the outset of his artistic practice, Charrière has shown an intense awareness of the impact that irresponsible human activity and ruthless plundering of the Earth's resources has had on the planet. Often focusing on remote regions, where such exploitation and experimentation are not readily visible nor easily reported, the artist questions whether we can afford to allow ourselves to think that the immensity of our planet's plains, mountains, lands and oceans are inexhaustible. Or, how far should the responsible and reasonable exploitation of its natural resources go? And, all the while, he calls upon his sense of aesthetic and deep philosophical reflection.

For this exhibition, Charrière presents two works. Projected inside the galleries of the Conservatorio di Musica Benedetto Marcello di Venezia, the stunning and powerful imagery of Charrière's film, *And Beneath It All Flows Liquid Fire*, 2019, [p. 67] leaves no visitor indifferent. The video work documents a night-time performance executed by Charrière for his solo exhibition at MASI Lugano in Switzerland. Having doused a neoclassical fountain in the centre of the town with a flammable liquid and setting fire to it, the artist recorded some utterly beguiling images of cascading flames and water – the result of combining two incompatible liquids. The work could be interpreted in many ways, but according to the artist himself, *deep beneath the Earth's surface, between its outermost crust and inner core, magma – the molten or semi-molten natural material from which all igneous rocks are formed – constantly churns.* Once it reaches the surface, the extremely hot molten mass of lava moves slowly across the surface until it becomes solid. But if a significant amount of the extremely hot pyroclastic flow were to reach an ocean, the effect could be disastrous for the planet. Knowing this, we see the playful and enticing imagery of Charrière's work very differently. *And Beneath It All Flows Liquid Fire* certainly questions the supremacy of humanity when faced with the power of Nature, which, needless to say, brings to mind some dramatic nineteenth-century landscapes in paintings by Caspar David Friedrich, Frederic Edwin Church, Fitz Hugh Lane and others. Yet, considering the time when they were painted, the vulnerability of human beings faced with the power of Nature is but a gentle reminder. In the twenty-first century, fully cognisant of the threats to planet Earth and its inhabitants, Charrière's work prompts some far-reaching thoughts.

Caspar David Friedrich, *Wanderer Above the Sea of Fog*, c. 1817
Oil on canvas, 94.8 × 74.8 cm (37 ¼ × 29 ½ in)

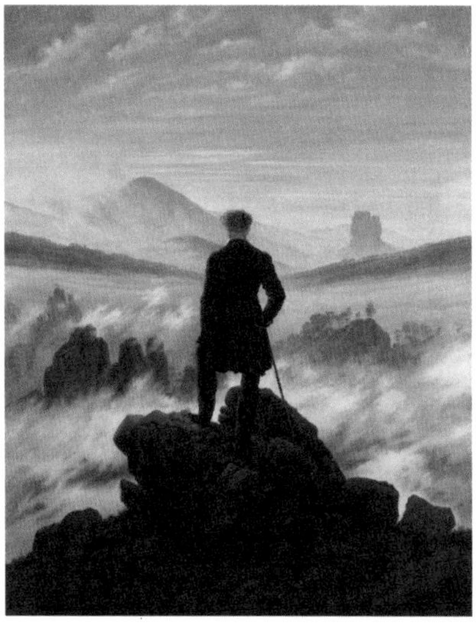

Exhibited in two outdoor courtyards of the Conservatorio di Musica, are four sculptures from Charrière's series *Not All Who Wander Are Lost*, 2019, [pp. 68–73] a title inspired by a line from J.R.R. Tolkien's 1954 book *The Lord of the Rings*. Charrière's exhibition and work titles, often based on poetic or philosophical quotes, give us a glimpse into his wide-ranging and thoughtful mind. In these four works, the so-called wanderers are simply glacial boulders, commonly referred to as erratic rocks. Such rocks are usually deposited during the movement of glaciers over many thousands of years and become visible only after the ice has melted. The boulders embody the history of planet Earth and its development but are equally analogous to much of humanity's movement – displacement and dislocation – within time.

Once installed, the perforated boulders, like ghosts of themselves, stand on a row of the core samples of stone extracted from them, some of which have had a metal section inserted. To make these works, Charrière drilled multiple core samples out of the rocks, a well-known process used to collect geological data and information about the Earth's climate over several million years. In itself, the act of repeated drillings signifies the taking away of natural resources from the planet. Sometimes, during the drilling and extraction process, a core sample breaks. In which instance, the artist usually replaces the original stone part with a fabricated precious or semi-precious metal – such as gold, silver, copper, aluminium or brass (alloy of zinc and copper) – thereby drawing attention to humanity's mining activities and by extension to other issues, such as racism, colonialism and other interventions. How much a single boulder can be core-drilled depends on how many cores can be taken before the boulder breaks. This is analogous to the plight of the Earth if we continue to consume its resources until it is irreparably destroyed.

Rayyane Tabet's, *Steel Rings*, 2013–, [pp. 120–123] from the series *The Shortest Distance Between Two Points*, 2007–, greets visitors to the exhibition in the impressive hallway of the *piano nobile* (noble floor, high-ceilinged and elaborately decorative) of the Conservatorio di Musica Benedetto Marcello. The installation convincingly illustrates the positive and negative aspects of entropy in life. The impressive 21 steel rings are exhibited standing directly on the floor. The rings, each engraved with a kilometre marker, longitude, latitude and elevation location, tell us the story of the 1,213-kilometre-long, 77-centimetre-wide steel pipeline that from 1950 to 1981 carried oil overland from Saudi Arabia to the Mediterranean Sea, passing through Jordan, Syria, the Golan Heights, and Lebanon.

The work brings up countless issues related to oil ever since the 'black gold' was discovered in the Middle East at the beginning of the twentieth century. The TAPline project itself was a successful undertaking that provided prosperity to the region and brought an entrepreneurial spirit to an entire population. Conceived of in the mid-1940s – with the idea of providing oil for European countries to rebuild their economies once the Second World War (1939–1945) had come to an end – construction of the pipeline was finally completed in 1950. Thus, the Trans Arabian Pipeline (TAPline) changed forever the northern region of Saudi Arabia. The project, which eventually became connected with Aramco, encouraged countless small businesses, and the creation of several new communities along the pipeline. After 31 years of operation, and the realisation of a new generation of super tankers that could transport considerable amounts of oil to Europe, the TAPline could no longer operate competitively and was finally decommissioned in 2001.

The story of oil is complex and is, to varying degrees, widely known. Every day, we see the far-reaching effects and ramifications of this precious substance, the use of which, like any other resource, started out as a positive benefit to humanity, but was soon weaponised or taken advantage of in various ways. This is no different to the excessive wealth creation we witness in the twenty-first century with global digitalisation. The problem seems to stem from humanity itself which must struggle always to maintain a decent balance.

The concept of entropy within life is of course very much intertwined with the existence of opposite phenomena, which makes the work of several artists in this exhibition particularly relevant for discussion. For example, Bharti Kher, an artist who is intensely preoccupied with the human body, primarily the female body, focuses frequently on issues of transformation and metamorphosis through time. In attempting to tangibly realise her ideas, Kher often strives to achieve harmony and a certain balance between different elements. This exhibition presents a large grouping from her series *The Intermediaries* [pp. 82–87] which the artist creates from found objects, that is a vast collection of painted clay figurines from southern India. As Kher beautifully explains in a filmed interview, she starts by cutting, breaking and dividing these figurines, which commonly represent humans, gods, goddesses, animals and imaginary beings. She then rearranges the parts, seemingly at random, and glues them together according to her own thoughts, fantasies and ideas. In this way the objects transit constantly between reality and illusion, the factual and imaginary, the possible and impossible. As the artist herself explains, these hybrid bodies reveal to us *an entire range and sources of life, from religious to secular.* In the incongruous and uncertain world in which we live these works more than ever remind us of the importance of not being shy about looking into new possibilities and hitherto unthinkable narratives.

The concept of balancing opposites within a system is equally intrinsic to the work of David Claerbout, albeit in a totally different way to that in the practice of Bharti Kher. His 24-minute, single-channel, colour video with animation, *Wildfire (Meditation On Fire)*, 2019–2020, [pp. 76–79] seems to be yet another visualisation of the recent wildfires around the world, but it is far more than that. Of this, Claerbout says, *Biological programming still exists in the living creatures of today and dictates a natural reflex to get away from any fire that cannot be contained. A 'meditation on fire' may therefore sound like an impossibility.* But a meditation is exactly what this video work is. Claerbout has subdued an element as devastating as fire – which by definition usually consumes all surrounding matter – into something solid, firm and fixed. This may be the power of digital technology but for Claerbout it demonstrates the power of compromise or the coexistence of opposites.

Wildfire (Meditation On Fire) is meant to be all-engulfing and mesmerising, therefore not only is the image projected on to a large screen of approximately five square metres but also, through some clever projection technique, the image appears to be three-dimensional, motionless and sculptural.

Sharing his thoughts on learning from artists of the past, Claerbout says, *From the painter Hans Memling (1430–1494), I remember the coexistence of hot and cool areas, respectively hell and heaven. This was the first thing that held my attention. The second being an interest in how spending time with a single image crystallises the matter that we perceive in it and how persistent looking can transform people of flesh and blood into sculptures carved from stone... To think of how an impression of fire – almost by definition fleeting – might transform into a solid building of flame.* It is utterly revealing to think of the work as being in a state of fusion between solid and fluid, confusion and clarity, randomness and predictability, but this too may be a way of unexpectedly bringing the reality of an image to the fore.

Darren Almond deals with the coexistence of opposites in a different way. As a young boy in his hometown, Wigan, in northwest England, Almond took up trainspotting to escape the claustrophobia of what was then a small coal-mining town. This interest and love of travel stayed with him and grew throughout his years at art school and, later, as a young artist. His work, *In The Between*, 2006, [pp. 44–49] a 14-minute, 3-channel, HD video with audio, is testimony to Almond's astutely thoughtful mind, always curious to expand his knowledge about the state of a world that he has by now frequently traversed. The subject of the video is the high-speed Qinghai–Tibet railway, completed in 2006 to connect major Chinese cities to Lhasa and other destinations in Tibet.

The video starts simultaneously on three screens with the central screen showing the interior of a Buddhist monastery, where monks, oblivious to the outside world, are chanting their daily prayer, while on the left screen we see strings of Tibetan prayer flags in red, yellow, blue, green and white and on the right screen we see a train advancing at dizzying speed. For much of the 14-minute duration of the video we follow the train's journey into a barren and mountainous landscape that for a few moments gives way to celebratory images of Tibetan prayer flags and brief impressions of the train stations. The uncompromising allure of the train indubitably proves its state-of-the-art technology and may convey the aggressive and domineering attitude of a superpower rushing to conquer its peaceful neighbour. Even so, the sympathy seems to be won by the peaceful Tibetan culture, and the joyful prayer flags that represent peace and universal compassion.

Clearly, and above all, the work reflects on a multitude of issues that are increasingly to be grappled with in our world, and are the topics of discussion in this exhibition, such as aggression, neo-colonialism, forced labour, and the human condition. The *In The Between* video could be seen as a metaphor for the intrusion of a superpower into the territories of a peaceful culture, but the underlying reality here could equally be the tale of the railway's construction. Indeed, it took almost 50 years to complete some 2,000 kilometres (nearly 1,300 miles) of track, half of which had to be laid at an altitude 4,000 metres above sea level. The construction took place in harsh climatic conditions with low oxygen levels, freezing temperatures, and ultimately claimed countless lives.

Returning to the topic of entropy in our world and with images of Almond's video work in mind, we can say that as much as we honour humanity for its genius ideas, hard work and remarkable achievements, indeed for building refined and complex civilisations over several millennia, we have to admit that they have also generated much chaos, damage, violence, atrocities and destruction, and today all these negatives seem to have reached saturation point and urgently require our undivided attention and action. Again and again, I have gone back to the concept of time appreciation and at each review I simply wonder whether the overly busy world we humans have constructed for ourselves allows us to have proper overarching insight into the realities of life and our own stance in the midst of it.

Looking back at human history and culture, one recognises, for example, that the last few decades have seen, among much else, an extraordinary ascendance of globalisation, with a largely positive response to it, as it has served well the interest of people in developed countries to purchase products more cheaply, while also providing development and financial resources to millions of people in the underprivileged countries of the world. It was only much later that the developed world realised the shocking implications of globalisation and the imbalance it has created in their own jobs market. Globalisation has caused devastating unemployment and the gradual closure of countless industrial plants and factories at home.

One of the major issues created by globalisation is the excessive production of consumer goods, including 'inexpensive' clothing, which is certainly central to the work of artist Si On. Indeed, few of us give more than a passing thought to the amount of clothing for sale in millions of stores worldwide, much of which is left unsold at the end of every season. In this exhibition, Si On's impressively large installation *Doomsday*, 2020, [pp. 104–109] clearly warns of the imminent danger to humanity. The 7-metre-high tsunami-like wave is frozen mid-roll, as if giving humanity time to take action to avoid catastrophe. Prophetically, the work was originally commissioned by the Mori Art Museum, Tokyo, and exhibited in 2020, ironically during the long pause for Covid-19 lockdowns.

Katsushika Hokusai, *Under the Wave off Kanagawa (Kanagawa oki nami ura)*, also known as *The Great Wave*, from the series *Thirty-six Views of Mount Fuji (Fugaku sanjūrok-kei)*, c. 1830–1832
Woodblock print; ink and colour on paper, 25.7 x 37.9 cm (10 x 15 in)

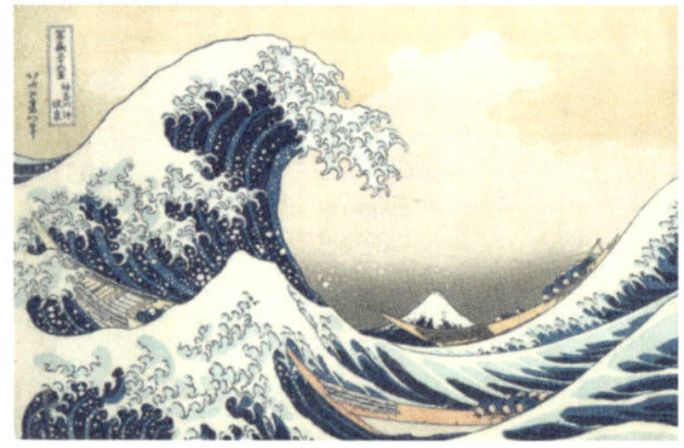

With obvious reference to Katsushika Hokusai's *The Great Wave off Kanagawa*, one of the most well-known images in the history of art, *Doomsday* is made of some three tons of clothing. The work expresses Si On's concern for the planet's fragile ecosystems and the growing threat of their destruction, which she calls *the revenge of Nature.* But this powerful, three-dimensional construction addresses above all the artist's concerns about the mass consumption of clothing and, by extension, other consumer products, all in the name of advancing the economy. Standing within the installation are several prominently displayed shrine-like statues reminiscent of those commonly seen in some parts of the world. Si On's use of these symbols might refer to naïvely begging for salvation or perhaps to assuming an opportunistic attitude at a time of threat and danger.

When it comes to war, violence and racism, the world and human civilisation has certainly seen enough of it. True, since 1945 our planet has not seen another world war, but there have been numerous localised conflicts, smaller wars in which world superpowers have not hesitated to exert their strength and authority, primarily to protect their own national interests. Operating within other countries requires at least a basic knowledge of their cultures, otherwise misunderstandings can lead to drastic consequences. Racism, to greater or lesser degrees, seems always to have existed in our world, but after the magnitude of atrocities perpetrated during the Second World War, the 'civilised world' would not tolerate any open repetition. It is then shocking to see the current regeneration of divisive racism which is at times encouraged by certain world leaders and other factions of society. If compassion is a human virtue, then our society seems to be forgetting its value. How can anyone close their eyes to images of thousands of refugees stranded at borders across the world or to the dead bodies of desperate migrants floating in freezing sea waters?

Our world has long been in thrall to greed and wealth accumulation and during recent decades such desires and intentions show little sign of abating. It is incomprehensible how some human beings can pursue with fascination the accumulation of enormous amounts of wealth, yet be apparently incapable of feeling or expressing compassion towards the countless individuals who need a mere fraction of it for their survival. A hallmark of our time is excess in many arenas but foremost is the exploitation of the planet's natural resources and the interconnected importance of all its ecosystems.

The opening up of communist blocs to the free-market economy in the last decades of the twentieth century has made a few people utterly and somewhat unjustifiably rich, while most of their population live in poverty. The twenty-first century and the dominance of digital technology has brought us many conveniences, but it has also coincided with ever greater levels of uncontrolled human activity that is intensively depleting much of planet Earth's natural resources. We may think we are saving the world by not printing documents stored on our computer, or that driving an electric car is being virtuous and 'green', but little is done to expose the true level of damage being done to planet Earth. For example, through the exploitation of lithium in the vast and remote Salar de Uyuni Salt Flat in Bolivia, and much else that Julian Charrière draws attention to in his works. Lithium is used in the batteries that power the ever-increasing amount of digital technology and electric cars.

Looking back at human history, our environment and activity, we see that the level of entropy has never been so high, and that the most urgent issue, global warming, is no longer the preoccupation of some teenagers but a serious global problem that requires urgent action if we are to hand on a better world to future generations. We, its inhabitants have, especially since the Second World War, been plundering Earth's natural resources, which has in turn endangered the survival of all living creatures and of planet Earth itself, almost to a point of no return – all without accountability or taking responsibility for the damage or its repair. With all these issues, one could say that our world has seen more than its share of wrongdoing and injustice. Fortunately, the world is also populated by some great people who are compassionate and generous, but still our society has much to do to make up for the shortfall of recent decades.

Probably more tactile and sensate than strictly cerebral is how Martin Puryear, one of the greatest living American artists, describes his unusual, impressive, philosophically laden, and sophisticated sculptures. *Shackled*, 2014, [pp. 112–117] shown in this exhibition is a relatively small work in his oeuvre, but it is no less intense or expressive. Dense, solid, mysterious, impermeable and obedient yet charged, this black cast-iron piece has a remarkably powerful presence which commands attention. Despite its small size, *Shackled* throbs with some 400 years of painfully unjust tales to be shared and to revivify a moral sense of abhorrence towards all human brutality.

Slavery and the need to dominate have existed in cultures throughout history. In Western culture, even before and including the Greeks and Romans and, later, in medieval Europe, slavery was common. Around the time slavery was about to end in north-western Europe, the encounter of Europeans with the American continents brought another surge of this practice, which ultimately became highly lucrative. It is not possible to be precise about the number of Africans taken as slaves to Europe and the 'New World'. According to Henry Louis Gates, Jr on *The African-Americans: Many Rivers to Cross* website, an estimated 12.5 million Africans were shipped to the New World, 10.7 million of whom survived the dreaded Middle Passage to disembark in North America, South America and the Caribbean.

Extreme tools of oppression, slave shackles are some of the most cruel and disturbing objects to behold. Nevertheless, it is surprising that the first public exhibition of *Shackled* occurred only in 2016. The choice of a shackle as imagery or object in Puryear's work is poignantly astute from an artist who has so intelligently embodied some of the most difficult areas of human history and done so always with grace and dignity.

Since at least ancient Greek times, *beauty* has generated much intrigue, conflict and even war. *The Judgement of Paris* in Greek mythology tells of a nobleman from Troy, Alexandros (Paris), who was called upon to decide who among the three goddesses, Hera, Aphrodite and Athena, was the most beautiful. All three goddesses offered bribes: Hera promised to give Paris kingdom over all men; Athena promised victory in war; and Aphrodite offered him Helen, the most beautiful mortal of the time. Paris selected Aphrodite, who rewarded him with Helen, wife of the King of Sparta. This led to the Trojan War being launched to rescue Helen from Troy, which has provided much material for discussion and literature, the most important being the *Iliad* by Homer, who wrote of this event in the eighth century BCE.

So, it is no surprise that the topic of the beauty pageant, with its potential for harm, has attracted one of the most vocal conceptual Mexican artists, Teresa Margolles. In her practice, the artist generally addresses the aesthetics of social causes and the consequences of violence and death. Trained in Forensic Medicine and Communication Sciences, Margolles believes that morgues reflect society, particularly when deaths result from drug-related crime, which is apparently rampant in Mexico. In a country beset in many parts by poverty, political instability and a lack of proper leadership, a significant proportion of the population sadly makes its living illegally, which must inevitably have a detrimental effect on the society. Revolted by such deaths, Margolles tirelessly focuses on various strands of crime and comes up with poignant artworks that speak out for the silenced victims. As a frequent visitor to morgues, Margolles often incorporates physical remnants of crime in her installations. For this exhibition, she has focused on beauty pageant events and their often dramatic consequences, a topic that is conveniently ignored and is not easily talked about. In reality, 'narco' people have such high standing in the society that naïve youths and young women, often under twenty, become infatuated with the glamour of 'belonging' to a 'narco' boyfriend. A quick Internet search reveals how quickly young beauty queens get involved in the violent world of drugs and too often killed in some related conflict.

The expertly made dress in *Blowback / The Power*, 2022, [pp. 98–101] which Margolles presents in this exhibition was designed and sewn with the help of specialist local dressmakers, who usually create glamorous attire for beauty queens in Mexico. Displayed proudly on an eye-catching pedestal, the dress glitters enticingly, but this gorgeous garment actually embodies a shocking dichotomy. While the meticulously embellished frock appears to be an object of desire coveted by many a young woman in Mexico, in that particular environment it would also come with the certitude of risk and danger. The many shiny and jewel-like decorative pieces on the sleeve of the dress are in fact glass shards which Margolles picked up from the street after the shootings (executions) that took place in her hometown on 17 October 2019, and which she then sewed, as an intervention, on to the dress.

Has our world gone badly astray? If I transpose Oliver Beer's theory that every object and every being has a specific resonance that keeps them in balance, then it seems to me that in our currently frenzied environment and time, humanity may have strayed way too far off its line of equilibrium. If I follow Arghavan Khosravi's philosophy of patience in difficult times as she expresses in *The Anatomy of A Woman* series of paintings, I understand that this shall also pass. But when?

Arghavan Khosravi's paintings are both compelling and uncanny, and their imagery inhabits a strange world that is simultaneously real and surreal. Often painted in vivid colours, these works intrigue us with their direct and realistic appearance. They promise easy access, yet their surreal aspect, which recalls the *trompe l'oeil* technique, leaves much to discover of a complex world beneath the surface. Khosravi was born in 1984, five years after the Islamic Revolution in Iran, and since 2015 has lived in the USA. Her paintings reveal something of the ideologies she has experienced, which collide with and fittingly incorporate her own natural reactions and reflections. Of her work, Khosravi says: *My practice is intrinsically linked to my life experience, yet opens a space to recast memories and process the paradoxes of my childhood in Tehran, while also grounding my perspective as an Iranian now living in the USA. I see my work as a vehicle for shifting power, validating personal storytelling, and connecting to universal messages about human rights.*

In Khosravi's series of paintings, *The Anatomy of A Woman*, 2019, [pp. 90–95] from which we have selected a few works for presentation in *Uncombed, Unforeseen, Unconstrained,* the artist's prime concern seems to be the situation of Iranian women in the current environment and perhaps, by extension, the challenges they face elsewhere in the world. This group of works was shown in Brussels in her 2020 exhibition, *This Shall Also Pass*, the title of which came from a well-known Persian proverb that calls for patience and discreet wisdom in times of crisis. In one painting, a woman looks anxiously out of a broken window. In another work, the front torso of a woman, bound over and over with red cord, also stands behind a broken window. Red cord appears frequently in Khosravi's paintings, metaphorically referring to acts of suppression and oppression.

Structurally, Khosravi's paintings are often intricate and employ several wooden structures that form multiple picture planes. Her three-dimensional constructions usually reference different stages or times within the narrative of a work. The artist constructs these pieces using shaped wooden parts on which she stretches a textile fabric before painting over them. An important source of inspiration here seems to be Persian miniatures which, although two-dimensional, are skilfully composed to show various stages and times within a narrative.

Oliver Beer opted to create a site-specific installation in a small, tucked-away chapel on the *piano nobile* of the Conservatorio di Musica. In his work *Little Gods (Chamber Organ)*, 2022, [pp. 52–55] objects, which Beer has selected with infinite care from various parts of the world are experienced in a wholly innovative way. Rather than focusing on their appearance as objects, in this installation we *hear* the sound of them and can distinguish each one specifically by its unique resonance. As the artist explains: *The installation is formed by an 'orchestra' of 32 vessels, each of which is selected for the precise frequency in which it resonates – unchanged since the day it was made.* Capturing their unique sound with tiny microphones in this installation, the artist *brings together vessels with potential animistic qualities – objects depicting and including faces, bodies or animals – as a reflection of the pan-historical, pan-cultural practice of animism as well as highlighting the innate musicality of the world around us.*

Building on his *Vessel Orchestra* exhibition which Beer created earlier and presented at the Metropolitan Museum of Art, New York, in 2019, *Little Gods (Chamber Organ)* is a playable musical instrument controlled by a keyboard. As he says: *The keyboard itself makes no noise, but instead acts as a controller that switches on the microphones inside the vessels when a specific key is pressed, allowing viewers to play and hear the resonance of each vessel in real time. In an institution which is constantly filled with music and musicians,* Little Gods *is conceived as a working musical instrument that allows visitors to the exhibition to play it themselves; or listen to others playing. The installation will also have its own musical life throughout the seven months of the exhibition, as the music students discover this unique and beautiful instrument hidden away in their school.*

Working on this exhibition with the eleven remarkable visual artists, I have, time and again, been surprised and inspired by their positive attitude towards the challenging issues facing humanity today. I understand that it is a privilege to exhibit works by these eleven artists, but many others are also working on equally complex and time-sensitive matters, yet all the while remaining admirably hopeful, positive and good-humoured. Faced with the need to find solutions to so many problems, this may indeed be the right attitude, because it is no longer helpful to merely complain and criticise. As we have seen demonstrated by several works in this exhibition, solutions can only be found by confronting a problem and getting to its central core. It will always surprise me, for instance, how David Claerbout could have identified destructive wildfire as a source of inspiration and meditation, or is it perhaps a sign of helplessness.

From devising measured and controllable entropy as Rana Begum has done in collaboration with Hyetal; to forcefully yet philosophically reminding ourselves of the damage humanity is doing to planet Earth, as manifested in Julian Charrière's work; to taking a measured stance towards entropy, as in the work of Rayyane Tabet; to the law of opposites seen in the work of Bharti Kher and David Claerbout; to reminders in the works of Darren Almond and Martin Puryear that colonialism and racism are not yet conquered, and that excessive consumerism in the name of advancing the economy is harmful, as Si On so eloquently expresses in her installation; to the necessity of seeing the atrocious realities of life and society, as illustrated in the work of Teresa Margolles; to the irony or deep philosophical thinking in Arghavan Khosravi's title *This Shall Also Pass*; to hearing in the work of Oliver Beer the uniqueness and content of life beautifully voiced as a personal resonance – all these significant revelations help to remind us of the precious and fragile nature of life. We need to live and continue to give the gift of life to future generations as well as to planet Earth. For the sake of all this, I believe it is our duty to find a balance between entropy and human activity. As we all know, the two are inseparable and therefore the answer must be in how we restore a viably co-existent balance. To me, much depends on educated and democratic societies that understand their civic responsibilities.

1 Coined as the second law of thermodynamics, entropy became known to us thanks to the work of physicist Rudolf Clausius (1822–1888) who in 1865, while working at the Swiss Federal Institute of Technology in Zurich, introduced the concept to the scientific world.

Entropisms

Julien Bismuth

Artist and Writer

A Measure of Disorder

Uncombed, Unforeseen, Unconstrained, hosted by Parasol unit at the Conservatorio di Musica Benedetto Marcello in Venice throughout the 59th Biennale Arte di Venezia, is an exhibition that has been conceived and composed in relation to the concept of entropy. The word *entropy* is used in a wide variety of fields, ranging from its origin in the field of thermodynamics, to its application in the fields of information science, anthropology, and ecology, among others. What it names is a quotient or measure of disorder, specifically within a closed system. The exhibition shows works by the artists: Darren Almond, Oliver Beer, Rana Begum with Hyetal, Julian Charrière, David Claerbout, Bharti Kher, Arghavan Khosravi, Teresa Margolles, Si On, Martin Puryear, and Rayyane Tabet.

Entropy

According to the *Oxford English Dictionary*, the word entropy names 'a degree of disorder or randomness in a system'. In the field of thermodynamics, a rise in entropy is also indicative of a rise in the amount of lost or unavailable energy for 'doing work' in a system. In information theory, entropy was used by Claude Shannon to denote the degree of uncertainty, unpredictability, complexity, or noise in the communication of information.[1] It plays a significant role, for example, in the compression of data files by reducing complex messages into more compact and efficient data files. As an aside, when Shannon started working on what he first called his 'uncertainty principle', the Hungarian-American polymath John von Neumann (who named another form of entropy after himself) suggested the word *entropy*, telling Shannon that, since no one really understood what the word meant, this would give him an advantage in any debate.[2]

One point or another

In the introduction to his paper on entropy in information systems, Shannon makes the following statement regarding information theory:

The fundamental problem of communication is that of reproducing at one point either exactly or approximately a message selected at another point. Frequently, the messages have meaning; that is, they refer to or are correlated according to some system with certain physical or conceptual entities. These semantic aspects of communication are irrelevant to the engineering problem. The significant aspect is that the actual message is one selected from a set of possible messages. The system must be designed to operate for each possible selection, not just the one that will actually be chosen since this is unknown at the time of design.[3]

In other words, it is not the meaning of the message that matters, but rather the communication of the message in question in relation to any possible form of interference or indeterminacy. It is not the communication of a specific message, but the communication of all potential messages in a system that has to be determined and ascertained. It is in this respect that the machine that I am writing on perfectly adheres to the constraints named by Shannon. It communicates a message faithfully, in part by defining that faithfulness at a distinct remove from the 'physical or conceptual entities' that it refers to. The text that I am writing is being simultaneously reduced to a sequence of binary code by the machine I am using, thus reducing its entropic quotient, while operating at a distinct remove from its semantic content. In doing so, however, in occulting the play of signification, Shannon loses sight of the most enduringly significant locus of entropy in linguistic communication. From rumour to 'fake news', it is in the relationships that words have to 'physical or conceptual entities' that disorder and uncertainty reside.

Dark Optics

David Claerbout's *Wildfire (Meditation On Fire)*, 2019–2020, [pp. 76–79] takes place in a rendered or simulated forest. The roving eye of the frame (this is a film whose enclosure is defined not by the eye of a camera but by the frame of a computer screen) starts by showing us the reflection of a greyish blue sky in what appears to be a lake. Lake and sky fade, giving way to a lush forest. We see leaves and plants moved by an otherwise imperceptible wind. We hear birds, and see flying insects, until those sounds and movements fade along with the simulated daylight. The wind abates, the sky darkens and reddens, and the forest is quietly overtaken by flames. Yet the engulfing flames do not move. Their static images neither billow nor warp but instead seem to float within the rendered layers of the virtual forest. As the film comes to an end, we move from a cloud of dark billowing smoke to the reflection of a forest in the rippling surface of a lake. The fire fades, replaced by what appears to be the reddish light of a sunrise. Birdsong returns, and we end where we started, with the same image of a reflected sky.

Digital eats all it can

The title of this section is a phrase in a drawing by David Claerbout. In a recent essay, the artist elaborates his theory of Dark Optics, of a world of hyperrealistic images in which the camera is absent, and the world is only present by means of its simulated digital rendering. He gives the example of a friend, who came to him with a 'magnificent picture of a sunrise she had taken with her iPad':

I asked her how much of the picture she thought she had taken herself. The vantage point is indicated by the IP address of the device. So is the weather, season, and time of day. Actually, algorithmic processes can 'guess' the ideal moment for photographing such a wonderful daybreak, so as to raise the mood of the average person. There was nothing of herself in what she showed me, beyond the coincidence of technology with itself.[4]

If Dark Optics names a world in which we no longer seize images of the world, but recreate it to our liking, what it describes is an information loop, the communication of expectations that are then precisely met by technology. Yet the loop is not closed, for what informs it is not a stable set of elements, but rather a disordered flux, which could potentially include Claerbout's recent works. *Wildfire (Meditation On Fire)* is itself a movie that loops, literally even, as its opening and closing sequences are identical. We end where we started, but what then do we make of the incendiary intrusion in between? The forest is invaded by fire but it is not consumed by its flames. The last trees we see in the reflection of the lake are just as green and lush as those in the opening sequence. The fire passes and passes through the forest, leaving only images in its wake. *Wildfire (Meditation On Fire)* can be seen as an allegory of capitalism, of a world in which we can consume everything without paying the price for the loss, nor for the entropy we produce in return; a world we can burn down without leaving any ashes behind, like the world of Disney, in which violence pits one immortal and elastic body against another, without consequences of any sort. Yet the inconsequence of the fire only makes it more unsettling, more uncannily disturbing than the images of wildfires we have come to expect in the press. The justifications that images provide for our interpretations are often most eloquent when they are indirect or even tangential. While looking at Claerbout's film, my thoughts kept turning to his visible dislocation of the rendered layers in his animation. There are moments in the film when these layers slip and dissociate from their background, like an afterimage or a reversed shadow. The familiar divide between depth and superficiality fades, losing its efficacy, giving way instead to the uncanny depth of a seemingly indefinite stack of more or less opaque or translucent surfaces, ending with that of the screen.

Turning in

The word *entropy* was coined as a counterpart to the word *energy* by the German physicist Rudolf Clausius. Both start with the Greek prefix *en-*, though entropy ends with a derivation of the Greek *trope* (turning, transformation) while energy ends with a derivation of the Greek word for *ergon* (work). There is a convolute or even involute resonance to the word *entropy*, and to its prevalent definition as a form of unpredictability or disorder in the interaction between discrete elements of a system. The determination of entropy entails the determination of the order or predictability that its disorder and unpredictability are measured against. It is at this point that the word starts to turn in on itself, spiralling and swirling ever more tightly into the coils of its own extensions and derivations.

Forms of entropy exist outside of the so-called hard sciences, in the field of the soft, the social, or the human sciences, namely anthropology. The anthropologist Claude Lévi-Strauss coined the word *entropology* to describe a potential field of study of human cultures in terms of their relative degree of entropy. Entropology would compare cultural groups along the following lines: their openness or closure to other cultures, their variability or invariability, the degree of equality or inequality of their respective subjects, as well as their scale and complexity. Far from being a more intricate form of evolutionism, Lévi-Strauss's hypothetical science leads him instead to outline a profound critique of so-called advanced or civilised societies:

. . . our societies not only make great use of the steam engine, but from the point of their structure, they themselves resemble steam engines. They function by using a difference of potential, which is actualised by different types of social hierarchy, whether it's called slavery, serfdom, or whether it consists in a division into classes has no fundamental importance when one considers things from such a distance, such a panoramic perspective. Such societies have managed to achieve a disequilibrium within themselves, that they in turn use to produce both far more order – we have mechanistic societies – and also much more disorder, much more entropy, even on the level of relations between humans.[5]

Darren Almond's *In The Between*, 2006, [pp. 44–49] provides a different perspective on the lethal consequences of such mechanistic societies. A three-channel video installation, its images alternate between footage shot in Tibet, with footage of the high-speed railway line built by the Chinese government to connect Tibet with major cities in China. In contrast to Lévi-Strauss's sophisticated approach to cultural differences, the high-speed Qinghai-Tibet railway operates along another, more brutal logic of cross-cultural interaction: one of assimilation, expropriation, and ultimately, destruction. The precisely staged interplay between the two streams of images and sounds embodies its stark disparities and its violence. There are moments when the three-screen projection becomes one single composed image, and others where the contrast between the two worlds becomes irreconcilably disruptive. A third of the way into the sequence, all three screens show the same footage of billowing colourful flags, accompanied by the sound of Tibetan ritual music. The next section shows a group of monks, praying and chanting in a temple, framed on both sides by symmetrically reversed images of the train moving past the camera from different angles. The trajectory of the train is mechanical and linear, in contrast to the slow, contemplative movements of the monks. Their unchoreographed gestures suddenly give way to music, as several monks pick up instruments and start to play. The ritual music continues as the image of the temple disappears, replaced by three identical shots of landscape filmed from the moving train.

Bricolage

In his book *La pensée sauvage*, Lévi-Strauss makes use of the untranslatable French word *bricolage*. The word designates a way of making things that in England might be described as 'cobbled together' and in the United States as 'DIY' (Do It Yourself). Yet neither of these translations are adequate. *Bricolage* is making do with the things you have available around you. It stands, according to Lévi-Strauss, in contrast to engineering. Engineers design tools, and find resources and materials to accomplish a project that they have conceived and designed from start to finish. A *bricoleur* responds to needs and circumstances by improvising tools and solutions with what is available, what is 'at hand'. As Lévi-Strauss points out, the original meaning of the word comes from hunting and billiards, and addresses a manner of responding to contingencies such as the swerve of a billiard ball, or the sudden movement of a dog or horse during a hunt to avoid an obstacle or adjust its course. Lévi-Strauss uses it more specifically in the sense of making-do, improvising a solution with the materials and resources one has available at the precise moment. Consequently, bricolage emerges as a manner of working and doing that is not unrelated to entropy, and in fact proposes an alternative perspective on its constitutive dichotomies, such as order and disorder, predictability and unpredictability, efficiency and waste. Bharti Kher's *The Intermediaries*, 2019, [pp. 82–87] is a series of works composed by means of bricolage. In keeping with the definition of the term in the O.E.D., she produces these collaged sculptures by 'appropriating a diverse miscellany of existing materials or sources, particularly ... found objects'. A *bricoleur* – or *bricoleuse* in Kher's case – is someone who works with contingency, rather than seeking to counteract or eradicate it with a preordained plan. Like the billiard players and hunters of the original definition, hers is not simply a reactive but also a creative gesture, transforming contingency into opportunity, found objects into the elements of an artwork, limitations into possibilities. Bricolage, in fact, can be seen as a potential way of living within an entropic landscape, finding the least disorder without aspiring to a perfect and thus static inert order, which, according to thermodynamics, is both the consequence and limit of perfect order, but also the ultimate state achieved by a rise in entropy, otherwise known as 'heat death'.

Hummin

Oliver Beer's work in this exhibition [pp. 52–55], like his previous installation *Household Gods,* 2019, plays on the phenomenon of acoustic resonance, by amplifying the sound contained and produced from an eclectic set of objects in a room. The sounds he amplifies are akin to the resonance one hears in seashells. His work calls to mind Alvin Lucier's seminal *I am sitting in a room,* 1969, in which the voice of the artist is gradually distorted and effaced by the ambient resonant frequencies of the room. While Lucier makes these resonant frequencies audible by means of a continuous recording and replaying of his initial speech, Beer leaves out any form of human agency, other than the installation of the objects, microphones, and sound equipment. The room is made to speak by way of the objects that sit within it. What emerges is a delicate and captivating aura of sound, understanding aura to mean both a 'subtle emanation', and – in the Benjaminian sense[6] – an index of haecceity, of the presence of a specific entity or object in a specific space and location.

By making us aware of the resonant emanations of quotidian objects, Beer not only engages with acoustic resonance, but also makes these objects more present. The thoughts spurred or inspired by an artwork are at times most fruitful when they are allowed to drift lightly, irresponsibly even, from their place of origin. While listening to a recording of Beer's installation, I became differently aware of the coffee cup that I was sipping from, the water bottle and cup in front of me, and even the discarded plastic container in the trash can at my feet. I wondered at the difference in resonance between a glass or plastic container. My thoughts strayed to the recycling bins just outside my window. I imagined a symphonic installation of all of the vessels it contained, and my thoughts turned to the absurdity of so-called 'single-use containers', and of the enduring waste that they produce. The vessels used by Beer range from museum artworks to objects taken from his own home, yet their resonant hum communicated to the vessels that surrounded me. Perhaps that is a form of semantic entropy, of the kind that Shannon immediately brushes aside in his introduction; or perhaps it is something else, something closer to the actual efficacy of language, and of its elusive relationship to ideas and things.

Florilège

Julian Charrière's *And Beneath It All Flows Liquid Fire*, 2019, [p. 67] shows a fountain on fire, a fountain that appears to circulate both fire and water. Rayyane Tabet's *Steel Rings*, 2013–, [pp. 120–123] consists of a row of metal rings that represent the first sixty-five kilometres of the unfinished and abandoned Trans-Arabian Pipeline, whose conflicted history reflects that of the region in which it was built. Each ring stands for a kilometre of the unfinished pipeline, and every one of them is marked with its specific geographical coordinates, as well as its distance from the point of origin of the pipeline. Like Charrière's other work in the exhibition, *Not All Who Wander Are Lost* [pp. 68–73], Tabet's piece refers to the drilling, prospection, and circulation of subterranean resources, from precious metals to oil, water, and gas. In recent years, videos of tap-water being lit on fire have been circulating online, their igneous state attributed to fracking. Though the claims have been contested, the videos continue to circulate, whether as actual documentation or as a metaphor for the numerous other uncontested dangers of fracking. In July 2021, television crews in Mexico filmed a fire at sea, apparently caused by an oil spill. The images show boats trying to put out the fire with water – water from the sea on which both they and the fire are floating. There are antecedents to such incidents – such as the Cuyahoga River fire of 1952 – yet the absurdity of the images they produce never fades.

Si On's installation *Doomsday*, 2020, [pp. 104–109], shows a different kind of lethal fluidity at work, namely that of the circulation of material goods, specifically clothing. In the aftermath of the Covid pandemic, the fashion industry's systemic overproduction of goods, and their customary policy of simply burning excess clothing items, came under closer scrutiny as a result of the increased amount of unsold merchandise. These facts and considerations link directly and indirectly to the works I have written of above, and all of them relate clearly and emphatically to the predominant form of entropy in modernity, namely the transformation of renewable and non-renewable resources into non-reusable waste. A polluted river on fire is not the same thing as a landfill, but both attest to the same stultifying logic of consumption, in which the water and earth we depend upon for our survival are literally made toxic by human industry. The machine that I am using to write this text, for example, is the result of a precisely imbricated set of ecologically ruinous processes, starting with the extraction of the rare-earth elements that allow it to run and, by making its screen glow, allow me to read the text I am writing.

Though the entropic fragments that make up this text were inspired by the works in this exhibition, they sit at a deliberate distance from them, allowing them to retain their autonomy. A similar sense of dissociative sympathy emanates from Rana Begum's collaborative work with the musician and composer Hyetal [pp. 60–63]. The reflected light and shadows of the coloured-Perspex panes and moving lights of Begum's wall piece, *No. 694 Hyetal*, move along invariable paths, yet their movement is constantly altered, inflected, and coloured by Hyetal's music.

In a similar manner, in Arghavan Khosravi's painting, *This Shall Also Pass (The Anatomy of A Woman Series #6)*, 2019, [pp. 90, 91] the different material elements of the work coexist while maintaining their distinction. 'This shall also pass', a Persian adage written in Farsi, floats above the surface of the painting, cut into the pane of frosted glass that is held within a wooden frame that partially contains it. A yellow string connects the top and bottom of the painting. The meticulous rendering of a woman, her hand resting against the wooden frame, her gaze meeting ours through a jagged hole in the glass, stands out against a plane of patterned cloth, the paint held within the outline of her body, leaving the rest of the decorated canvas intact. The violence contained in the shattered glass reverberates within the gaps between the different elements it is intended to contain.

In the works of Martin Puryear [pp. 112–117] and Teresa Margolles [pp. 98–101], more explicitly lethal forms of violence are evoked without being directly named. The form of Puryear's sculpture, *Shackled*, 2014, recalls that of a body, whether human or animal, yet the iron ring that encircles it bears an unmistakable relationship to its title. The glittering stones that adorn Margolles's recreation of a beauty queen dress are fashioned from glass collected from crime scenes related to the drug trade in Mexico. Margolles transforms this morbid residue into gemstones, that she then uses to adorn her faithful replicas of the diverse regalia of Sinaloan drug cartels, in this case, the dresses worn by beauty pageant contestants, which have been closely connected to the drug cartels for years.[7] In doing so, she recycles yet another form of waste, waste being another name for the material by-products of societal entropy.

Disaggregation

The difficulty of properly understanding entropy has to do with the fact that all of its applications are grounded in the complexities of its associated discipline. Just as Claude Shannon's definition rests on his preliminary conceptualisation of information, so Lévi-Strauss's *entropologie* is anchored in his structuralist approach to the comparative study of human cultures. Yet, whether in the realm of thermodynamics, information, or culture, the underlying concern of entropic studies has to do with a determinate relationship between order and disorder, predictability and unpredictability, certainty and uncertainty, a relationship often expressed as a numerical measure, a degree, an extensive rather than intensive difference in the vocabulary of philosophers Bergson and Deleuze. If entropy is reduced to a measure on a linear gradient, then its cipher, the null number [zero] that anchors its gradient of values, is the human subject. In order to properly engage with the concept of entropy, one has to call into question its underlying premises, as can be seen in the work of contemporary thinkers such as Donna Hathaway and Isabelle Stengers. To cite the latter, in order to provide concrete alternatives to the increasingly entropic logic of the Anthropocene world, one has to cease thinking of nature in opposition to culture, but rather as a realm in which *. . . if we were to give it the attention it deserves, we would find more, and we would refuse to find less.*[8] To do so, and thus, to pull the delineation between nature and culture to its point of indistinction, would perhaps even allow one to have a similar perspective on humanity, and give it a similar attention, so that we might also 'find more and refuse to find less' within ourselves.

The shame of being human

In the passage on entropy at the end of *Tristes Tropiques*, Claude Lévi-Strauss deploys the concept to formulate a virulent critique of humanity:

Man has never – save only when he reproduces himself – done other than cheerfully dismantle billions of structures and reduce their elements to a state in which they can no longer be reintegrated [...] As for the creations of the human mind, they are meaningful only in relation to that mind and will fall into disorder as soon as it will have disappeared. Taken as a whole, therefore, civilisation can be described as a prodigiously complicated mechanism: tempting as it would be to regard it as our universe's best hope of survival, its true function is to produce what physicists call entropy, or in other words, inertia.[9]

The book ends with a tenuous dissipation of this pessimistic overview by means of a turn of the author's gaze towards the realm of the extra-human, finding respite in the beauty of a crystal, the scent of a lily, and ultimately the sense of 'patience, serenity, and reciprocal forgiveness' produced by a chance exchange of glances with a cat. This turn away from the human and subjective calls to mind the words of a thinker who is often defined in contrast to Lévi-Strauss, that is, Gilles Deleuze. There is a distinction to be made of course between these two thinkers, but it is far from simple. Something of it comes through, however, in the following passage, taken from a series of interviews of Deleuze conducted by Claire Parnet. In it, Deleuze formulates a response that in fact does not contradict so much as it intensifies and displaces the conclusion of Lévi-Strauss's impassioned critique, in part by retrieving something of the potentiality of art, in its capacity to reveal other perspectives and other forms of resistance to the entropic tendencies of humanity:

I think that the man who said it, the writer who said it most profoundly is Primo Levi. He said, 'when I was liberated, what dominated was the shame of being a man.' So, that's a phrase that's both incredibly splendid, I believe, very beautiful, and [...] it's not abstract. The shame of being human is very concrete. But it does not mean all of the nonsense that it's been made to mean [...] it doesn't mean that we're all assassins. It doesn't mean that we're all guilty. [...] I think that, at the basis of art, there is the idea, or the very vivid sentiment, a certain shame at being human, which makes art then consist in liberating the life that man has imprisoned. Humanity never ceases to imprison life. It never ceases to kill life. The shame of being human. The artist is one who liberates a life, a powerful life, a life that is more than personal. It is not his life. Liberating life, liberating life from the prisons that man [...] that's resisting. That's what resisting is [...] it is, we can see it clearly in what artists do, I mean, there is no art that is not a liberation of a potency of life. There is no art of death for a start.[10]

Epilogue

There is a phrase I wanted to use to describe the interaction between the works on view in this exhibition. It is *disparate harmonies*. The art of negotiating entropy is an art of disparate harmonies.

1 Claude Elwood Shannon (1916–2001). American mathematician, electrical engineer and cryptographer, known as 'the father of information theory'.
2 John von Neumann (1903–1957). Mathematician, physicist, computer scientist, engineer.
3 Claude Shannon, 'A Mathematical Theory of Communication'. *The Bell System Technical Journal*, Vol. 27, 623–656, July, October, 1948, p. 623.
4 David Claerbout, 'The Silence of the Lens', *e-flux Journal*, Issue #73, May 2016, at https://www.e-flux.com/journal/73/60460/the-silence-of-the-lens/
5 Claude Lévi-Strauss (1908–2009), *Entretiens avec Georges Charbonnier*. Paris: Belles Lettres, 2017, p. 34. Quoted text translated by Julien Bismuth.
6 Walter Benjamin (1892–1940), German philosopher, cultural critic and writer.
7 Emma Coronel, wife of the infamous El Chapo, is a former beauty pageant winner, and numerous other incidents have revealed the close and complex ties between these pageants and the cartels. https://www.washingtonpost.com/news/morning-mix/wp/2016/08/10/miss-world-mexico-pageant-director-abducted-shot-dead-in-targeted-sinaloa-attack/
8 Isabelle Stengers, *Résister au désastre*. Paris: Wildproject, 2019, p. 34. Quoted text translated by Julien Bismuth.
9 Claude Lévi-Strauss, *Tristes Tropiques*. Paris: Plon, 1955, p. 496. Quoted text translated by Julien Bismuth.
10 Gilles Deleuze and Claire Parnet, 'R comme Résistance' in *Abécédaire*. Quoted text translated by Julien Bismuth.

Julien Bismuth is an artist and writer, currently living and working in New York.

The Hole

Tom Morton

Miss Clara Lambert, early as usual, stepped briskly across the green towards her low red schoolhouse, where she had taught the children of the small village of Brightbury these past seven years. While the morning sun promised that the day would be warm, feeling closer to summer than late September, it had not yet steamed the dew from the grass, and she was pleased that she had taken the precaution of wearing her thick leather boots.

As she neared the centre of the green, Clara's thoughts of her first lesson – and of young Rory Rawlinson's struggles with the letter 'r', which he would always pronounce as a soft wet 'w' – were interrupted by an unexpected sight. A few steps ahead of her was a hole, perhaps a yard wide.

She was sure it had not been there before. Clara crossed the green at least twice daily, often enough that its features – the church on its east side, the inn on its west, the oak stump that clung to the grass a short way from the hole – were as familiar to her as those of her own neatly pretty face. Hoisting her skirts, careful not to trip, she moved towards the hole, and took a closer look.

Clara encouraged her students to believe in the evidence of their own eyes. This, she told them, was the basis of all knowledge worthy of that name. Trust only in what could be observed, verified, measured – otherwise, what separates you from those dull, suspicious folk who imagine there is a sprite in every hedgerow, an augury in every magpie or falling star? Nevertheless, there on the green, peering down towards her feet, it was a principle she found difficult to apply.

Her eyes told her that the hole was round – no, not just round but perfectly circular – and so intensely, irresistibly dark that the autumn sun, strong as it was, failed to illuminate even the first fraction of its depth. No tool she knew of could dig with such precision. No void she'd ever encountered admitted so little light. Somehow, it felt less like an empty space than a substance, even an object. A spill of oil, of ink. An ancient mirror, blinded by tarnish, its silvery backing oxidized to an unremitting black.

At the same time, something within her protested this image, redrafting it as a shallow, rough-edged pit, dug with a blunt shovel and rimmed with turned earth, in which pink worms – she could see them clearly now – flexed, probed and shuddered, appalled by the glare and space of the surface world. Clara closed her eyes, opened them, and the perfect circle reasserted itself. Another blink, and she was looking at the worms again. Try as she might, she could not fix the hole in her mind. She had an uneasy sense that, having been discovered, it would rather be forgotten, and if not forgotten, then carelessly ignored.

'Have you lost something? An earring perhaps?'

Relaxed, amused with itself, and accustomed to being listened to, the voice at Clara's shoulder belonged to Alexander Umber, the local squire and owner of a large hilltop estate overlooking the village. Unbidden, her hand travelled to her left earlobe, squeezed the plump, unpierced flesh.

Receiving no further response, Umber coughed once, twice, and finally touched Clara just above her elbow.

'Miss Lambert, are you quite all right?'

'Ah, Mr Umber, it's you. I was just examining—' She gestured towards the hole. 'It seems to have appeared overnight. Surely it isn't the work of an animal?'

'Indeed not, dear lady. If only! A rabbit of that size would feed one of our village families for a week. Allow me to inspect it.'

Umber moved forward, his right arm brushing momentarily against Clara's left. Bending at the waist, he glanced down into the hole, frowned, then prodded at it with his cane. Clara saw the tip disappear into immeasurable darkness. She saw it press into grey, pliant soil.

Seemingly satisfied, Umber straightened and said, 'Miss Lambert, when the burden of my estate allows, I spend my leisure hours in study. The wisdom of the ages, of course, but also our new sciences, which I think may guide us here. As you have suggested, no creature native to these parts digs so broad a burrow. Likewise, the geology of our landscape precludes the possibility that this is a sinkhole. Brightbury rests on a bed neither of limestone nor of chalk.

'I fancy that what we have here is the impact crater of a small meteorite – the skies were unusually lively last night – although the meteorite itself was, of course, reduced to dust when it struck the village green. Pity, I would have liked to keep it for my collection of curiosities. You must come up to the house to see them. Only last week, I acquired a narwhal's tooth, although my dealer in the city would have me believe it is a unicorn's horn.'

Clara regarded the squire – his glossy auburn whiskers, his square white teeth. It was said in the village that Alexander Umber would soon require a wife. It was said, too, that he admired Brightbury's young schoolmistress, that he found in her plain-speaking practical manner not a deficit of adornment, as many did, but rather a bracing charm. How Clara felt about this was not yet quite clear to her. Of all the things the squire possessed – lands, fortune, pleasing looks, a measure of dilettantish learning – the most abundant was his certainty, something she felt might answer her every question, or else swallow her whole.

Behind Umber, some distance away, several children began to make their way across the green. The Cole twins Jude and Jethro. Daisy Fletcher and Maisie Farrow. The unfortunate Rory Rawlinson, his red knees blazing on his thin, white legs. All at once, Clara imagined the boy slouching home from the schoolhouse, distractedly mumbling 'r, r, r' to himself, and stepping straight into the hole, his pale limbs disappearing into its dark mouth. She blinked. No, impossible. Surely the hole was barely a foot deep? The worst Rory could do was turn an ankle. She addressed the squire.

'Mr Umber, meteor crater or not, I believe this hole represents a danger to the children of our village. A trip, a fall. One of my students might sprain a wrist, break a tooth. I would feel so much more at peace if someone were to—'

'Fill it in? I'll set a couple of my men to it directly. Come lunchtime, you'll never know it was there. Now, you go off to your lessons. I'll make sure your pupils find their way to you without coming to any harm.'

Thanking him, Clara departed. A coy glance back over her shoulder, she knew, was what Mr Umber was hoping for, would push things on and up. But this was not her way, and besides, something had stirred a dim restiveness within her, a muffled animal instinct, so she walked forward, eyes fixed on the schoolhouse, into the new day.

All that morning, Clara found herself distracted by thoughts of her discovery. Setting her class a writing exercise that would keep them busy at their desks, she monitored the green from the schoolroom window, through which the hole appeared not as an opaque black disc, or a grey and earthy cavity, but as a slender, shadowy ellipse, some five yards from the oak stump.

As Mr Umber had promised, two men – the squire's hulking steward Phipps, and mute Will Cole, older brother to Jude and Jethro – duly arrived with a brimming barrow of earth and emptied it into the hole. From the puzzled looks on their faces, however, this quantity was insufficient to the task, and they soon loped off, and returned with a second load. This barrowful, too, proved inadequate, and so did the third, the fourth, the fifth. By the eighth load, their labours had attracted the attention of the village drunk, Old Eli Sullivan, who sat down on the stump to watch them as he slugged from a bottle of blackberry wine. Through his purpled lips, he offered up unwanted advice and brief bursts of rowdy song.

Returning from lunch, Clara put her class to work at their arithmetic books, and took up her station by the window. Now accompanied by Mr Umber, the men were once again wheeling the barrow across the green, which now held not a load of earth, but a great coil of jute rope. Shooing Old Eli from his seat, they tied one end to the stump, and the other around Will's slim waist. With Phipps taking up the slack – knees bent, the heels of his huge boots digging into the grass – and the squire issuing instructions, Will lowered himself into the hole. Old Eli watched intently.

Hand over massive hand, Phipps paid out the rope. It was slow work, but as the seconds turned to minutes, and the steward still showed no signs of stopping, Clara began to wonder just how deep Will had descended, how much longer it might take before he reached the bottom of the hole, and stood gazing up towards a distant circle of blue, cloudless sky.

But then Phipps stumbled.

The rope fell from his grasp, and with sickening speed it was yanked across the grass by the weight of Will's body. Clara watched helplessly as yard after yard of slack whipped by, vanishing into the hole's dark, implacable throat. Stretched to the very limit of its length, its fibres straining against the intransigent stump, the rope at last grew taut, thrumming and then stilling like a struck piano string.

Umber raced towards the hole, followed by Old Eli and the winded, grass-stained Phipps. As the three men stared down into its depths, Clara heard a small, humid voice issue from her schoolroom. Rory Rawlinson.

Ignoring the boy, she kept on looking out over the green. The tautness of the rope meant that Will was still suspended from its other end, that he had not fallen the full depth of the hole, smashing himself into a paste of meat and bone and hair. The shock of his sudden plummet might have stopped another young man's heart, but Clara knew Will from his time as her student, and something – perhaps his dead tongue, silent from birth – had gifted him an uncommon resilience. He would emerge shaken, yes, but otherwise entire. And yet, something still troubled her. The rope was, what, at least twenty yards long. How deep then was the hole?

A tug at her sleeve.

'Miss, Miss. I've finished my arithmetic.'

That wet 'w' sound. Rory could have simply said maths, but the boy really was a trier.

Clara turned back to her class.

An hour later, the bell rang, and having instructed her students to walk the long way home today ('I'm sure you would not wish to disturb the squire's men at their work.'), Clara left the schoolhouse, and hurried to the centre of the green.

Will Cole sat slumped against the barrow, his dark eyes staring straight ahead. The squire paced around the hole, his face puckered with irritation, now and then muttering something inaudible to Phipps, while Old Eli, back on the stump, blew a low, solemn note over the lip of his bottle.

'Oh, for heaven's sake stop making that noise, man!' barked Umber.

Spotting Clara, he quickly composed himself.

'Miss Lambert. Young Will here took a closer look at our hole, and it appears it's a little deeper than we bargained for. Now, I've thought it over, and tomorrow morning I'll see to it that a fence is placed around its perimeter. That should make it safe for your children until we can find a more permanent solution. For tonight, duckboards will have to suffice. My man Phipps was just on his way to fetch some planks.'

The steward glanced towards the barrow, and Will's unstirring form.

Clara was just about to thank Phipps for his efforts, when from the stump Old Eli spoke. His voice was firm, deliberate, yet unmistakably slurred.

'No need for duckboards, Sir – and Miss. Old Eli will keep a watch on things this night through.'

'But you're—' Umber did not want to say the word drunk to his face, at least not in front of a lady. 'What I mean to say is, won't you fall asleep?'

'Reckon I can wait out the morning. Got my grog to keep me warm.'

'That's very gracious of you, Mr Sullivan', said Clara. It was one of her articles of faith that chances should be given, that people – adults as well as children – would rise to her good opinion. Besides, Old Eli had proved himself useful to the village on more than one occasion. Chasing crows from the fields for a handful of coins, suggesting remedies for minor ailments (thyme tea for coughs, cherries for gout), finding Maisie and Daisy that time they'd got lost in the woods.

'Well,' said Umber doubtfully, 'that's settled. Thank you, Eli. Um, Mr Sullivan. Phipps, Will – I think that's enough for today.

The potato harvest begins tomorrow, so get some rest. Miss Lambert, may I walk you home?'

Without waiting for a response, the squire took Clara's arm, and steered her across the green. Behind her, she heard Old Eli blow another note across the top of his bottle, low and long.

When Clara awoke the next morning, the sun through her thin curtains was unusually high in the sky, and she realised, with mounting panic, that she had overslept. Hurrying across the green towards the schoolhouse, where several of her students were already milling about its doors, she saw Mr Umber and Phipps driving thick, wooden fenceposts into the ground around the hole. Slowing to a stop, it seemed to her that the black disc – right then, that's what it was – had grown during the night, its diameter now spanning close to a yard and a half. Old Eli was nowhere to be seen. The only sign of him was a drained bottle of blackberry wine, standing upright on the stump.

'Looks like our sentinel abandoned his station,' said Umber, mallet in hand. 'Probably crawled off to one of my barns to sleep off last night's debauch. Or maybe he decided to head south for the winter early this year. When there's frost on the ground, Brightbury's no place for a man without a hearth to call his own. Poor devil. Drink's a terrible mistress.'

Clara was about to ask if there wasn't a chance that Old Eli might have taken an inebriated stumble into the hole, but something stopped her. Partly, it was the squire's confidence in his own hypothesis, and the blithe way he stood so close to the hole's edge. Then there was the fact that the thought of Eli – of anybody – disappearing into that beckoning darkness was one her mind refused again to fully countenance. Somehow, it felt that to follow it to the end would be to will it to happen, would admit it from the chaos of the imagination into the village's calm well-ordered reality.

So, instead, she said, 'You and your steward are to be congratulated on your industry, Mr Umber.'

'Yes, dear lady. Soon have this up. I fear it might be a rather unsightly addition to our village. But, as you so wisely reminded me yesterday, the safety of our young folk is paramount.'

Clara looked at the squire, handsome in his shirt sleeves. Was his participation in putting up the fence a little pantomime, played for her benefit – a sign of how highly he valued her good graces? Alexander Umber, after all, was not known for getting his hands dirty with physical labour. Perhaps it was wrong to flatter herself so. Nevertheless, it was a pleasant thought.

'I do believe you have given me an idea, Mr Umber. I must make haste to my class, but if you can spare me a moment tomorrow after school, I'll be waiting here with a surprise for you.'

'Gladly, Miss Lambert.'

Umber struck his post with another blow from his mallet. Smiling, Clara bade him good morning, and set off across the green.

By midday, the squire's work was done, and he and his steward departed. True to Umber's word, the fence was not attractive. Taller even than the looming Phipps, and starkly utilitarian in design, it resembled a military fortification, or the pen of some captured, feral beast. Still, it seemed sturdy enough, and its appearance was something Clara planned to change.

Leading her class out of the village to the woods and hedgerows beyond, she had them gather great armfuls of autumn wildflowers – teasels and devil's bit, sneezewort and pennyroyals – with which to adorn the fence. The result was – Clara told herself as Maisie Farrow fixed the last stem of yellow toadflax in place – pleasing, and the children had seemed unbothered by the sudden appearance of the hole, accepting her assurances that it was nothing to worry about, was perfectly normal, just nature unfolding another of its knowable mysteries.

Only Rory Rawlinson appeared in any way perturbed, but perhaps that had more than anything to do with the nettle stings he'd suffered during the afternoon's gleaning. He would crash so recklessly through the woods, never looking where he was going, and with his short trousers, what else could he expect?

When Mr Umber joined them at the end of the school day, he was all smiles. Passing among the children – ruffling hair, handing out pennies – he had the air of a man for whom a troubling question had been decisively resolved, and all in his favour.

'Why Miss Lambert,' he said, as the last of Clara's students skipped off across the green, 'it's as though this little puncture in our world was never there at all.'

That night, attending to her needlework in her cottage across the green from the schoolhouse, Clara's thoughts turned to the fence, and how sorry it would look when its covering of wildflowers faded and died. Winter was coming, and soon the countryside would be bare and colourless, and she would have to think of some other way of masking the severity of Mr Umber's construction. A coat of cheerful paint, perhaps? Or hang its posts with corn dollies? That would certainly be a good project for her class.

Rising, she opened her front door, and looked out over the moonlit green. A dog was sniffing at the fence, the village innkeeper's spaniel Nelly, nosing out information among the stink of cut teasels. Satisfied, Nelly turned, cocked a leg, and began urinating against the fence. But her arcing stream met no resistance. Right before Clara's eyes, in the time it took to blink, the fence had fallen clean out of sight.

With a yelp, Nelly scrambled away from the hole, and began barking wildly. No creak or crash had accompanied the fence's disappearance. It had been subtracted, silently and utterly, from the realm of visible things. Above, the moon beamed down, bright twin of the dark consuming disc at the centre of the green. Throwing on a heavy shawl, Clara ran out.

Responding to Nelly's protestations, a second dog began to bark, over by the church. Soon, every dog in Brightbury was howling, a chorus of animal panic urging itself on to greater and greater volume as though, if it only grew loud enough, big enough, blared out every thought, it might prevail against the unknown, unseen threat.

Driven from their tankards by the noise, people came pouring out of the inn, among them – Clara noted – the grave-faced figure of Mr Umber. Seeing that the fence had vanished, they gathered around the hole, staring, pointing, shouting out in bafflement and fear. Finally, the dogs began to quiet. By the time Clara reached them, the innkeeper had led Nelly off by her collar, trailing her last, desolate whimpers behind her, and the squire was addressing the crowd.

'. . . So, there it is. Really nothing to worry about. Return to your ale. I'll join you shortly. The next round is on me.'

The people began to walk back to the inn. Whatever Mr Umber had said had pacified them, at least for tonight, and they seemed cheered by the promise of a free drink, but still, now and then they stole a look back at the green and murmured uneasily to one another in the crisp autumn air.

Noticing Clara's arrival, the squire said, 'A cold night to be walking the village, Miss Lambert, even in that cosy shawl. It seems you've caught me on one of the rare occasions I look in at the Crossed Keys. Good to show my face once in a while, I'm sure you understand. I gather you saw—' He nodded at the hole.

'Yes, Mr Umber. Our fence has gone, and the hole appears to be growing.'

The squire smiled. He had, thought Clara, a certain innocence. Or at least a belief that he couldn't be hurt. She glanced sideways at where the fence had once stood, only minutes before. Black disc. Grey cavity.

'The question is when will it stop? It's already nearly a yard wider than it was this morning. At this rate—' She paused, performed the mental calculation. 'Well, the green is two square acres, give or take, so by Christmas it will be nothing but a crater. Come Lent, the village will be swallowed whole.'

'Bless you, Miss Lambert, always the schoolteacher! My governess used to set me problems like that when I was a boy. If a dairymaid has a bucket of such and such dimensions, and a cow that gives so much milk a day . . . well, I forget the rest, but I suspect it comes down to the strength of her grip. No, I'm afraid all this is a result of my shoddy workmanship. Put the posts in too close to the edge, in loose soil, and the whole thing collapsed in on itself, along with those delightful flowers. Serves me right for trying to impress a lady.'

Clara blushed. Irritated with herself, she glanced at the hole again. There was something almost cleansing about the intensity of its darkness. Black disc. Black disc. Her next words came out harder and hotter than she intended.

'Mr Umber, you have the great gift of a plausible bearing. Nevertheless, I am an educated person, with eyes in my head, and while my prognosis was extreme, and in time may well be proved false, I know as well as you do that this is not simply a case of a few misplaced fenceposts. I insist that you call a village meeting where this matter can be discussed frankly and in full. More than that, I demand that you present the people of Brightbury with a plan for the coming days and weeks. They look to you for leadership, Mr Umber, and it is my fervent hope that you will provide it before panic grips the village, and every man, woman and child is howling like those dogs.'

Moonlight shone down on the squire's bland, handsome face. Whatever he was feeling – astonishment, fury, even perhaps an odd arousal at her impertinence – he was keeping it in check.

Umber held Clara's gaze for a long, searching moment, then gave a sudden laugh.

'Miss Lambert, you are quite correct. We need to look this thing straight in the eye. Honesty, that's what is called for. Honesty and action. Now, can I offer you something warming at the Crossed Keys to take the chill off? Not in the public bar, of course, but the saloon is perfectly respectable, even on a Friday night. We can discuss what

I'm going to say at this meeting. I have long thought you the most clear-headed person in Brightbury. I am sure that you will help me find the right words.'

As they walked towards the inn's amber lights, Clara considered asking the squire what he saw when he looked into the hole. Was it the same restless, mutable form that flashed across her eyes, her mind, or was it something stable, ordinary, really no different from any other (how did he put it?) puncture in the world. And yet, his arm in hers, so warm, so sure of itself, the question died on her lips.

Still, there remained something fiercely urgent within her that demanded to be answered – or obliterated. When they had finished shaping Umber's speech for the village meeting – both of them giddy with the realisation that these words, delivered in this tone, were the only ones that would do – he walked with her to her door, and asked if he might kiss her. Clara closed her eyes.

Cavity. Cavity.

Then she told him yes.

By next morning, the hole had swallowed the oak stump.

Held in the church, the meeting began in an atmosphere of fractious accusation. A veteran infantryman claimed the hole was a plot by foreign powers. Daisy's mother, Ma Fletcher, stood up to say that this was what happened when good people neglected their faith. The innkeeper told how his dog Nelly now refused all food, yes even a chop from his own table. Will Cole's uncle bellowed that since Will's misadventure in the hole, his nephew would stay awake all night, a candle burning at his bedside. Only when the sun rose would the lad finally close his eyes and even then he was plagued by bad dreams, screaming silently into his pillow at the terrible darkness in his head.

When the villagers had finally exhausted themselves, Mr Umber got up to speak. Seated beside him, Clara cast her mind back to what she had told him at the inn. *Think of them as children. What children need isn't the truth – nobody knows that anyway, not about this – but reassurance. As long as they feel there are adults in place who've got the measure of things – that's you and me, Alex – they'll accept just about any situation. What they want is a good reason not to think about it. Take it from me as a schoolteacher.* And he had.

Spreading his hands, the squire said, 'Thank you, friends, for sharing your feelings with us here today. I must confess that I, too, was momentarily alarmed. But then it came to me. Everything in creation has its natural limit, which it does not – it cannot – outgrow.

A bean sends up a stalk, true, but it is only in fairy tales that it penetrates the clouds. An infant might develop into a great burly fellow, like my steward Phipps, there.' Umber gestured towards him, to scattered laughter, then continued. 'But into a giant? No. There is nothing in this world, after all, too big for it to comfortably contain.

'My point is that while the hole in our green is, uh, expanding, this is only its current course, and one that may in time reverse. Why, if you'll forgive my cheek, there are those among us now, advanced in years no less than wisdom, who lately appear to be shrinking!'

Umber bowed gallantly towards the village's only nonagenarian, the tiny, wrinkled Widow Pugh. There was more laughter. He had warmed them up. Now, the big finish.

'The plain fact of the matter is that while the hole is in its, ah, dynamic phase, putting up a second fence only risks wasting good timber. So, what should we do? The answer, friends, is to monitor the situation – our estimable schoolteacher Miss Lambert has volunteered for the task – and to continue as normal, as best we can. We are all aware of the potential dangers the hole poses at present, and we are all, when it comes down to it, capable of making the right choices to keep ourselves and our families safe.

'Yes, you should avoid the hole. Avoid the whole green for now, if that feels right for you. But ask yourself – ask the doughty Widow Pugh – has Brightbury never weathered a passing storm before? Have we not come – together – through droughts, through floods, through fire? I look around me, and here we all are. Friends, we cannot allow this . . . this temporary phenomenon to disrupt our way of life!'

For a moment, there was silence, and then the cheers started.

Umber sat down. Clara squeezed his hand.

'I feel rather empty,' he said. 'Live with it. Is that really all there is to say?'

'Yes,' said Clara. 'What else can we do?'

For most inhabitants of the village, living with the hole meant – while never wholly forgetting it was there – pushing it to the back of their conscious minds, which was in some senses surprisingly easy to do. Level with the flat green, from the right distance it presented little to the eye, and as September gave way to October, and social life disappeared indoors for the rest of the year, there were no cricket matches for it to mar, no picnics it might spoil. Yes, there was still the forthcoming winter fair to consider – some time ago, Mr Umber had promised a travelling circus would pitch up on the green this year, a keenly anticipated treat that now seemed in doubt. Yet, perhaps by then the hole would, as the squire suggested, have reached its manageable maturity.

Then there were the villagers who discovered that the hole, for all its inconvenience and sullen threat, had at least one use – as a place to dispose of unwanted things. Into its broad nothingness were tipped the contents of commodes, a dead goat fallen to blackleg, even the wedding ring of the village carpenter, Ned Tuttle, after he discovered his wife had cuckolded him with the blacksmith.

It was speculated that plump, blubbering Ned might soon throw himself, or his rival, after his tarnished gold band, but this proved wide of the mark. The Tuttles came to an accommodation, and the blacksmith moved into their cottage. Soon the three of them were walking about grinning like newly-weds. In earlier times, this would have provoked widespread public censure, but since the meeting there was a new, if still intangible spirit abroad in Brightbury. When Ma Fletcher made a disapproving remark about the trio one Sunday after church, the Widow Pugh was heard to tell her, *Oh hush now. Life is short, let them enjoy it while they can.*

All the while, and as Mr Umber had pledged, Clara tracked the hole's growth. This she did by placing large white pebbles at one-yard intervals from its edge, stretching in a line to the north corner of the green. Clara checked these markers every morning on her way to the schoolhouse, and after a few days discovered that there was no discernible pattern to the hole's expansion. One morning, it had grown by less than a quarter of a yard, the next by almost two (swallowing a pebble), and the next by nothing at all. In her tidy script, she posted a record of each day's findings on the noticeboard outside the church, where anybody might consult them, although after a week it was only Alexander Umber who appeared to do so with any regularity.

What contributory factors accounted for a period of rapid or paused acceleration? Weather conditions? The swellings of a subterranean river? The grinding together of continental plates? Really, Clara supposed it could be almost anything, excepting the prayers Ma Fletcher sent up into the sky, beseeching her lord and saviour to tame His unruly Earth.

One Saturday, lunching with the squire in the saloon bar of the inn, it occurred to Clara that it would be all too easy for some mischief-maker to move her pebbles when she wasn't looking – placing, say, those near the green's north corner incrementally closer together, and those near the hole a little further apart – giving her a false reading. But then again, as Mr Umber had argued, who would this profit? The villagers were all in this together, whatever *this* actually was.

By the first day of December, the hole could have easily accommodated the little red schoolhouse – indeed, any of Brightbury's buildings save the inn, the church, Mr Umber's barns and his home up on the hill. According to Clara's calculations, it grew no further on the second day of the month, nor the third or fourth, and on the fifth she reported, having checked her measurements twice over, that it had apparently contracted by a yard and a half. Three more days of contractions followed, and while these were more modest, they nevertheless confirmed a promising trend – the hole was gradually closing up. Umber was delighted, and quickly called another village meeting to announce the good news. There and then, among jubilant celebrations, it was decided the winter fair would go ahead on the green as usual. The squire sent a notice of engagement to the travelling circus. To applause, Phipps gathered up Clara's pebbles in his barrow, and tipped them into the hole.

The day of the fair arrived. The inn's long trestle tables were hauled out on to the green, the villagers roasted chestnuts over crackling braziers and turned a fat hog on a spit, and the circus folk – with their harlequin costumes and dark, desert faces – arrived in their caravans, parking them in horseshoe formation around the hole. As Clara watched them ready themselves – the clowns applying their make-up, the fire-eaters gargling cold milk and tying back their hair – she felt carefree, truly carefree, for the first time in weeks. The black disc was gone. The grey cavity was filling itself in.

She wandered across the green in search of Mr Umber, finding him bobbing for apples in a barrel, surrounded by several of her class, who squealed in delight every time he plunged his sleek, auburn whiskers into the water. Emerging sodden, his mouth stoppered with fruit, he looked ridiculous, yes, but also heroic and triumphant. Rory Rawlinson stood beside the squire, holding his frock coat. The boy was making real progress with his speech. Yesterday, he had pronounced his own first name with only one wet 'w'.

Presently, the circus headman beat his gong, and the villagers began to assemble a short distance from the hole, which now had a long rope strung across its diameter – the same rope, if Clara was not mistaken, that Phipps had used to lower Will Cole into its depths. On the grassy stage of the green, tumblers turned their somersaults, jugglers spun their clubs, and a conjuror plucked a handkerchief from Mr Umber's breast pocket, made a complicated fold, then opened it to reveal a startled woodpigeon, which she released flapping into the air.

The gong sounded once more, and the headman announced the show's finale. On the far side of the hole, where the rope was staked to the cold earth, stood a girl, young enough to be one of Clara's pupils, dressed in white, her bare brown feet planted on the grass.

With a nod to the headman, she stretched out her arms, and took her first step along the rope's length, her toes gripping its fibres, her eyes staring straight ahead. Another step. The villagers held their breath. Two more. She was speeding up now, gathering momentum. Beneath her, the hole beckoned.

Cavity. Disc. Cavity.

Clara reached for Umber's hand.

The girl was almost halfway across when Clara became aware of a commotion behind her. Turning, she saw mute Will Cole stumbling his way through the crowd, his face bleary, a stained nightgown flapping around his bare, bony ankles. The girl's eyes flickered, her steps slowed to a stop, her brown toes gripped the rope so hard they turned white. Nearing the front, Will lunged forward, waving his arms, mouthing silent syllables, but Phipps blocked his path.

'Lad's not been sleeping,' said the steward, pulling Will towards his massive chest. 'Enough to give anybody a turn, that. Come on now, let's get you home to bed.'

For a moment, Will struggled. Then, the last of his energy seemingly expended, he went limp in Phipps' arms, and allowed himself to be bundled, not unkindly, back through the parting spectators. Umber frowned, then nodded. The circus girl closed her eyes, opened them, and walked on.

As she stepped off the near end of the rope, and gave a dainty curtsy, the crowd erupted into cheers. Wives and husbands hugged one another. Children crammed their mouths with chestnuts, and cried happy tears. It was as though it was not this foreign girl at all, but rather the whole village who had faced down their fears, and passed through danger to a place of greater safety. Mr Umber ordered the innkeeper to fetch out a fresh barrel of ale. As the crowd broke off, and headed towards the trestle tables, Clara saw the squire pass a heavy bag of coins to the circus headman. The girl –

was it his daughter? – was slipping her bare feet into a pair of shoes.

Setting a teacherly smile on her face, Clara approached her.

'That was very brave, what you just did.'

The girl glanced up. Her eyes were not the eyes of a Maisie, a Daisy. They were as strange and old as the stars. Getting no response, Clara continued.

'I'm sorry, perhaps you don't speak my language. Only I was wondering, how do you bear it? The fear I mean. I suppose the trick is not to look down.'

The girl pulled at a shoelace. Grunted.

'I understand what you are saying. No, you can look down, if you like. The trick is to persuade yourself there's nothing there.'

That night, the village went to bed late, with swimming heads and mouths smeared with hog's grease.

By dawn, all that remained of the circus folk were the tracks of their caravan wheels, pressed into the grass around the hole.

At seven o'clock, Will Cole's younger brothers noticed he was missing from his bed. At ten, Phipps found him hanged from a beam in Mr Umber's hayloft. Silent to the last, Will left no note.

Three days later, Will's funeral service was interrupted by the reappearance of Old Eli. Dressed in fine clothes, looking ten years younger and vigorously sober, he threw open the church doors, marched down the aisle past the pews of mourners, took to the pulpit and proclaimed in a bright, steady voice that he had returned to the village with a wonderful message. The hole had called him to its depths, and then the hole had delivered him back to the village, transformed. There were riches down there, beyond their wildest imaginings, if only they were brave enough to claim them. Clarity. Truth. A new and abundant life.

Will, Eli said, had been called too. That's why he volunteered to go down there on that rope. But that was the coward's way, and the hole has its own plan for cowards. Live in fear, die in fear. You want to rise up with its treasures? First you've got to let yourself fall.

As the mourners stared in numb disbelief, Eli descended from the pulpit, marched back down the aisle and out of the church door. Jude and Jethro let out twin howls, and Will's uncle staggered up from his pew, fists bunched, his cheeks plum with rage. Umber appealed for calm, and sent Phipps out after Eli, but the man was nowhere to be found. He would not be seen in the village again.

In the days that followed, there were more disappearances. The Widow Pugh. The whole Fletcher family. The innkeeper and his dog. The remaining villagers told themselves there were ordinary reasons for all this. Hadn't there been an invitation from distant relatives, talk of a pilgrimage, some business about unpaid tax? Publicly, Clara nodded along in agreement, but alone in her bed one night, she began to nurse a private doubt. If the hole was closing – slowly, yes, but surely – then so too was the possibility of emulating Old Eli's apparent rebirth.

She imagined throwing herself into that black nothing, falling for what felt like forever, and then – what? Emerging in silks and gemstones, blissfully proclaiming that she finally saw the world as it really was, and that the world was good?

No, the drunkard's claims were absurd, she knew that, and so did her fellow villagers. Whatever personal disequilibrium was ultimately responsible for his rant in the church, or indeed for poor Will's suicide, it surely long predated the appearance of the hole. All that had done was tip the scales still further, leaving mania with no effective counterweight. Even if what Eli had said was somehow true, she would not be following him into the darkness. Alexander Umber had asked for her hand in marriage on the afternoon of the Cole boy's funeral, and that held its own, transformative promise.

Christmas came and went, and the New Year brought ferocious winds to the village, which blew across the fields and houses for hour after hour, day after day, ripping scarecrows from the earth, laundry from sagging washing lines, and sending the weathervane on the church spinning in an endless, exhausting cycle. Worst of all, the winds blew across the hole – now a seemingly stable eleven yards in diameter – sounding a low, insistent note that reverberated in the windows of every building, the bones and teeth of every man, woman and child. The villagers took to stuffing their ears with cotton, candlewax, gobbets of clay. Still the noise persisted. To Clara's mind, it resembled the sound made by Old Eli as he blew across the opening of his bottle, only hugely amplified, as though it were meant to wake dormant gods from their slumbers, and put them to new and terrifying work.

When news of this development reached the squire up at his manor house, he rode down to Brightbury and invited Clara to stay with him as his guest until the winds stopped. Over the hole's moans, she told him no, and explained he should be flattered. She was sure his intentions were nothing but honourable, but away from the village, her bed beneath his roof, she feared she could not refuse herself certain matrimonial pleasures before their wedding night. Besides, there was another consideration. To break ranks with her neighbours now, to pull the cotton from her ears and head to high, hushed ground – hadn't he said that the villagers were all in this together?

Mr Umber laughed, and said that since Ma Fletcher had taken off on her pilgrimage, Clara ranked as the most virtuous woman in Brightbury. She slapped him playfully on the chest, and said there was one small favour he might grant her. Teaching at the schoolhouse was impossible under these conditions. Might he allow her to relocate her class ('A temporary measure, that's all it is.') to his library?

Next morning, leading the children up the hill, battling against the winds, knowing that each step drew them further away from the hole and its ceaseless, maddening lowing, she imagined herself the prophet of some lost tribe, guiding them towards a promised land.

At the gates of the manor house, she was met by Phipps.

'Miss Lambert.'

'Yes,' she smiled, 'for a few weeks yet, and then I suppose I shall be Mrs Umber. I'm not sure I'll ever quite get used to that. Anyway. You've been told about the arrangement? My children, the library? Perhaps Mr Umber can spare them a few moments to give them a tour of the house's public rooms. They would be so grateful, and I've made sure all their hands are squeaky clean.'

'Mr Umber is not here, Miss. Nevertheless, he's left instructions that you will have the use of his library, until all this passes.'

Clara blinked. Alex had not told her he'd be away today.

'Remind me, when is your master returning?'

'Didn't say, Miss. Now, please follow me.'

Phipps led Clara and the line of village children up to the house, through the grand entrance hall, along long lamplit corridors and into the vaulted library. Already dazed by the squire's sweeping staircases, his moon-white statuary, his elegant furniture tottering on thin, gilded legs, her class stared open-mouthed at the great shelves of leathery volumes that reached up to the ceiling, the narwhal's tooth mounted on the chimney piece, the huge windows that looked out on to a terrace, and beyond that, to the distant village below. Clara had been here before – oh, those afternoons when she had wanted to lose herself completely, to feel every fence she had planted fall away – but never had she felt such a sense of possession. Glancing through the panes, she saw that the wind was still blowing dark clouds across the sky, but here in this sumptuous, muffled space, the hole's terrible music could not be heard.

'I'll take my leave,' said Phipps, and without waiting for an answer, walked out of the room.

At the centre of the library stood a long mahogany table, covered with books stacked in chaotic, teetering piles. Titles on geology, topography, and astronomy. Treatises on metaphysics. Volumes of myths. Heavy world atlases, and a cartographic survey of Brightbury and its surrounding region. Holy texts, major and minor. Knowledge old and new. Here and there, bookmarks protruded from between the pages. Clara allowed herself an indulgent little grin. Her gentleman scholar. Alexander must have forgotten to have his servants clear the table in preparation for their arrival. Well, her children would need it for their schoolwork.

'Class, we're going to begin by shelving Mr Umber's books. A demonstration of our gratitude for his kindness in allowing us to study here today. Now first, the natural sciences. Yes, that's right, the volumes over there.'

Would Alexander be annoyed at her presumption? Perhaps, but he'd be too gallant to show it. Anyway, when whatever frenzy of dilettantism he was currently experiencing abated, he'd see that having a well-ordered library was to his advantage.

'Not you, Rory,' she said to Rory Rawlinson, as the boy moved towards the table. 'Come sit with me by the window, and we'll work on your pronunciation. I think we're almost there, now. Just one more little push.'

The boy followed her to the window-seat. Gingerly, he sat down.

'Now then, repeat after me: *round and round the rugged rock . . .*'

An hour passed.

'*. . . the ragged rascal ran!*'

The boy sat back, staring at the space in front of him, as though marvelling at the sounds – the seven hard, rolling 'r's – that had issued from his mouth.

'Rory you've— you've done it! Oh, this is wonderful. And see that,' she said, feeling the warmth of a sunbeam on her cheek, filtering through the window behind her, 'the storm's finally turning. Let's step out on to the terrace. I think we've earned a stretch of our legs. Class, I'll be back in a moment. Please carry on quietly with your work.'

Outside, the weather had indeed improved. Bright, clear, windless, the only sound a distant cooing. It couldn't be, could it? The woodpigeon released by the circus conjuror?

Rory tugged at Clara's sleeve. Panicky little jerks.

'Miss, Miss, look down the hill. The village.'

Clara trained her gaze downwards. The green was gone, and then so was the inn and the church and the little red schoolhouse. The hole swallowed every cottage on her street, and the next, and the next. On it went, consuming yard after yard of ground, subtracting everything the villagers had ever built or cultivated, everything they'd ever cherished or despised. Still the black disc grew.

She scooped Rory up. Tears were coursing down the boy's cheeks. In all his young life, he'd never travelled more than a mile beyond Brightbury.

'There's no use running, is there, Miss?'

The hole had reached the bottom of the hill now. Clara wondered briefly where Alexander was. Sitting up last night in his library, had one of his books told him what was about to happen, or had he been granted some dark flash of intuition? Had he ridden for the green, determined to stare fate in its vast blind eye, or scurried off like a rat? Wherever he'd gone, it hadn't been to her, but the end result was just the same. Soon, there would be nowhere left to go.

'No, Rory, no use at all.'

'It's not fair, Miss Lambert. I'm not ready.'

Those hard 'r's. Clara smiled. Another distant coo, high up in the sky.

And then nothing.

And then the thing after that.

Tom Morton is a writer, curator and Contributing Editor for *frieze* magazine, based in Rochester, UK.

Works in the Exhibition

Darren Almond

Lives and works in London

01, 02, 03
In The Between, 2006
3-channel HD video with audio
14 min., 3 screens
Installation views at *Uncombed, Unforeseen, Unconstrained,* Conservatorio di Musica Benedetto Marcello, Venice, 2022

01

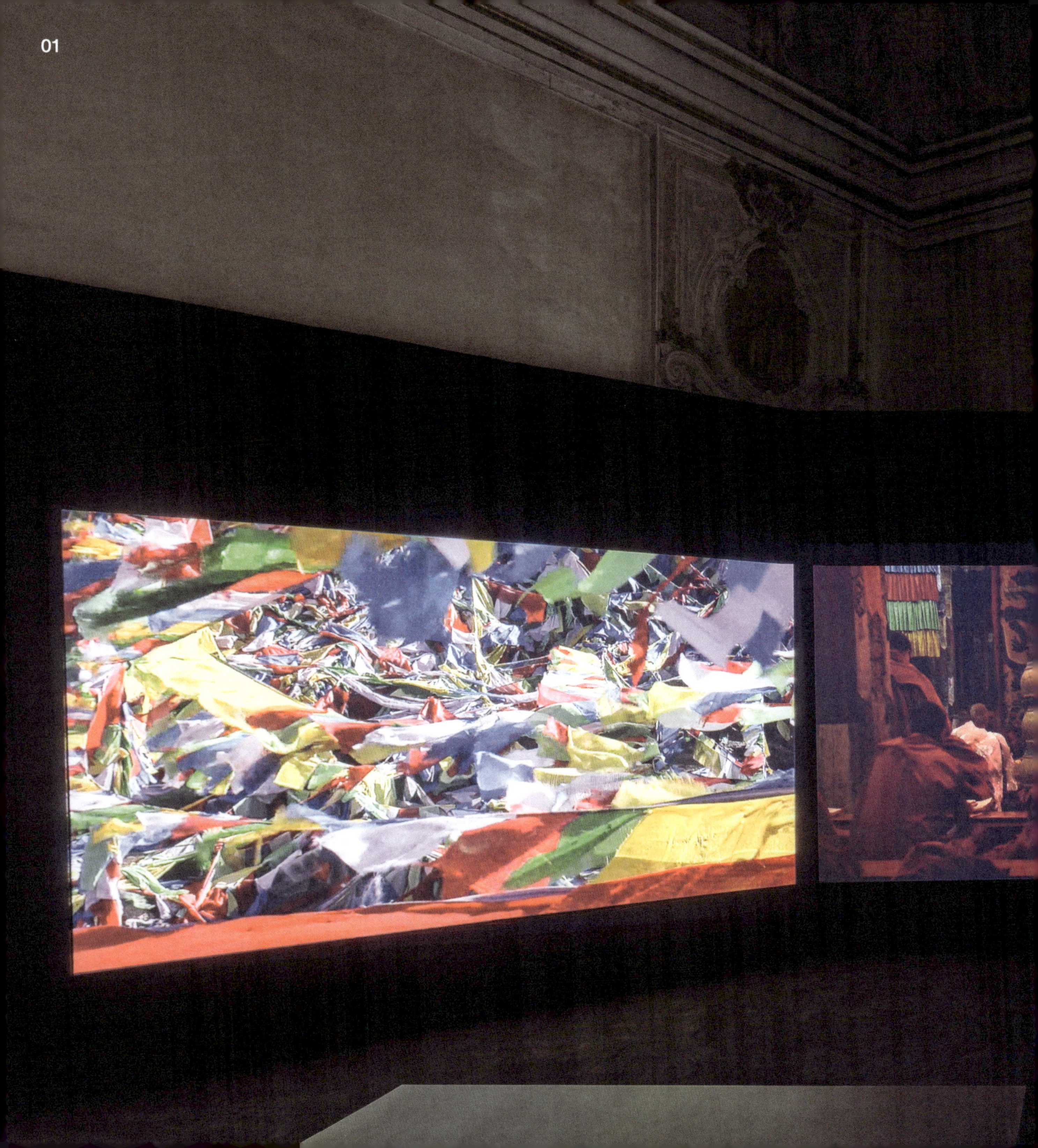

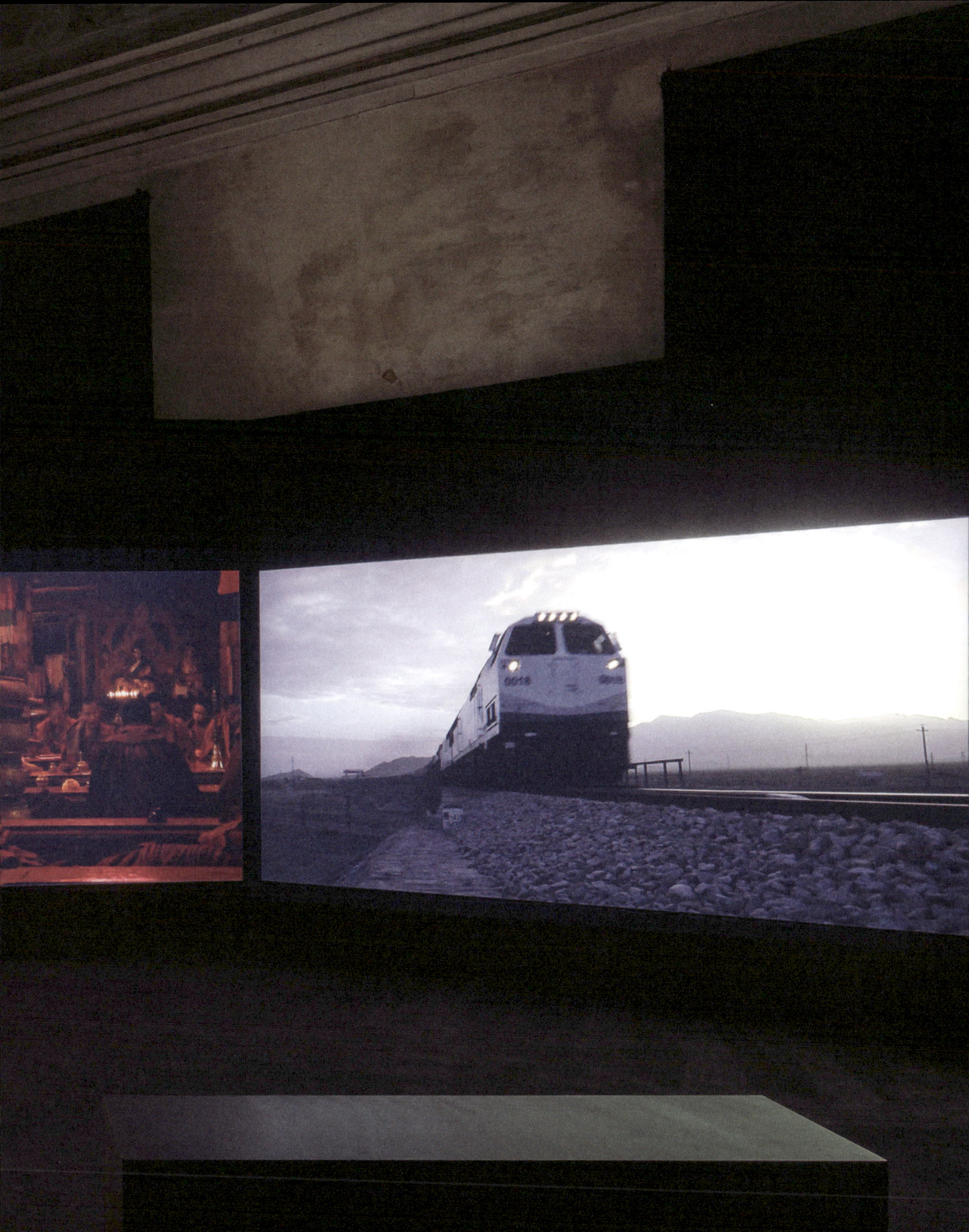

02

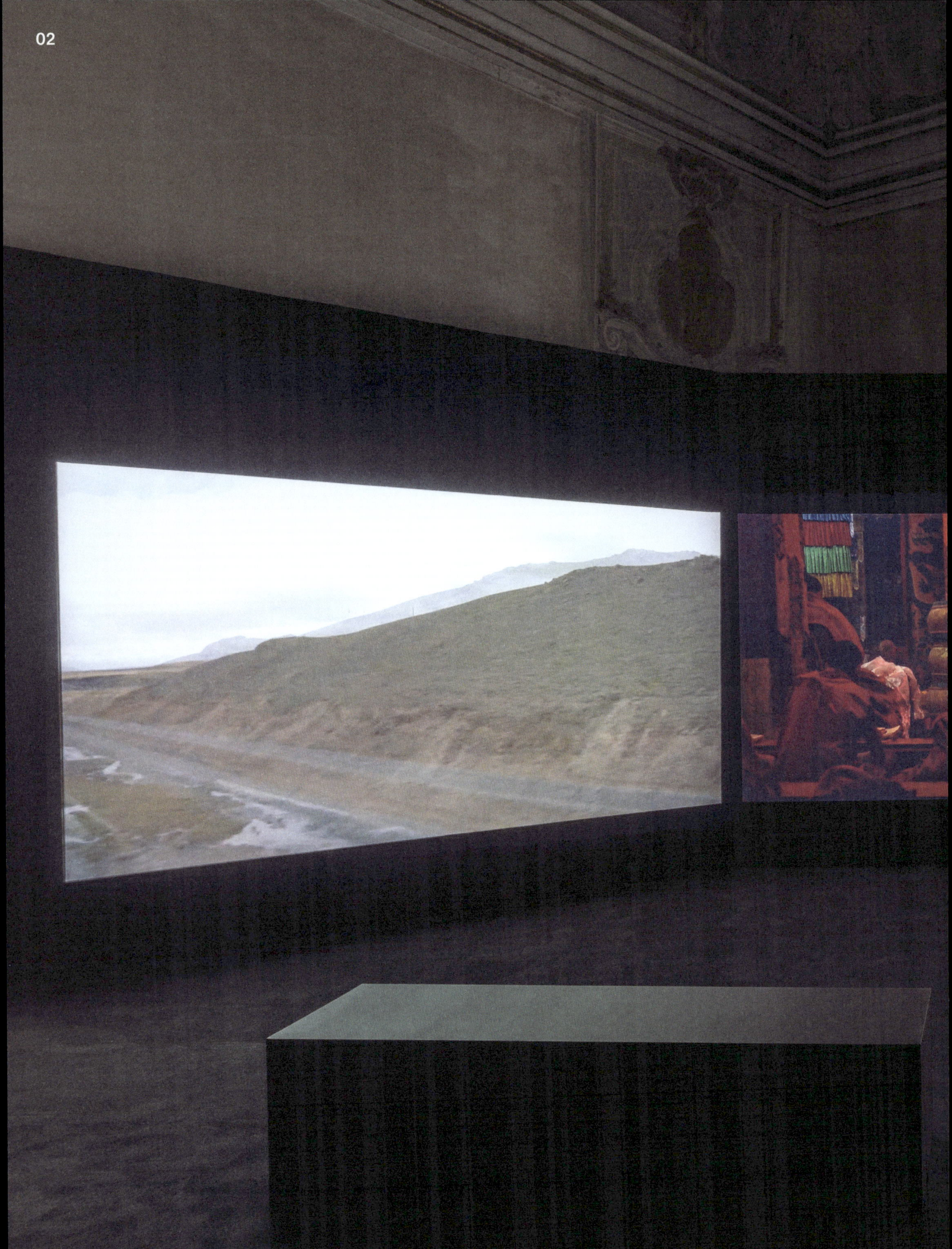

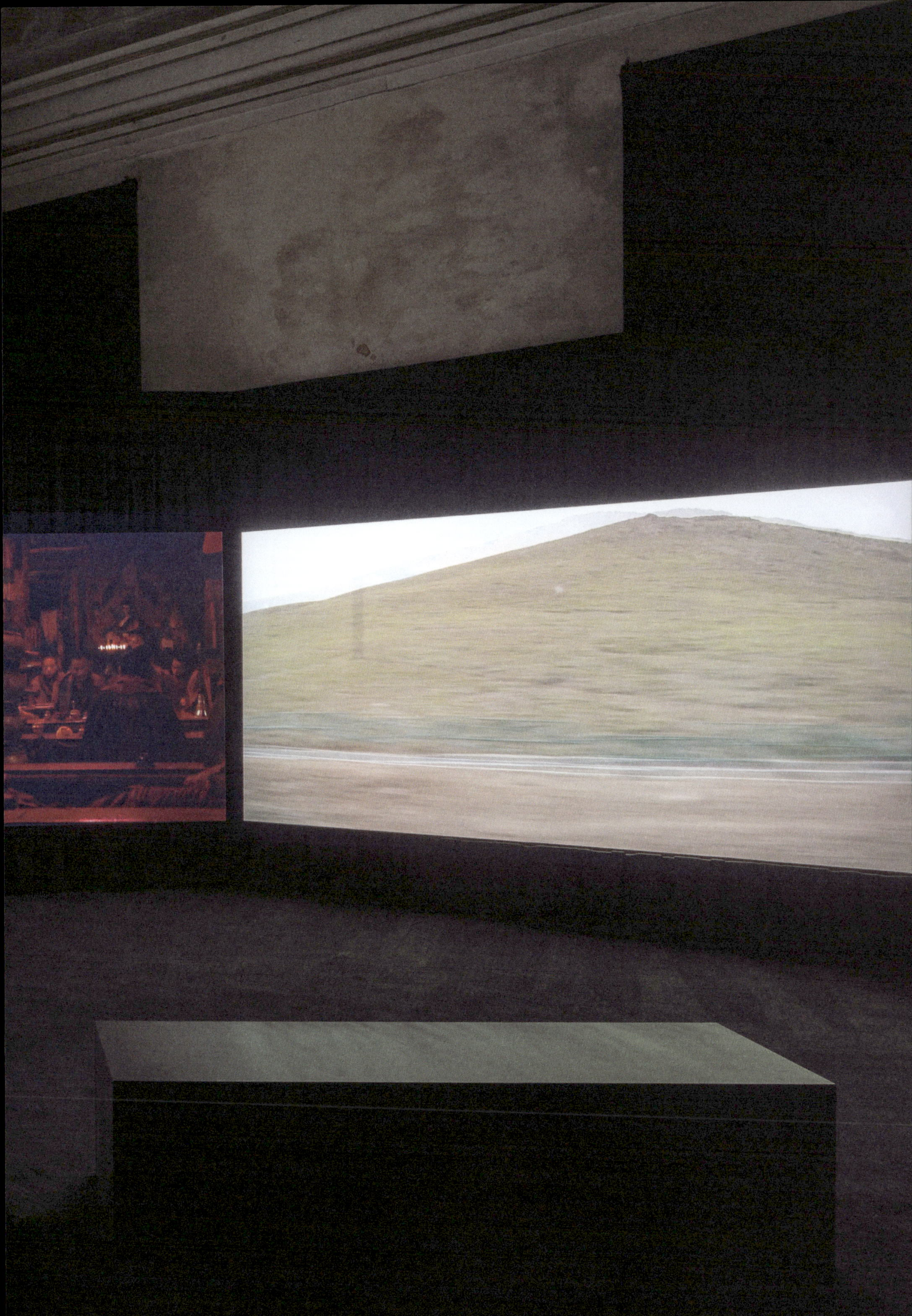

03

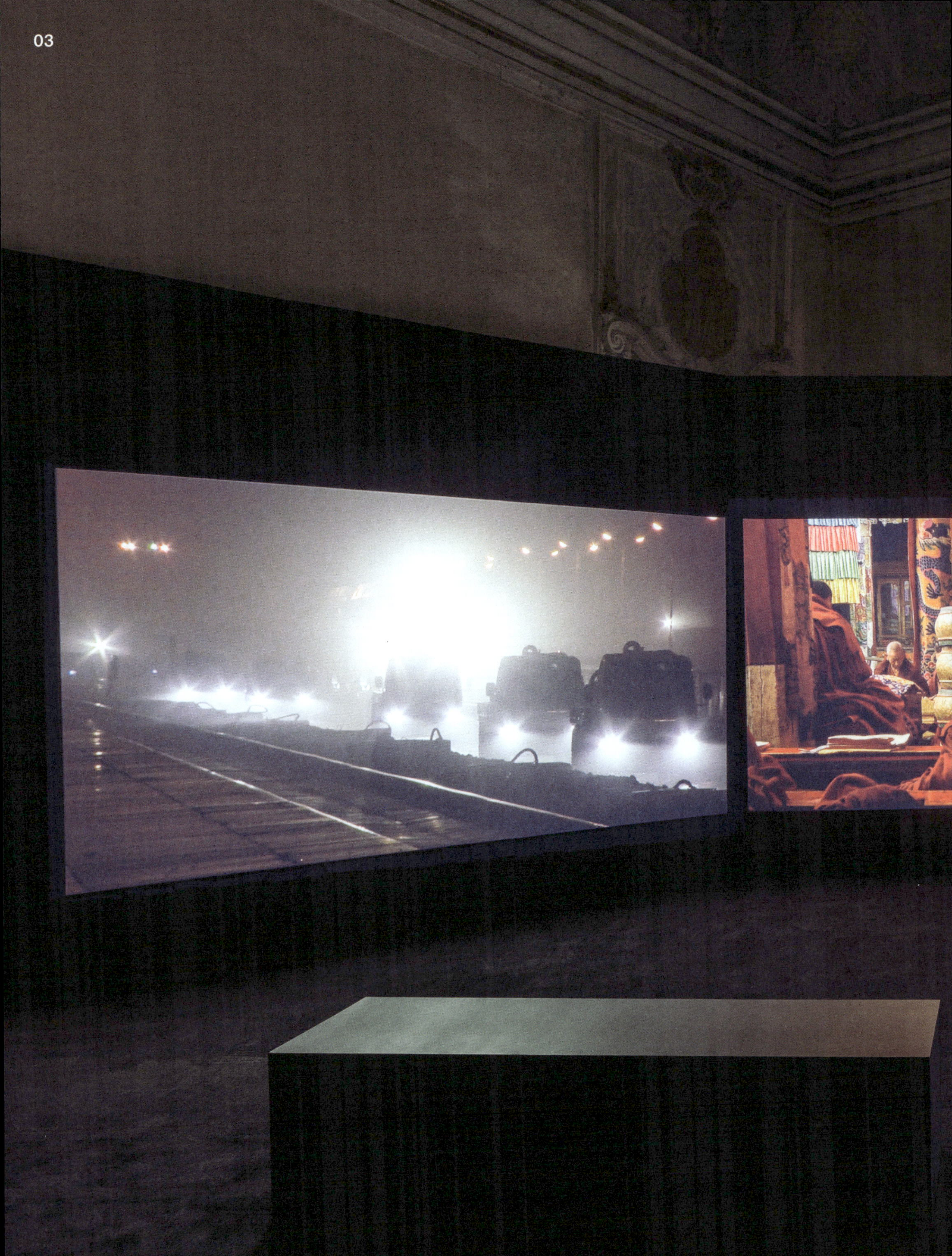

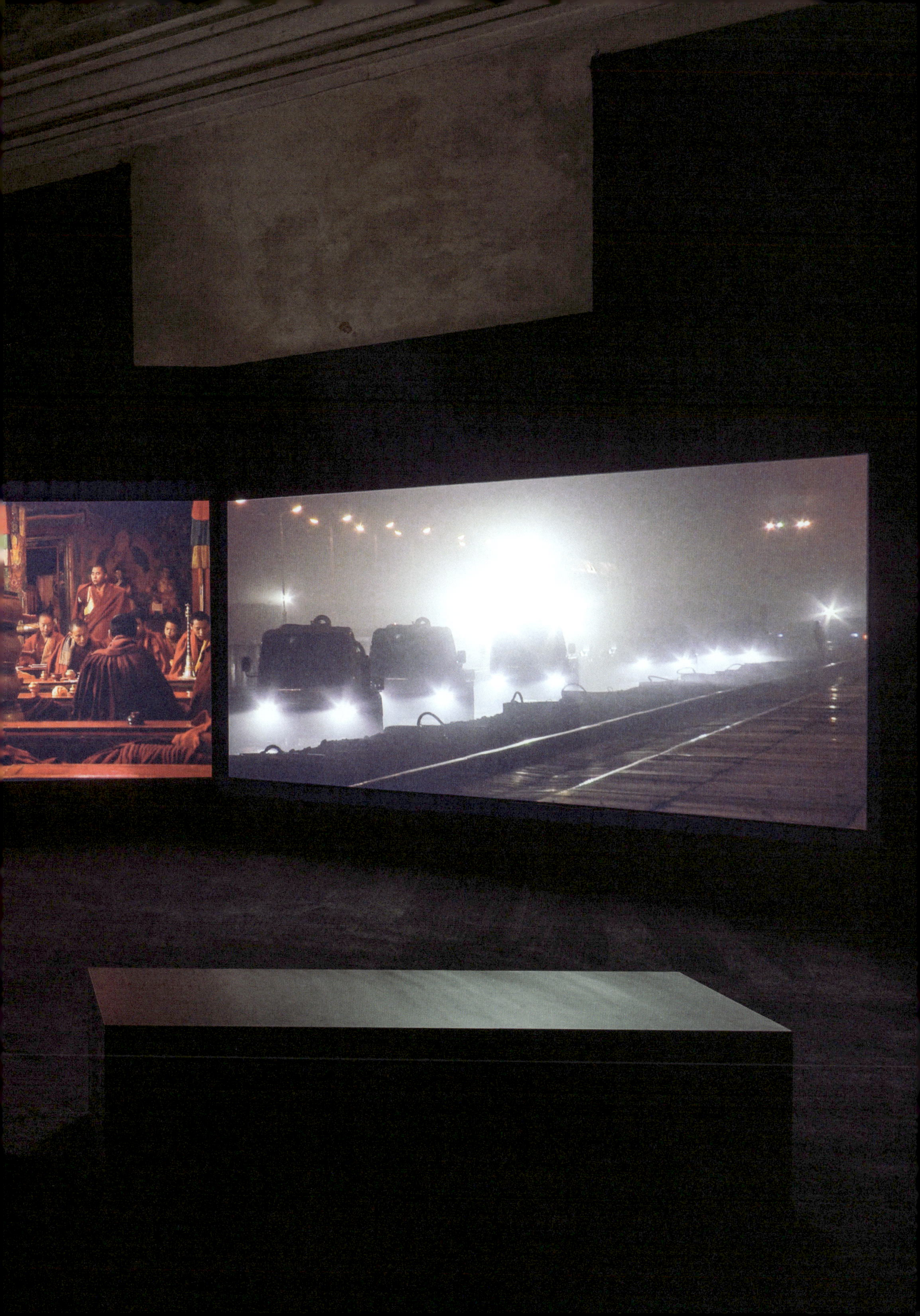

Oliver Beer

Lives and works in London and Paris

04, 05, 06
Little Gods (Chamber Organ), 2022
32 vessels, 32 microphones, speakers, plinths, audio equipment
Dimensions variable
Installation views at *Uncombed, Unforeseen, Unconstrained,* Conservatorio di Musica Benedetto Marcello, Venice, 2022

07
Cyanotype Drawing for Little Gods (Chamber Organ), 2022
Cyanotype, white ink and chalk
61 × 86 cm (24 × 34 in)

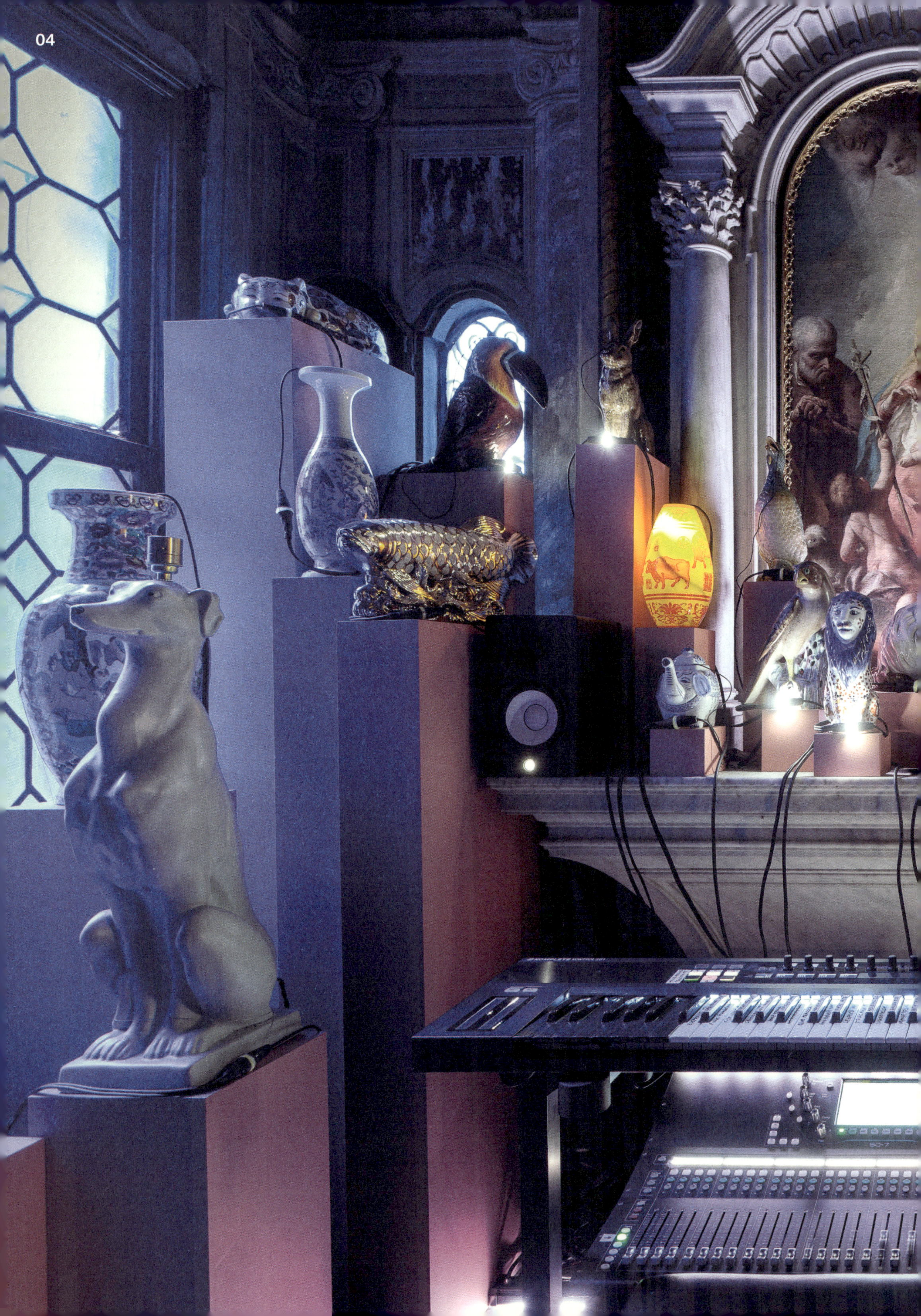

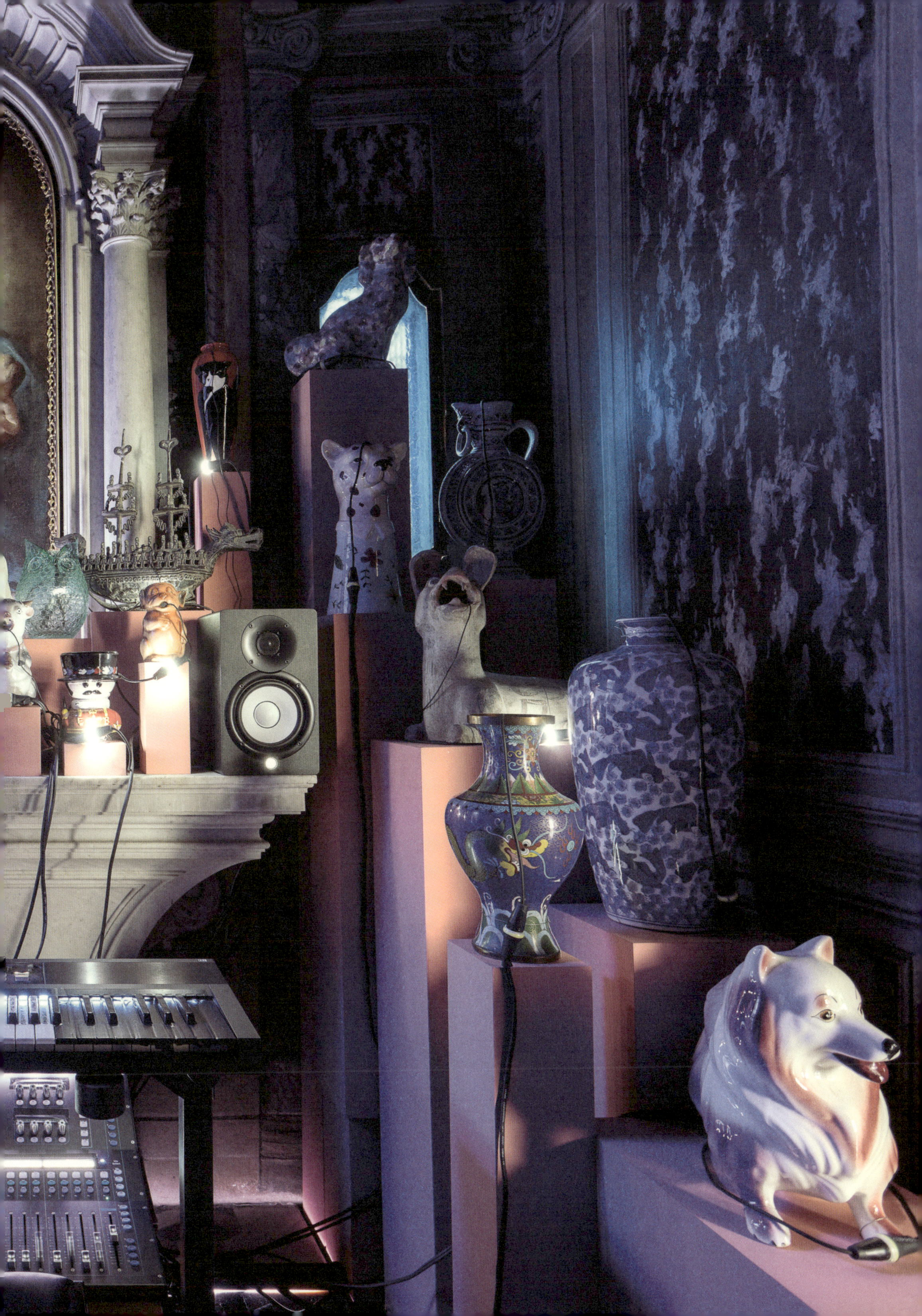

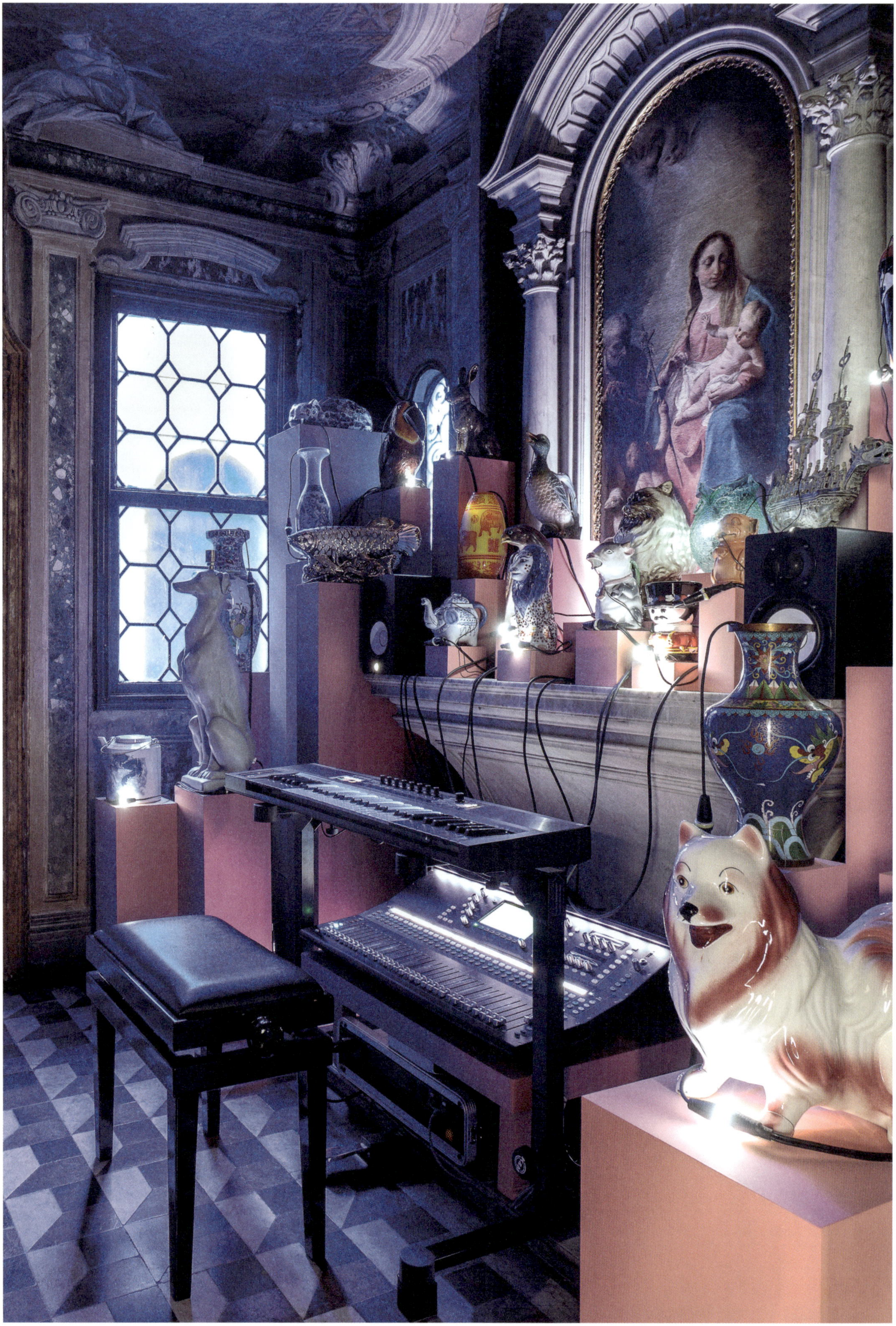

06

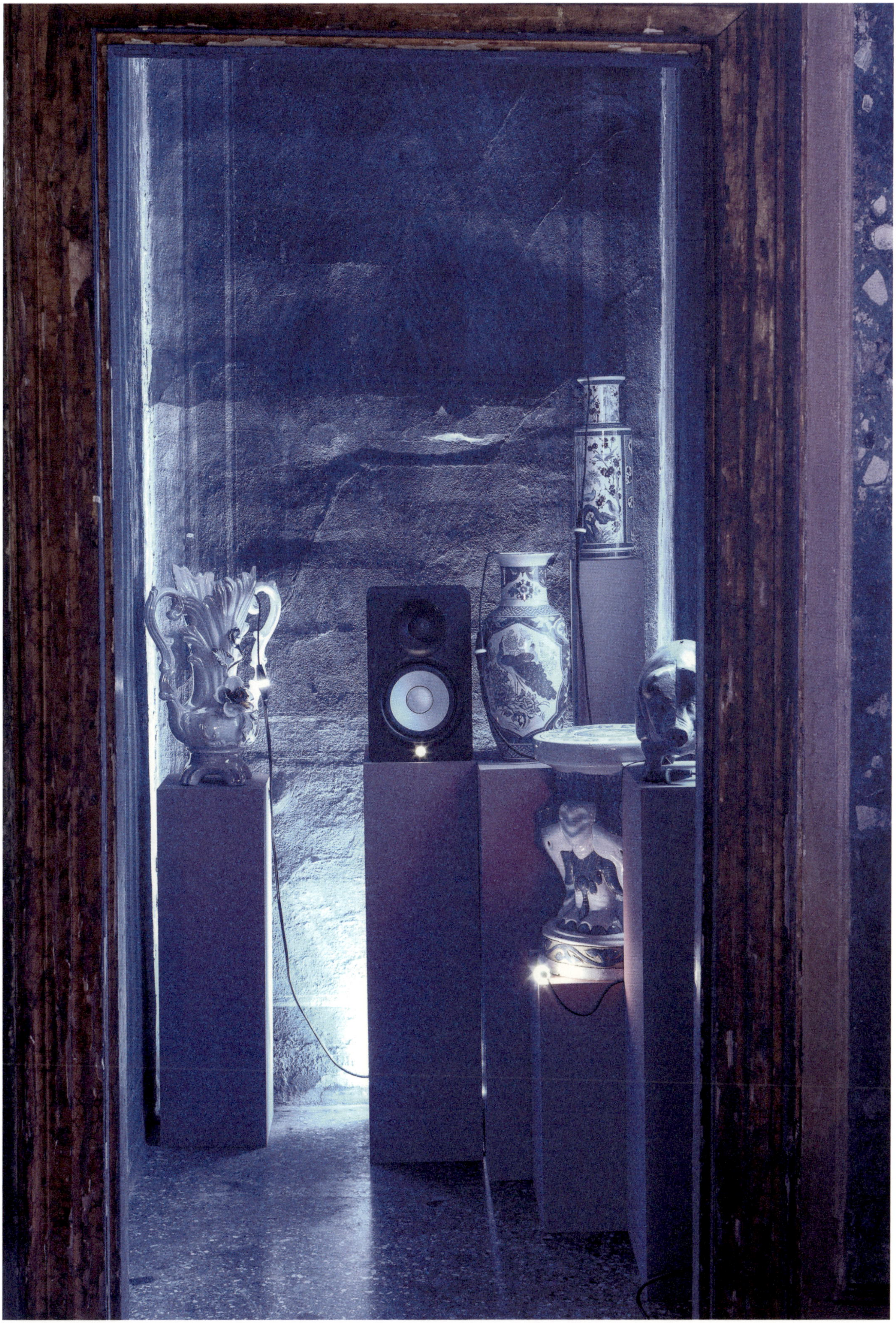

07

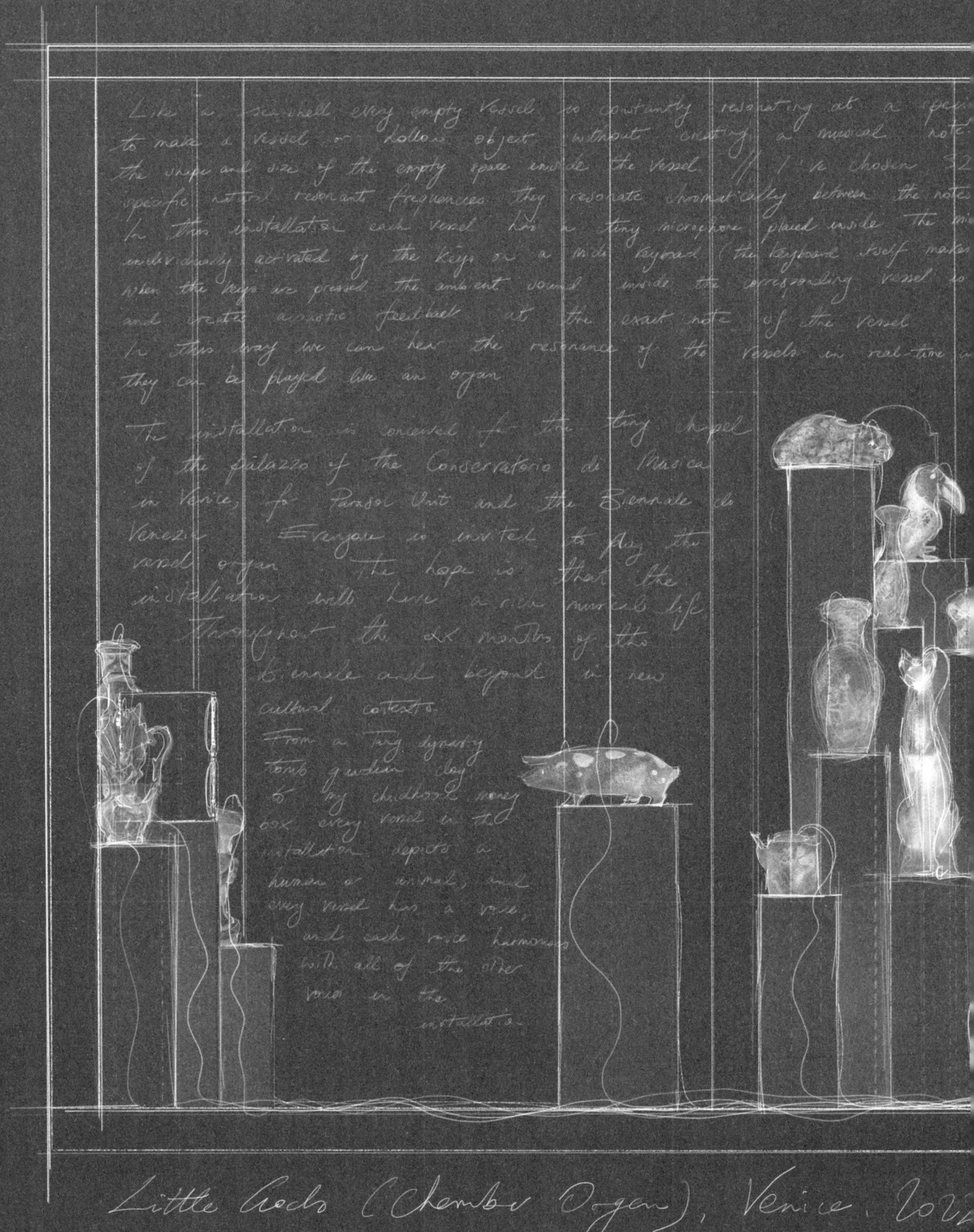
Like a seashell every empty vessel is constantly resonating at a
to make a vessel or hollow object without creating a musical
the shape and size of the empty space inside the vessel. // I've chosen
specific natural resonant frequencies they resonate chromatically between the
In this installation each vessel has a tiny microphone placed inside. The
individually activated by the keys on a midi keyboard (the keyboard itself
When the keys are pressed the ambient sound inside the corresponding vessel
and create acoustic feedback at the exact note of the vessel
In this way we can hear the resonance of the vessels in real-time
they can be played like an organ
The installation is conceived for the tiny chapel of the palazzo of the Conservatorio di Musica in Venice, for Parasol Unit and the Biennale di Venezia. Everyone is invited to play the vessel organ. The hope is that the installation will have a rich musical life throughout the six months of the Biennale and beyond in new cultural contexts.
From a Tang dynasty tomb guardian clay to my childhood money box every vessel in the installation depicts a human or animal, and every vessel has a voice, and each voice harmonises with all of the other voices in the installation
Little Gods (Chamber Organ), Venice.

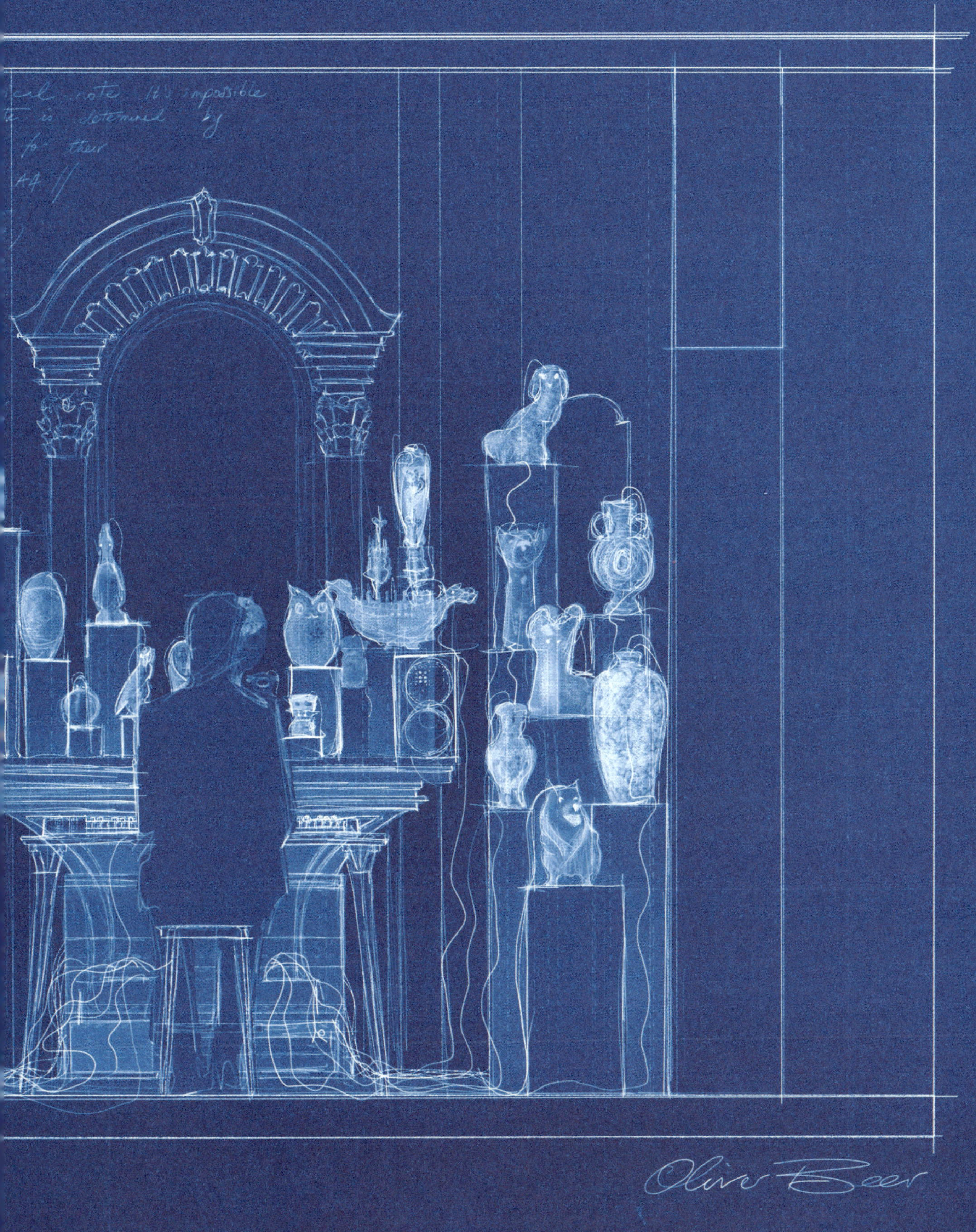

Rana Begum in collaboration with Hyetal

Both live and work in London

08, 10
No. 694 Hyetal, 2016
2 MDF panels, 46 coloured mirror Perspex, 2 vertical lights. Audio 10:10 min.
240 × 240 × 12 cm (94½ × 94½ × 4¾ in)
Installation views at *Uncombed, Unforeseen, Unconstrained,* Conservatorio di Musica Benedetto Marcello, Venice, 2022

09, 11
No. 694 Hyetal, 2016 (details)

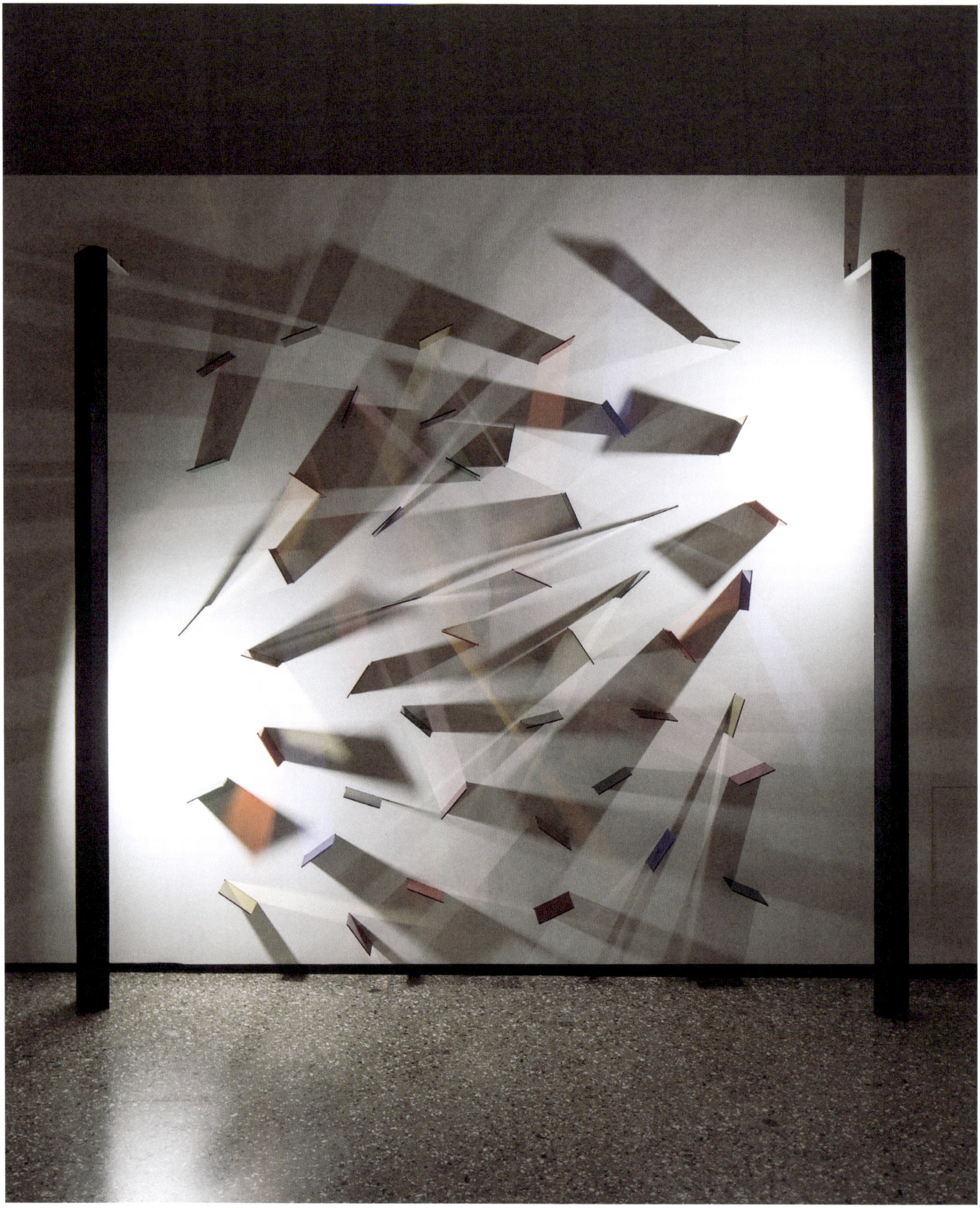

09

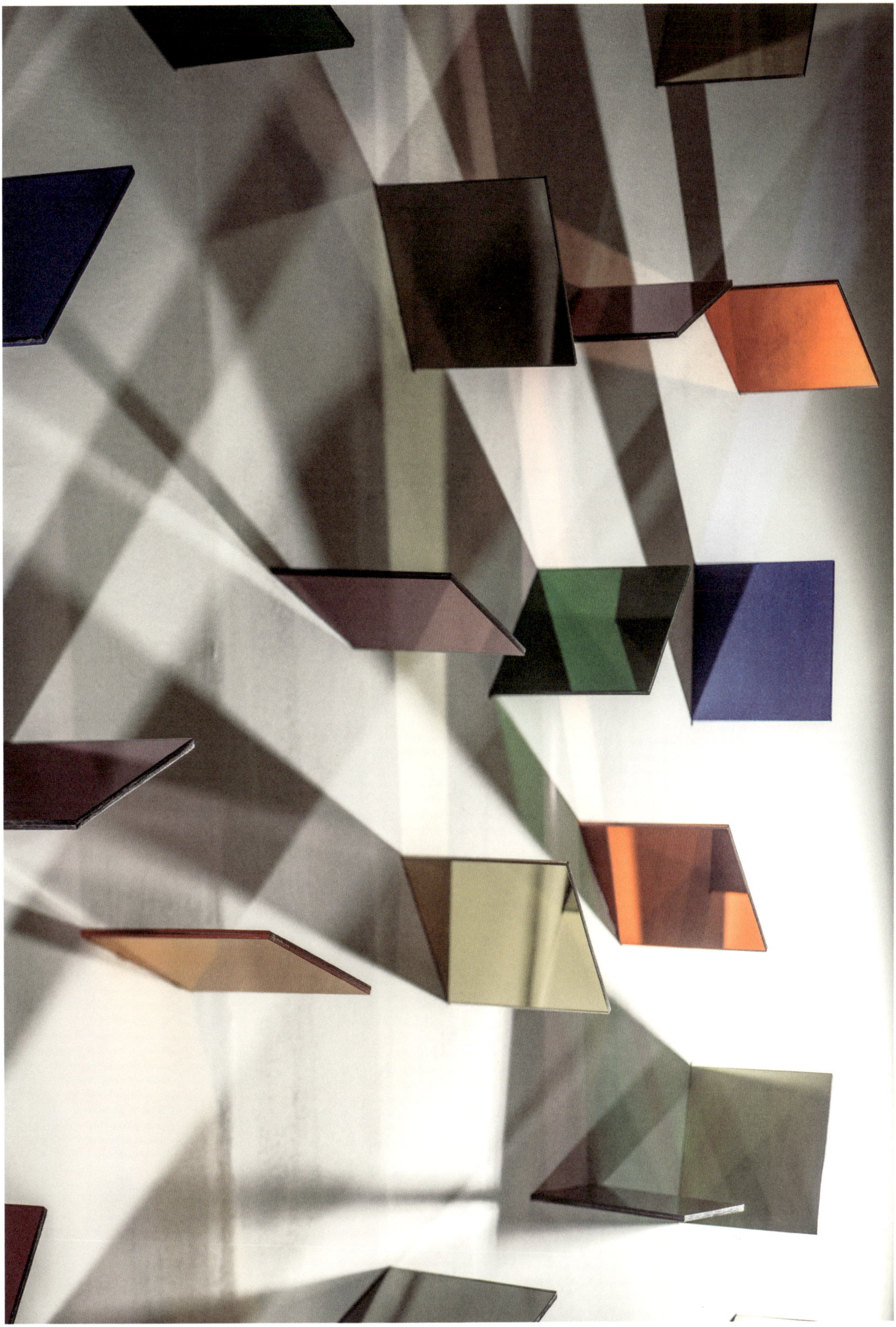

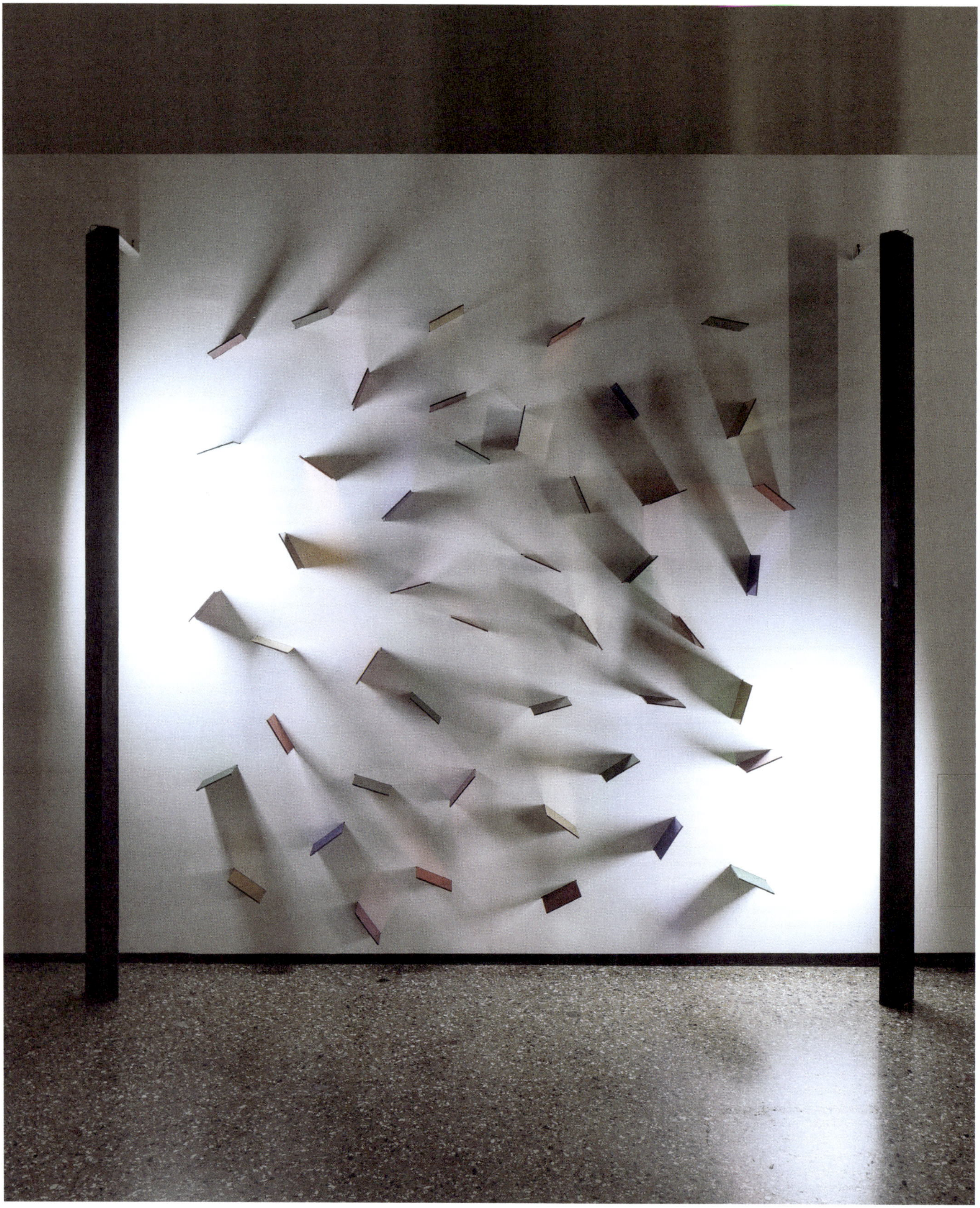

11

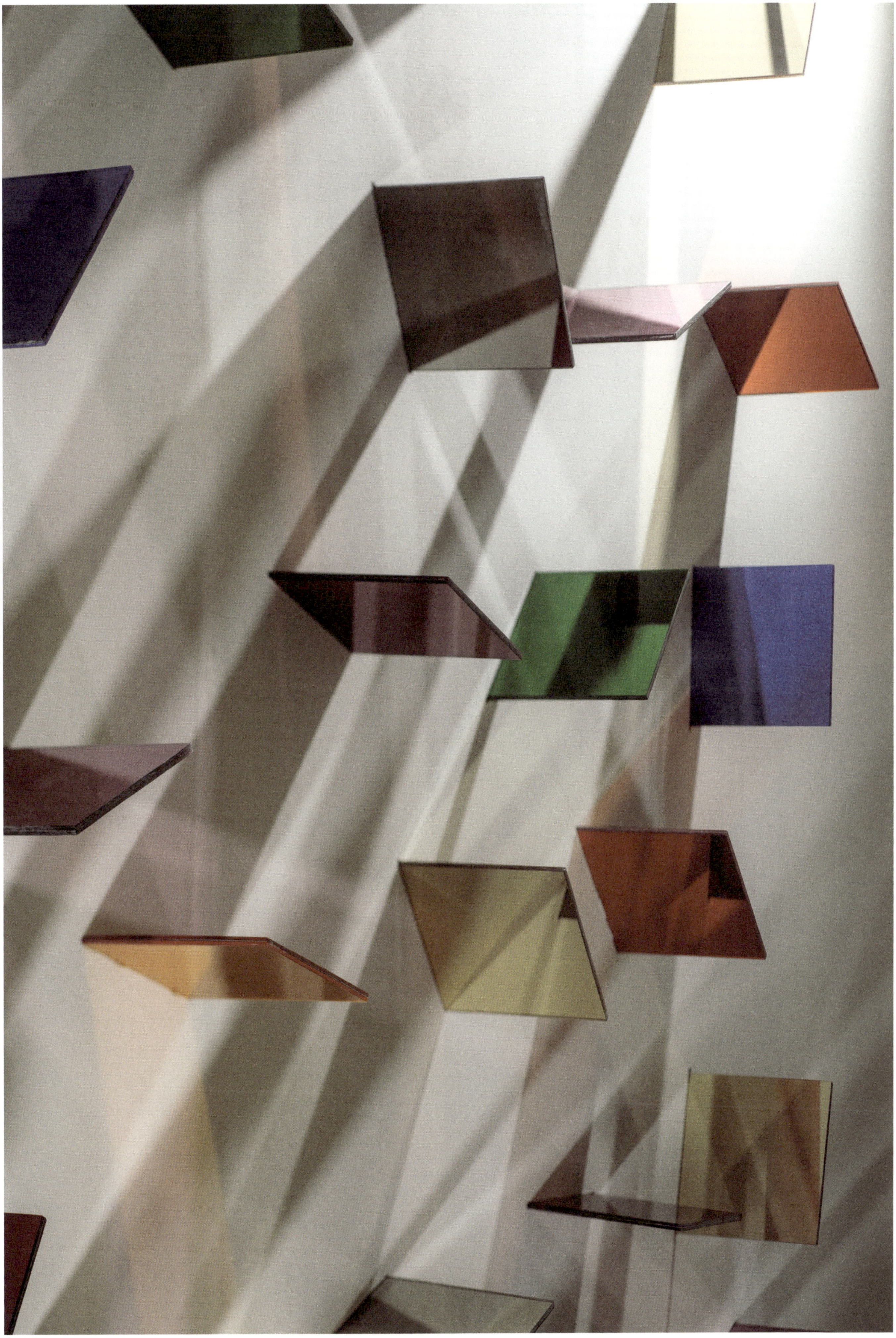

Julian Charrière

Lives and works in Berlin

12
And Beneath It All Flows Liquid Fire, 2019
UHD colour video, 16:10 aspect ratio, stereo sound
Continuous video loop
Installation view at *Uncombed, Unforeseen, Unconstrained,* Conservatorio di Musica Benedetto Marcello, Venice, 2022

13, 14
Not All Who Wander Are Lost, 2019
Four unique pieces: glacial erratic rock, drill cores, aluminium, brass, copper, stainless steel
135 × 100 × 682 cm (53¼ × 39½ × 268½ in)
99 × 100 × 435 cm (39 × 39½ × 171¼ in)
150 × 120 × 525 cm (59 × 47¼ × 206¾ in)
120 × 100 × 738 cm (47¼ × 39½ × 290½ in)
Installation views at *Uncombed, Unforeseen, Unconstrained,* Conservatorio di Musica Benedetto Marcello, Venice, 2022

15, 16, 17, 18
Not All Who Wander Are Lost, 2019 (details)

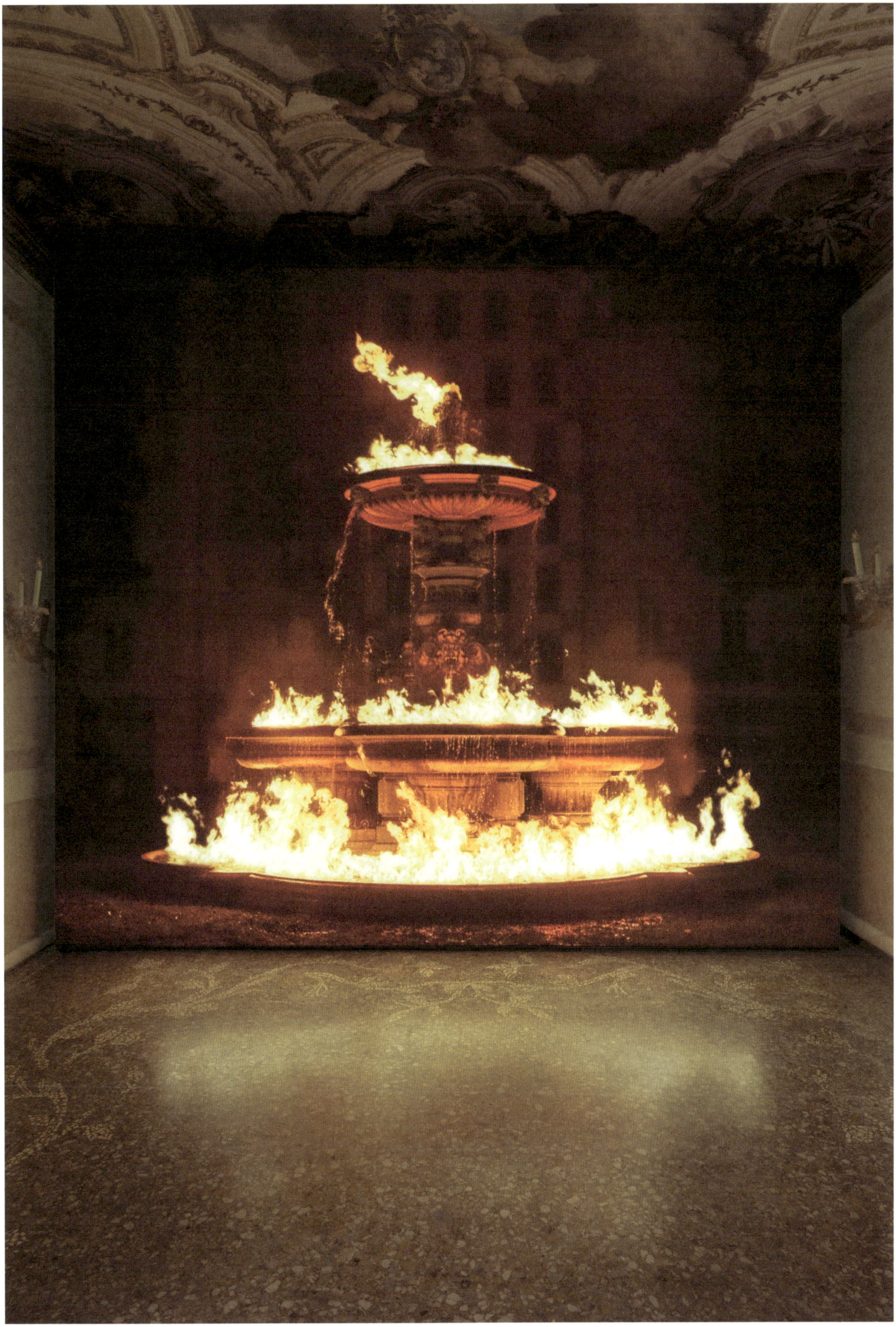

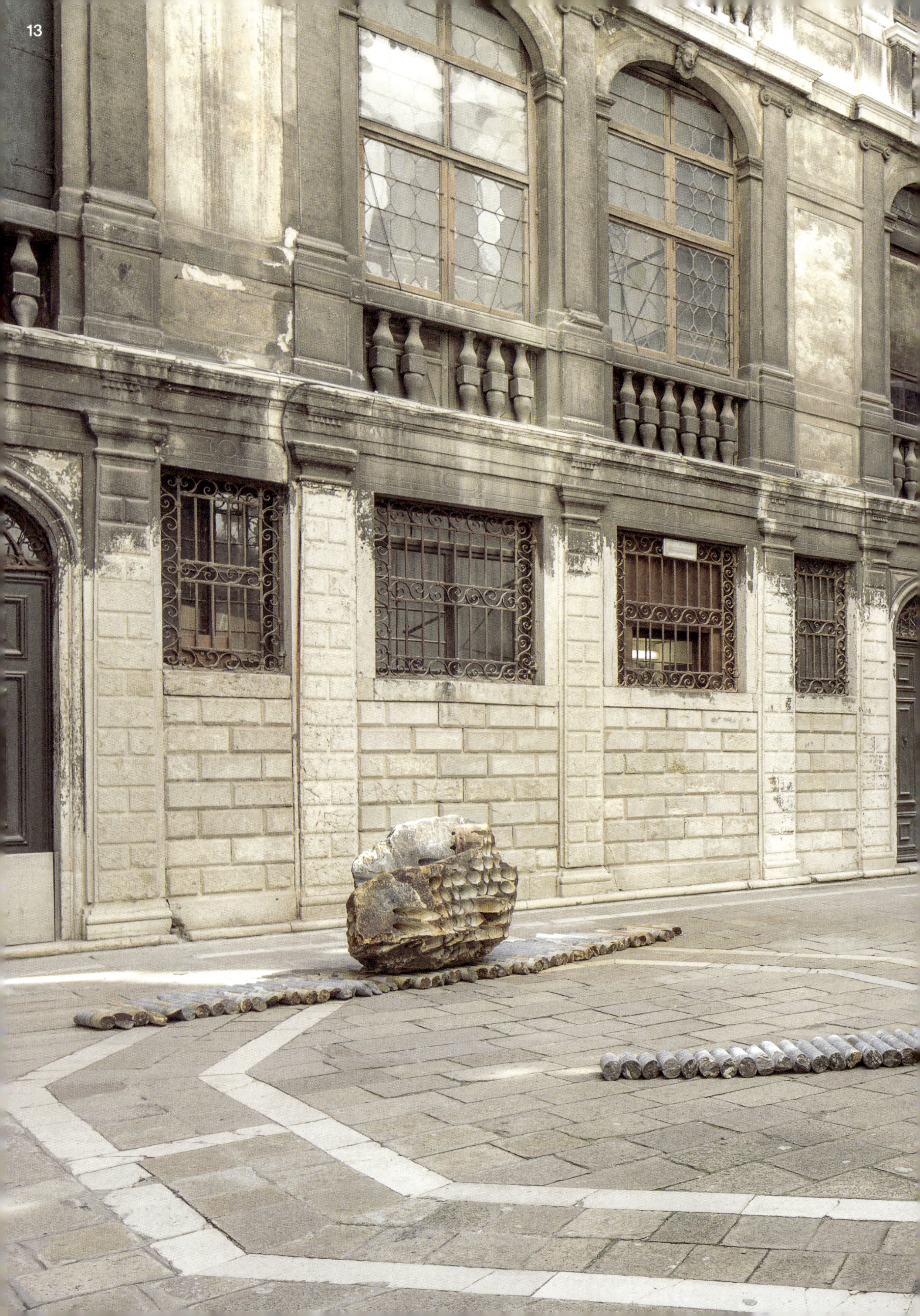

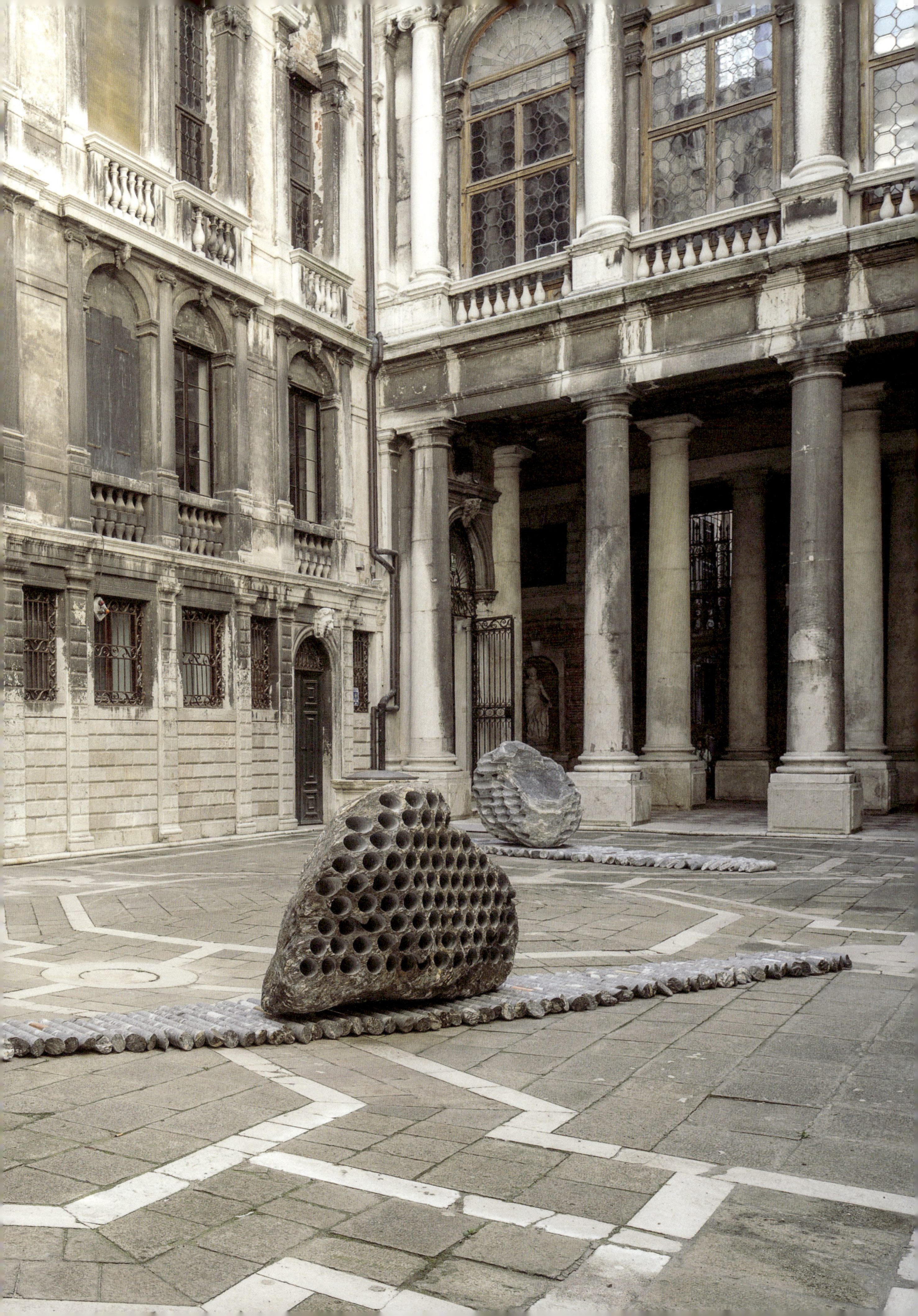

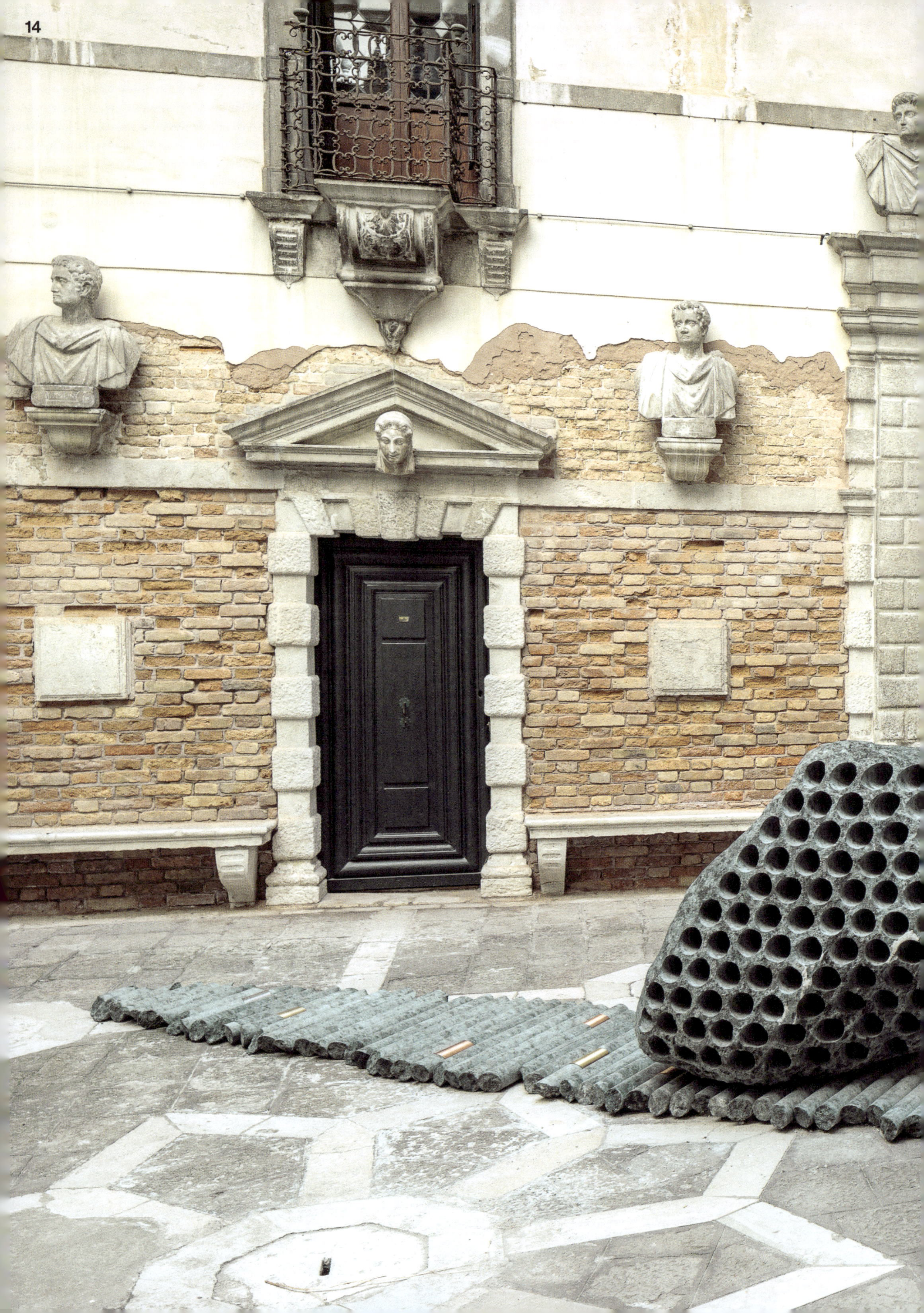

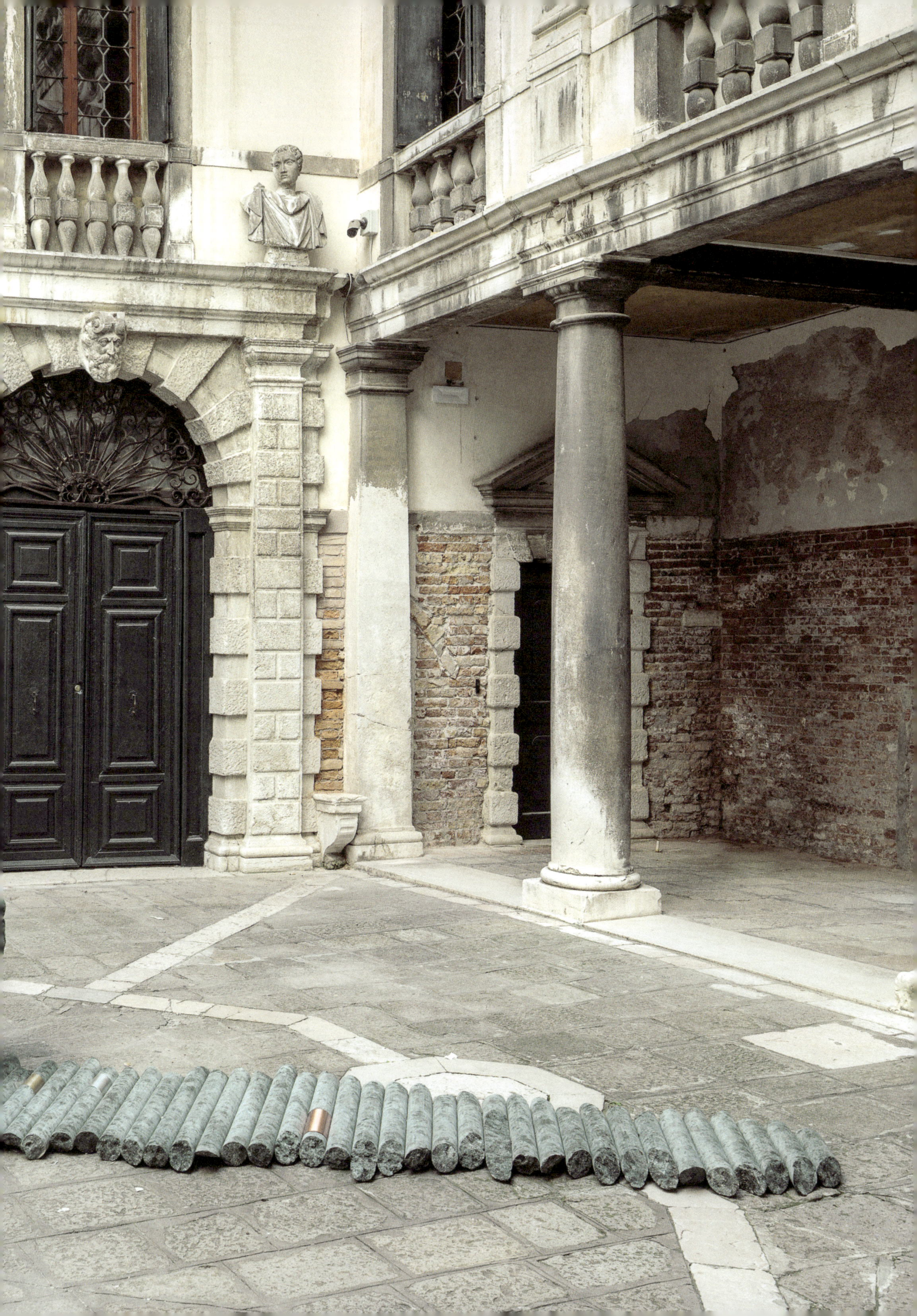

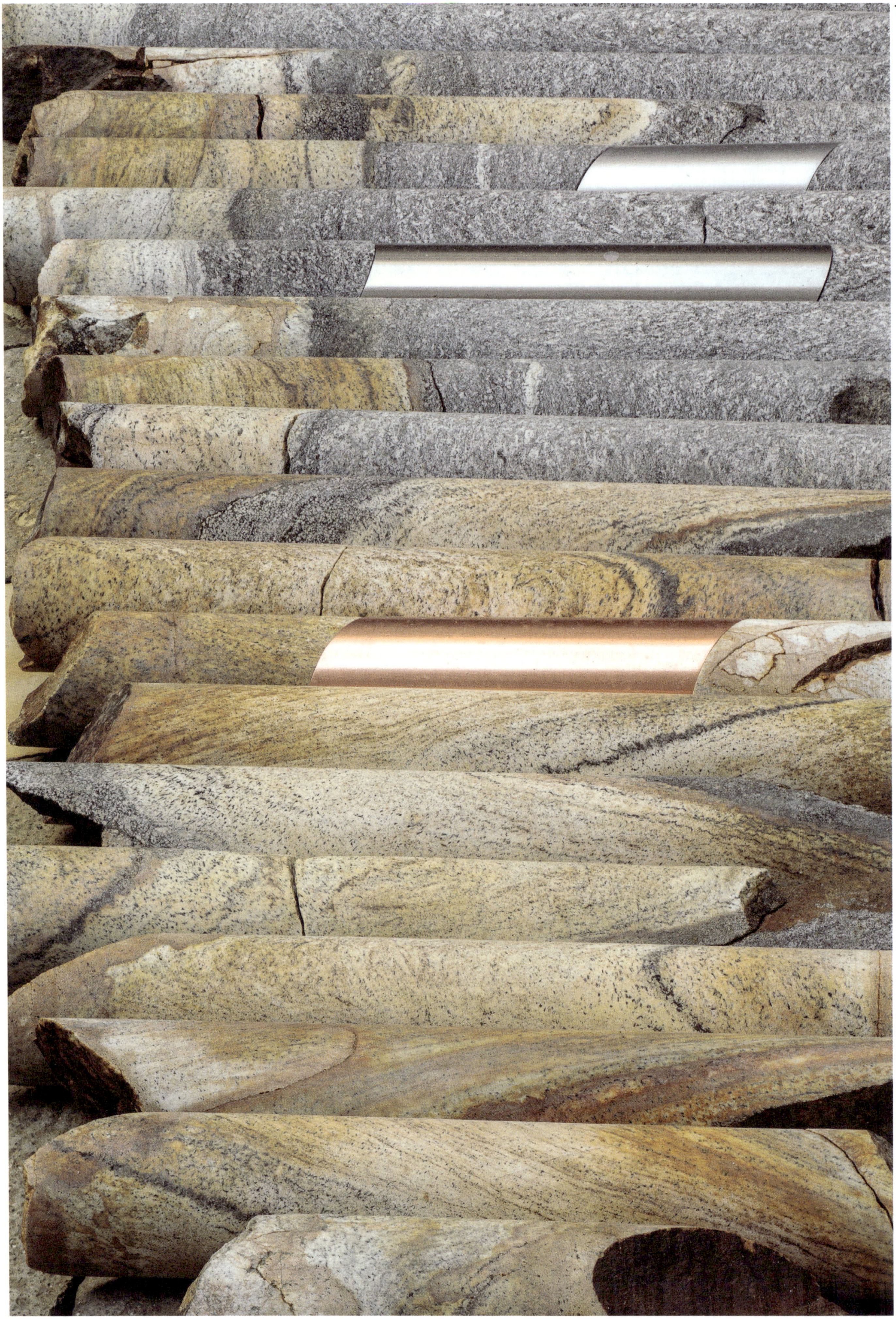

16
17
18

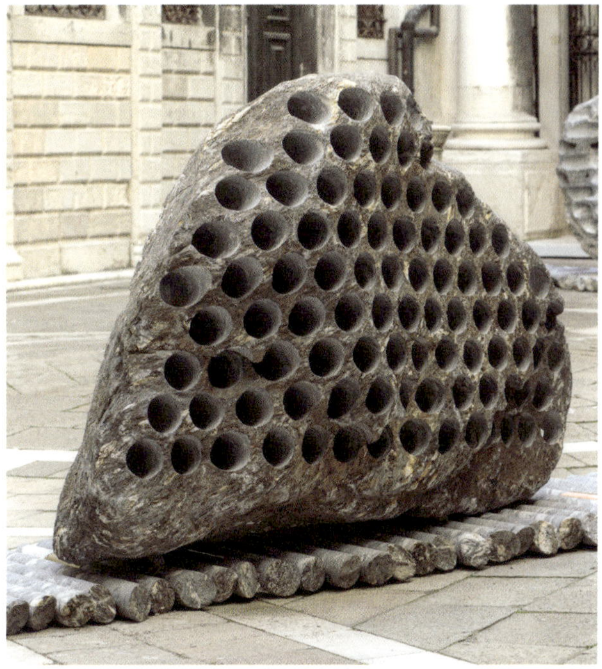

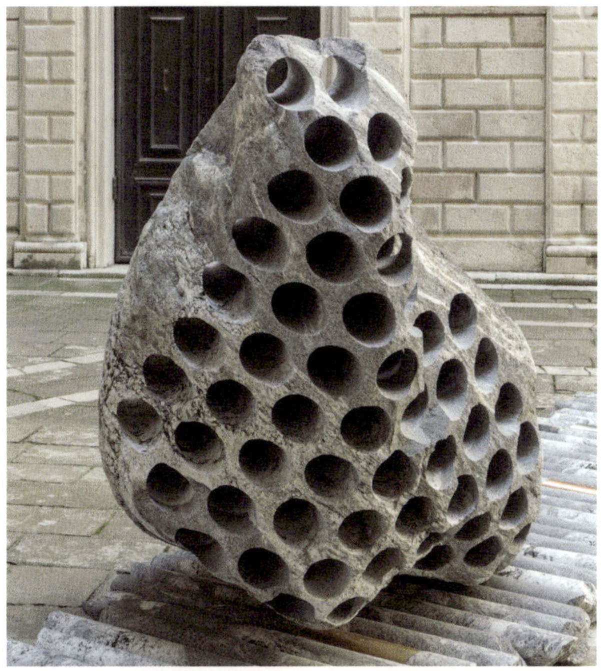

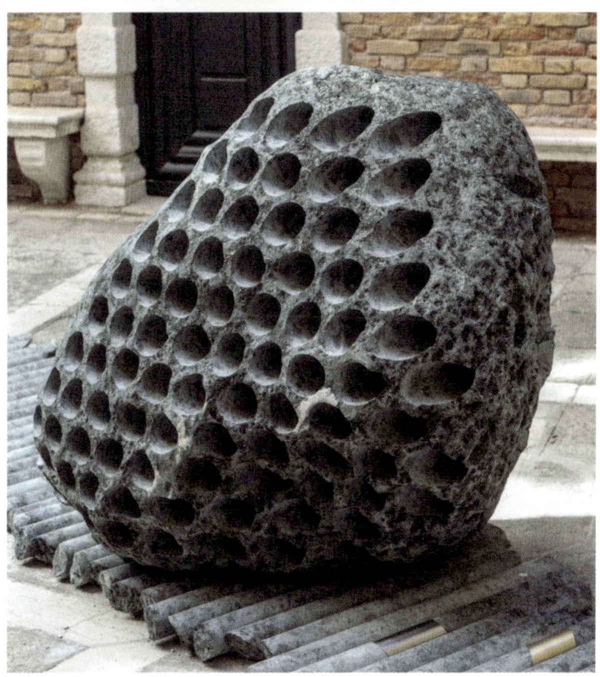

David Claerbout

Lives and works in Antwerp and Berlin

20, 21
Wildfire (Meditation on Fire), 2019–2020
Single-channel video projection, 3-D animation, stereo audio, colour, 24 min.
Installation views at *Uncombed, Unforeseen, Unconstrained,* Conservatorio di Musica Benedetto Marcello, Venice, 2022

19, 22
Wildfire (Meditation on Fire), 2019–2020
Video stills

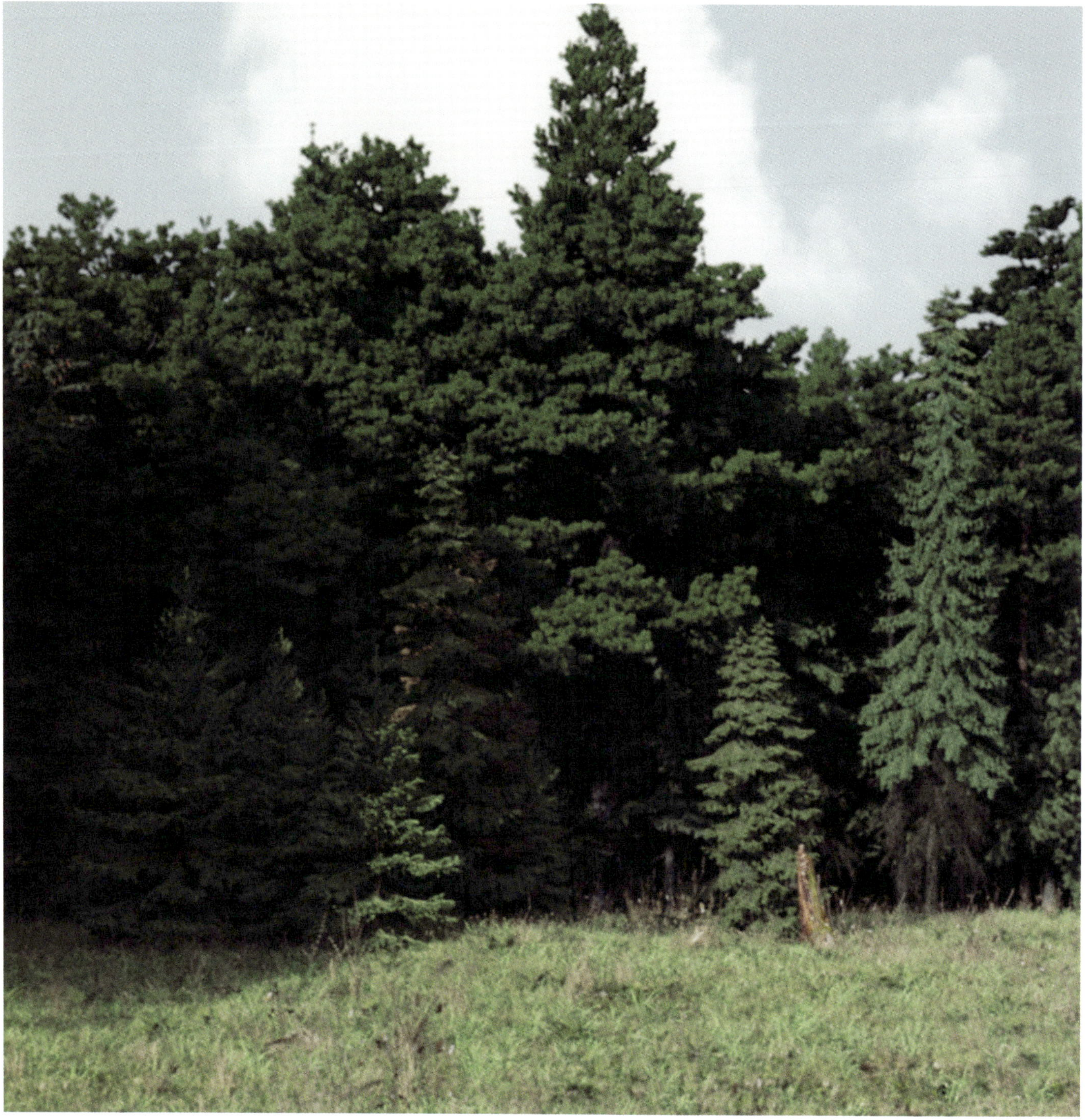

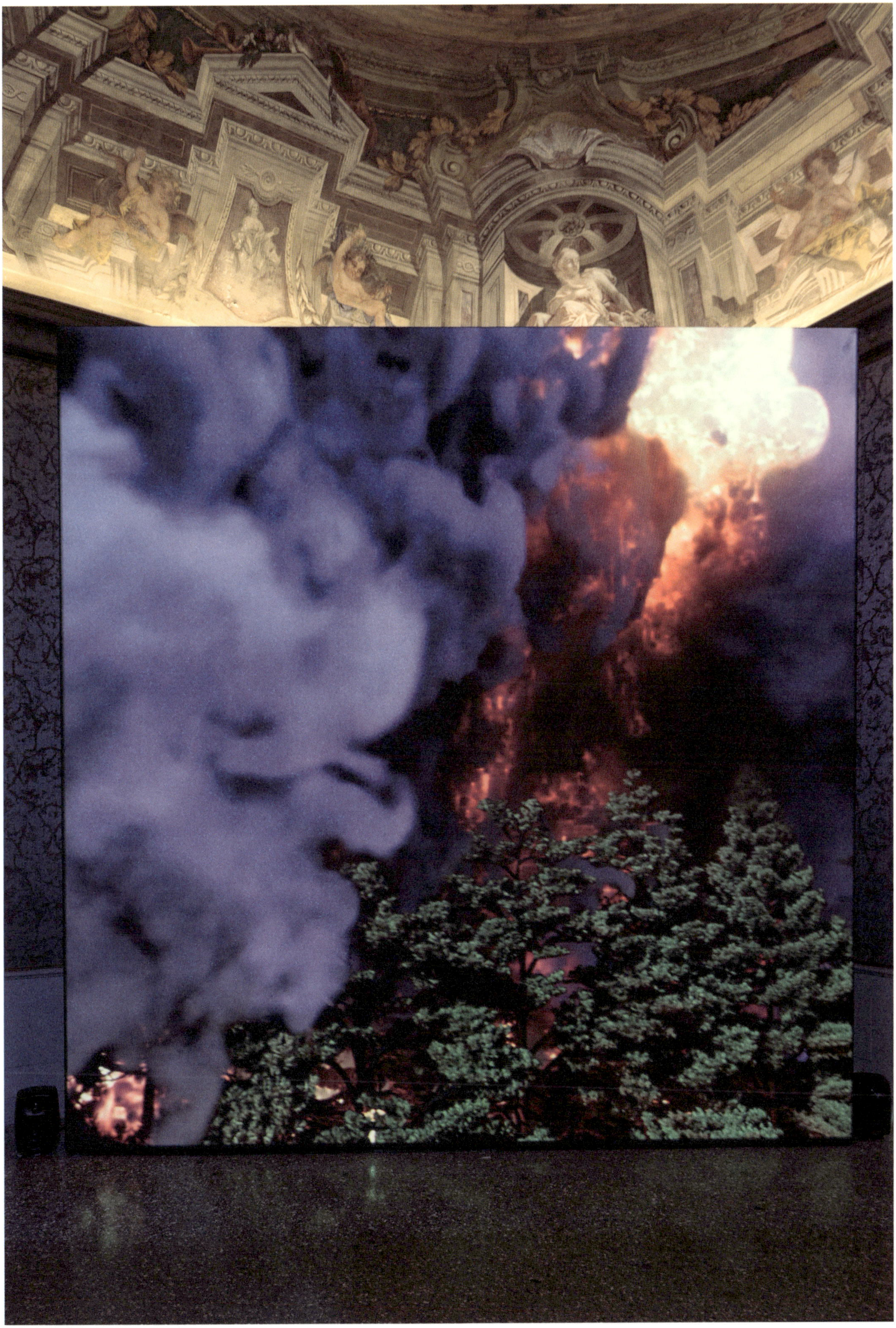

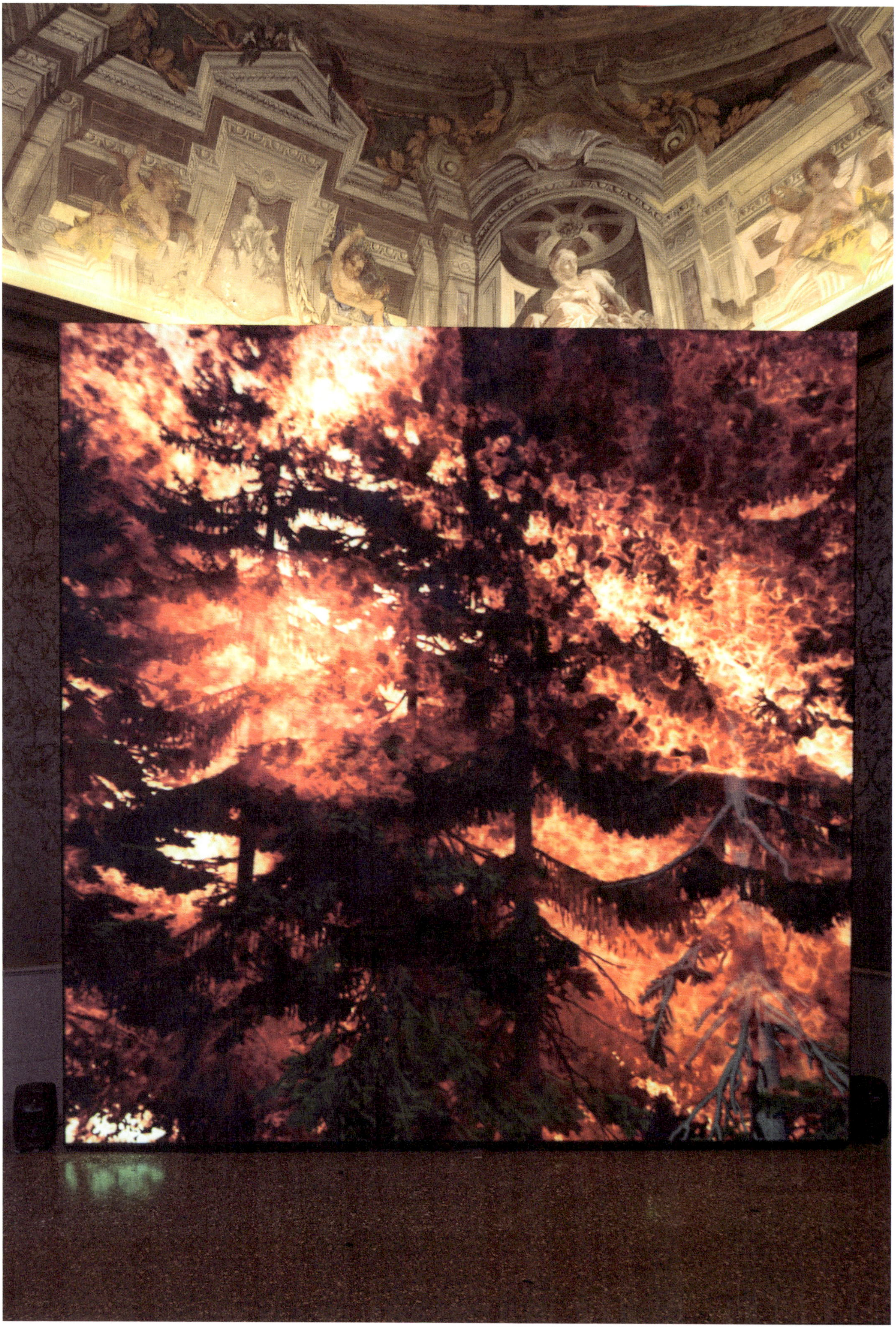

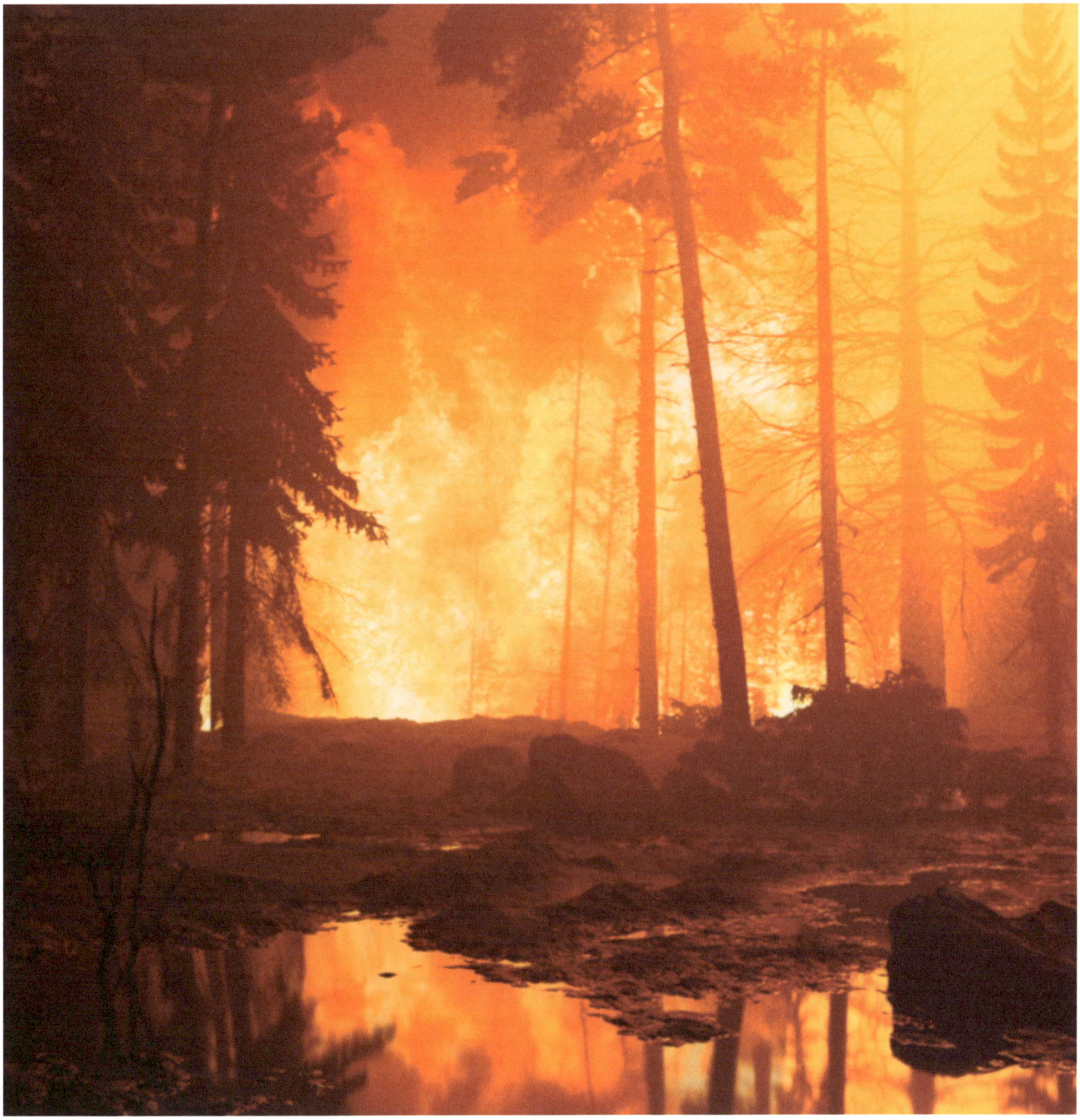

Bharti Kher

Lives and works in New Delhi

23, 24
The Intermediaries (series), 2019
Mixed media, unless otherwise noted:
clay, wax, brass, copper, cement
Dimensions do not include base or plinth
Installation views at *Uncombed, Unforeseen, Unconstrained,* Conservatorio di Musica Benedetto Marcello, Venice, 2022

25
Ship of Fools, 2019
38 × 26.5 × 26.5 cm (15 × 10½ × 10½ in)

26
Sisters, 2019
31.6 × 11.5 × 20.3 cm (12½ × 4½ × 8 in)

27
As Dangerous as an Albatross, 2019
26.4 × 10.1 × 20.3 cm (10½ × 4 × 8 in)

28
Talisman for September, 2019
19 × 12.7 × 26.4 cm (7½ × 5 × 10½ in)

29
The Great Seat of Learning, 2019
63.5 × 15.2 × 25.4 cm (25 × 6 × 10 in)

30
Bird Girl, 2018
Clay, cement, wood, paint, wax, brass
36 × 13 × 10 cm (14¼ × 5 × 4 in)

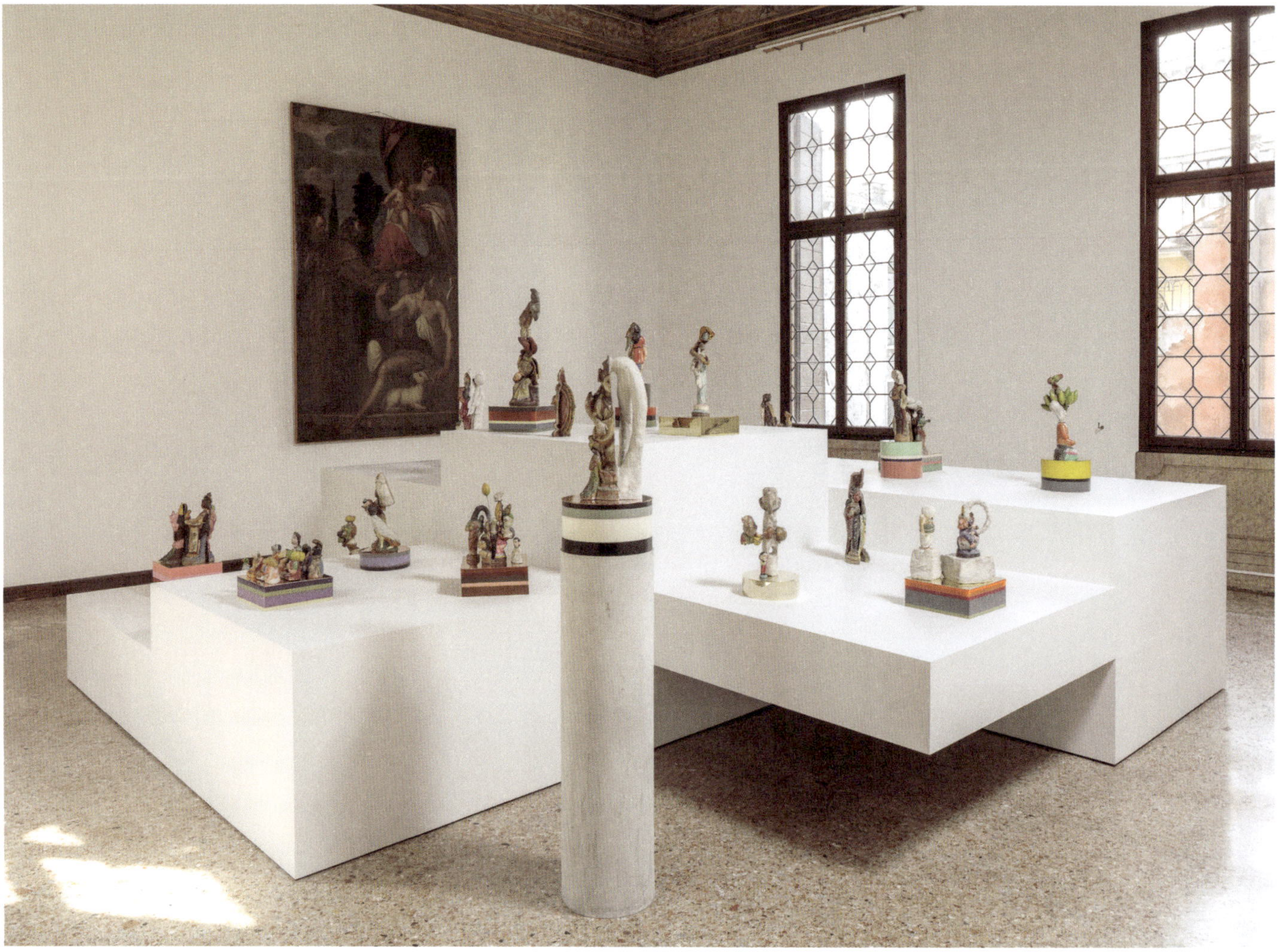

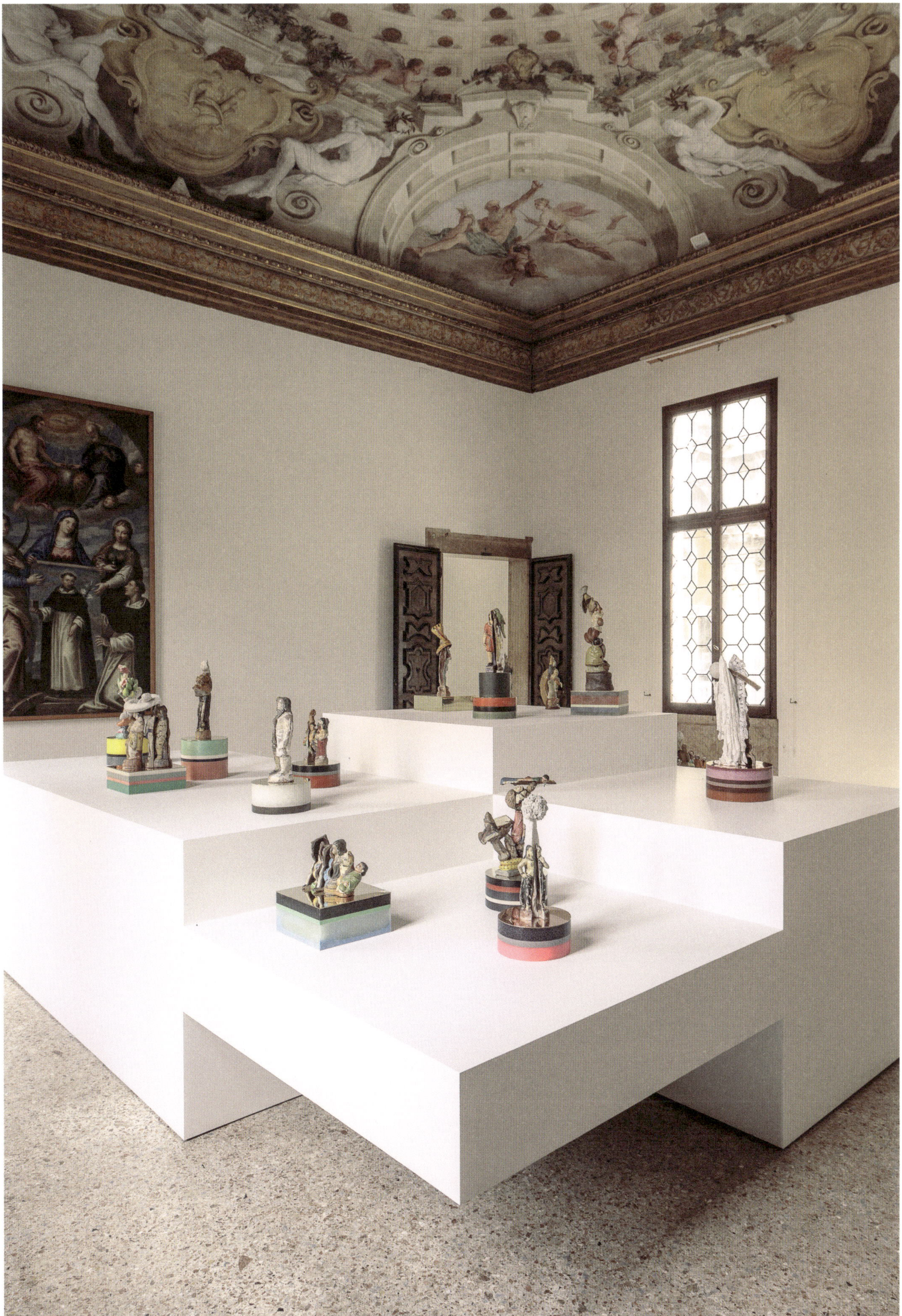

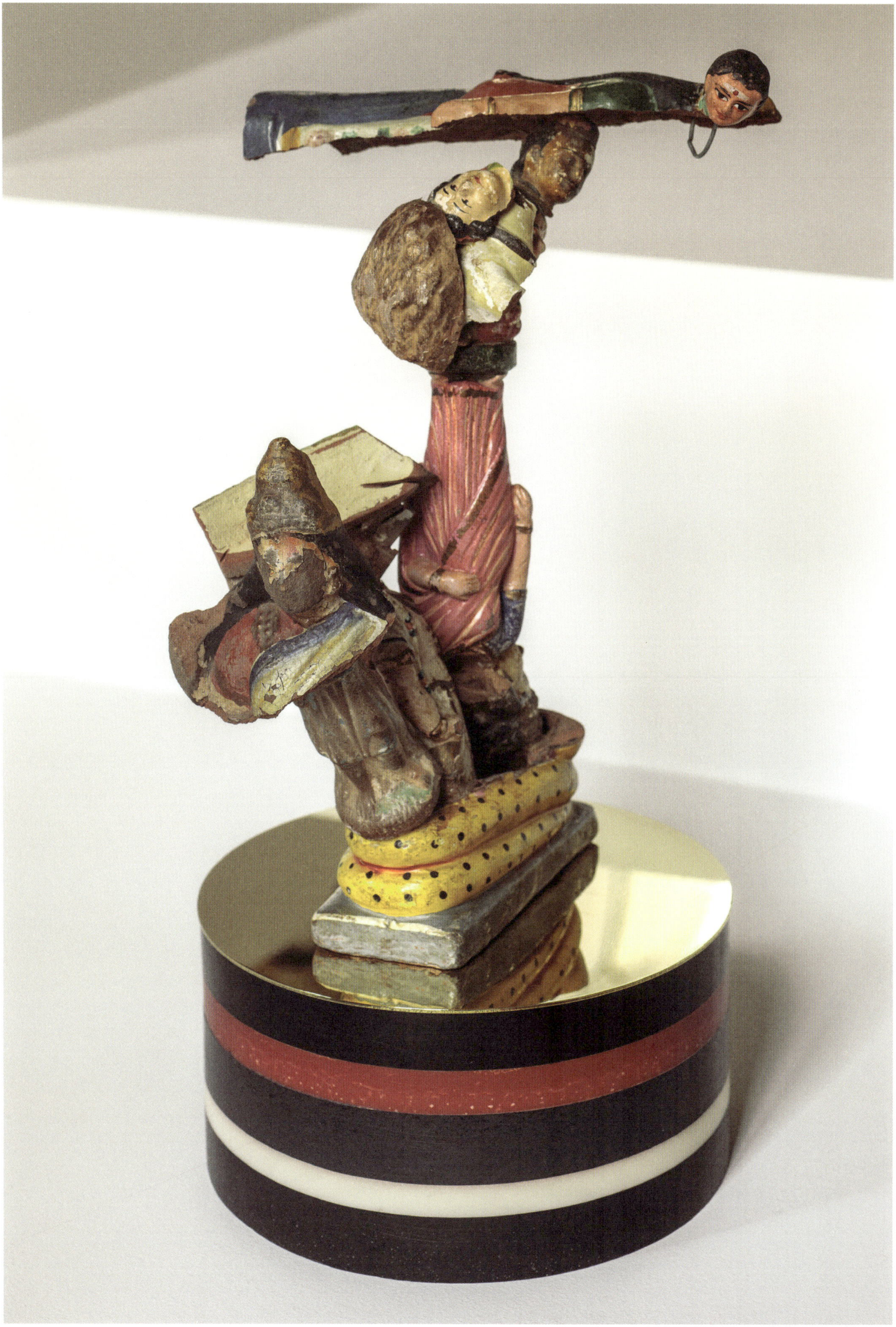

26
27
28

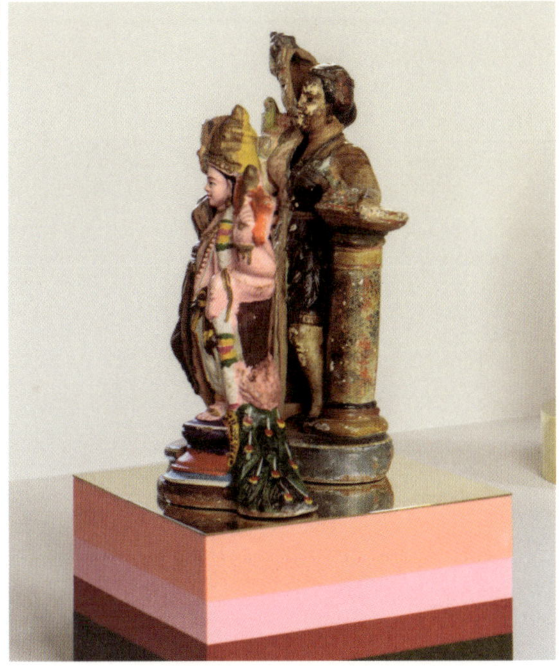

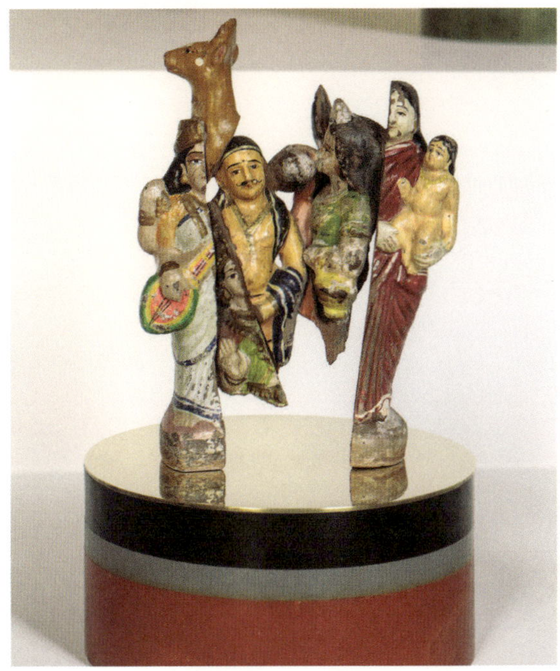

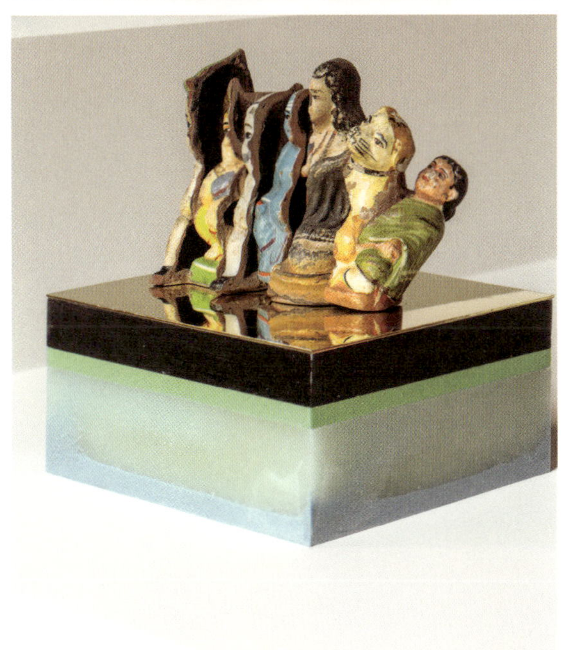

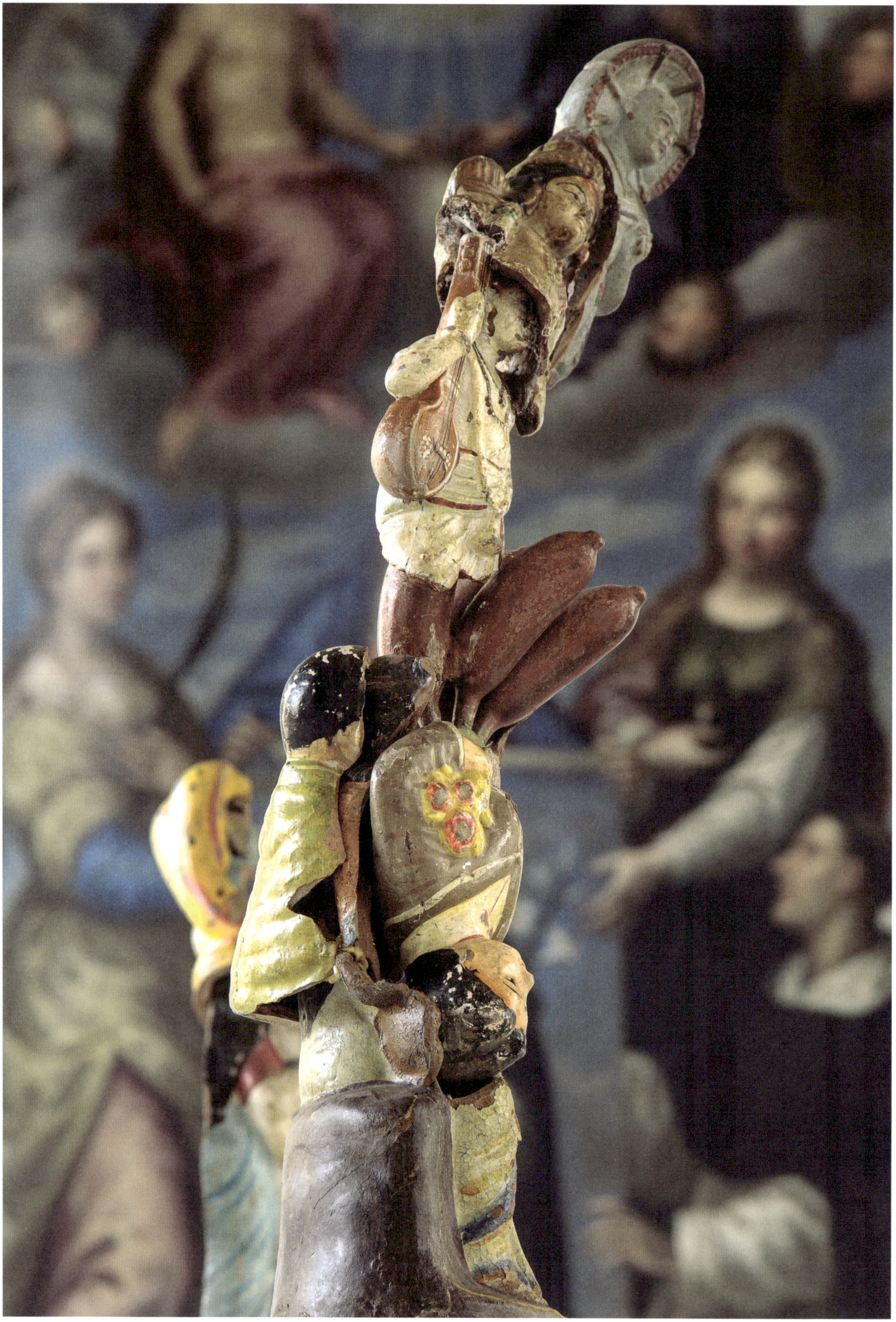

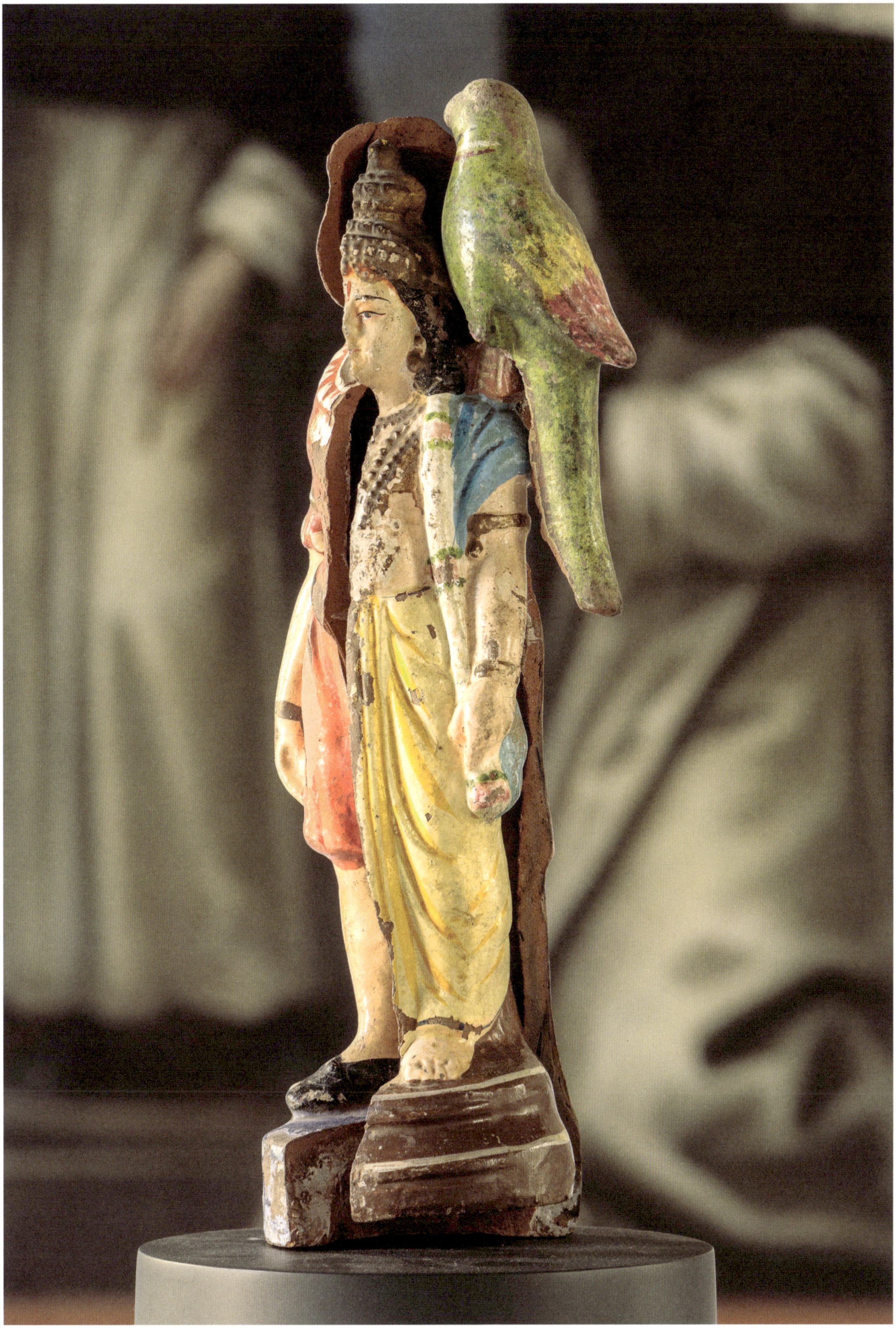

Arghavan Khosravi

Lives and works in New York

32, 33, 34, 35
The Anatomy of A Woman (series), 2019
Installation views at *Uncombed, Unforeseen, Unconstrained,* Conservatorio di Musica Benedetto Marcello, Venice, 2022

31
This Shall Also Pass (The Anatomy of A Woman Series #6), 2019 (detail)

32
This Shall Also Pass (The Anatomy of A Woman Series #6), 2019
Acrylic, found textile, wooden panel, Plexiglas, thread, wooden cut-out
94 × 48 cm (37 × 19 in)

33
Quite Determined (The Anatomy of A Woman Series #4), 2019
Acrylic, cotton canvas, found textile, wooden panels, rope
94 × 43 cm (37 × 17 in)

34
The Anatomy of A Woman Series #5, 2019
Acrylic, cotton canvas, found textile, wooden panels, thread, mirror
96.5 × 78.8 cm (38 × 31 in)

35
The Anatomy of A Woman Series #2, 2019
Acrylic, cotton canvas, found woodblock-printed textile, wooden panels, thread
137 × 63.5 cm (54 × 25 in)

36
The Anatomy of A Woman Series #2, 2019 (detail)

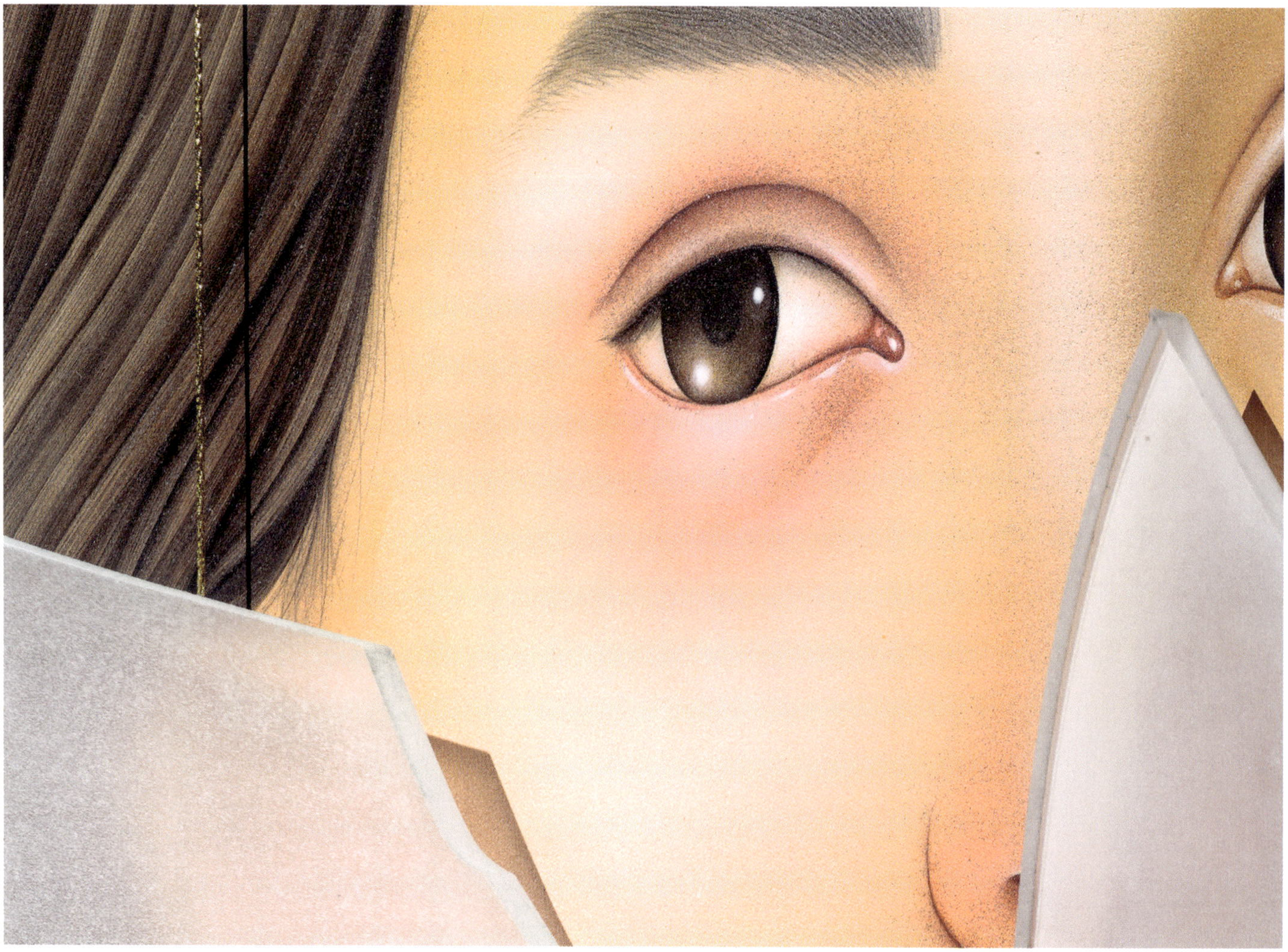

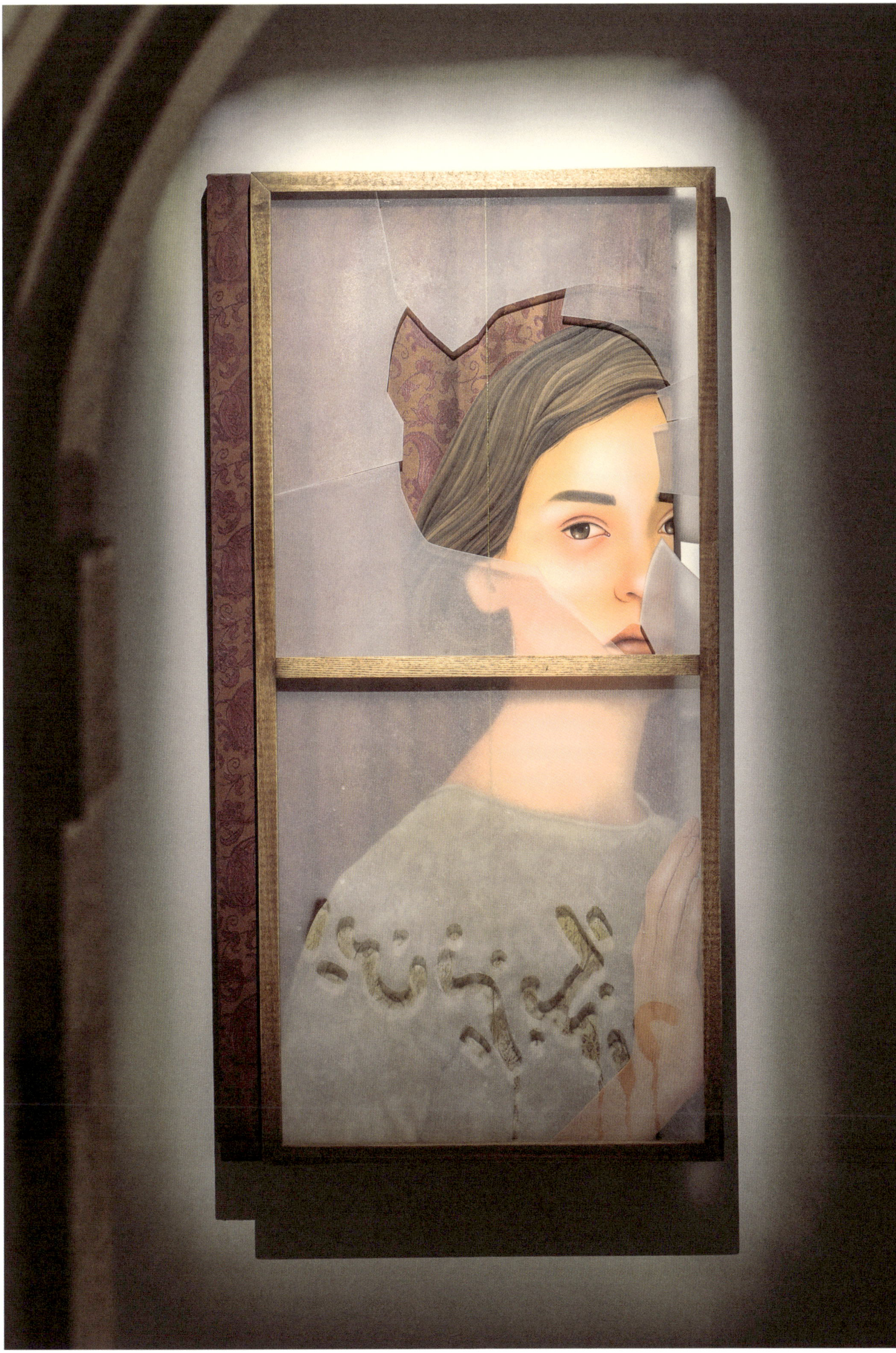

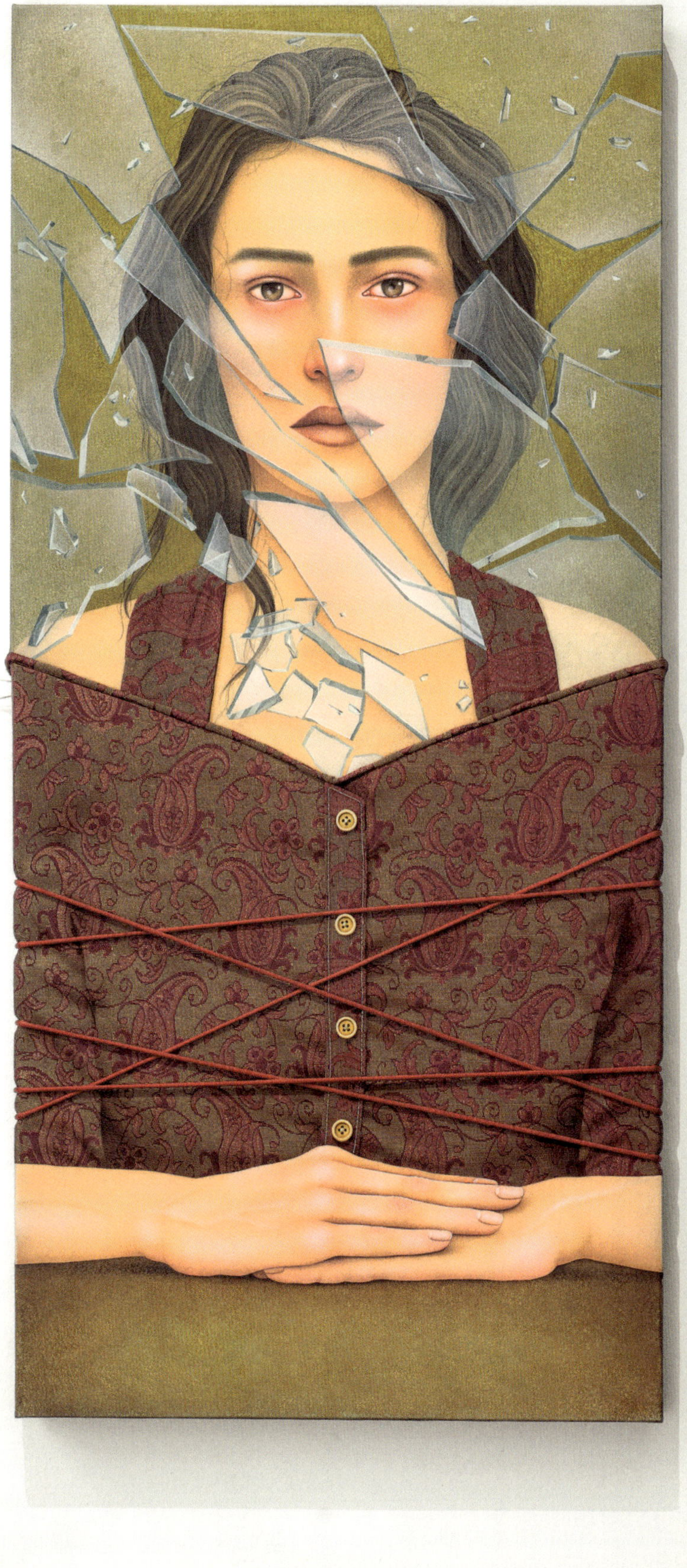

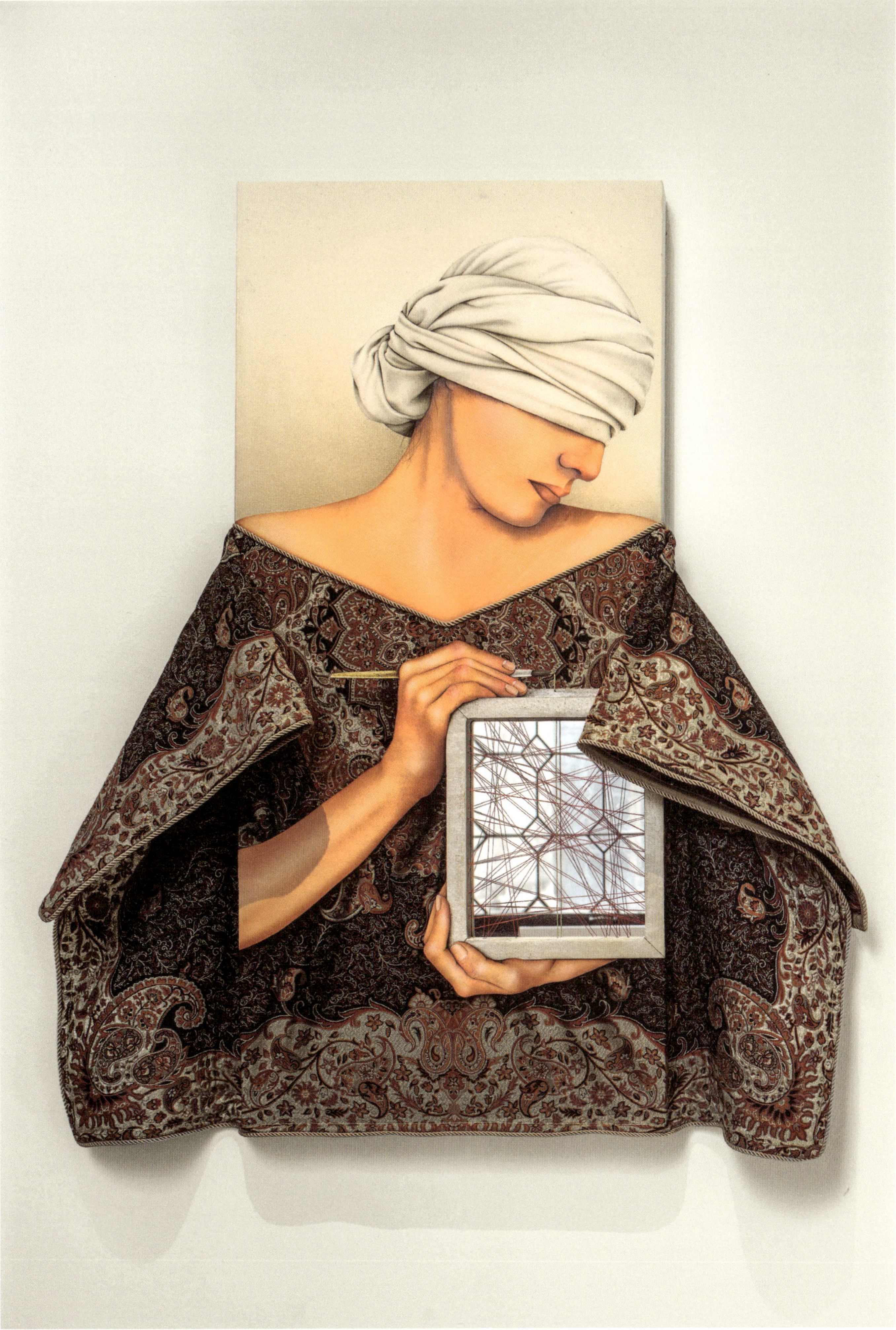

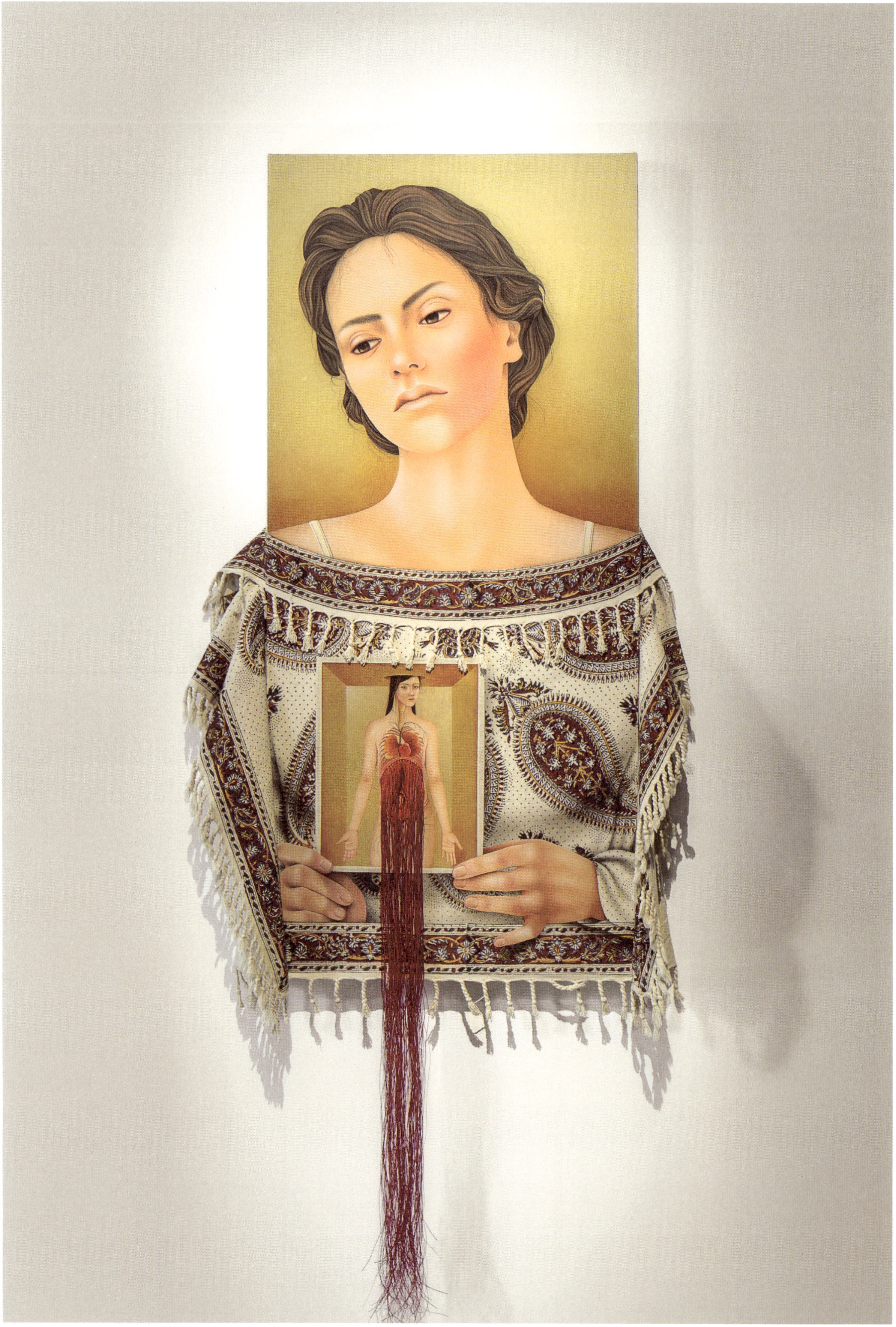

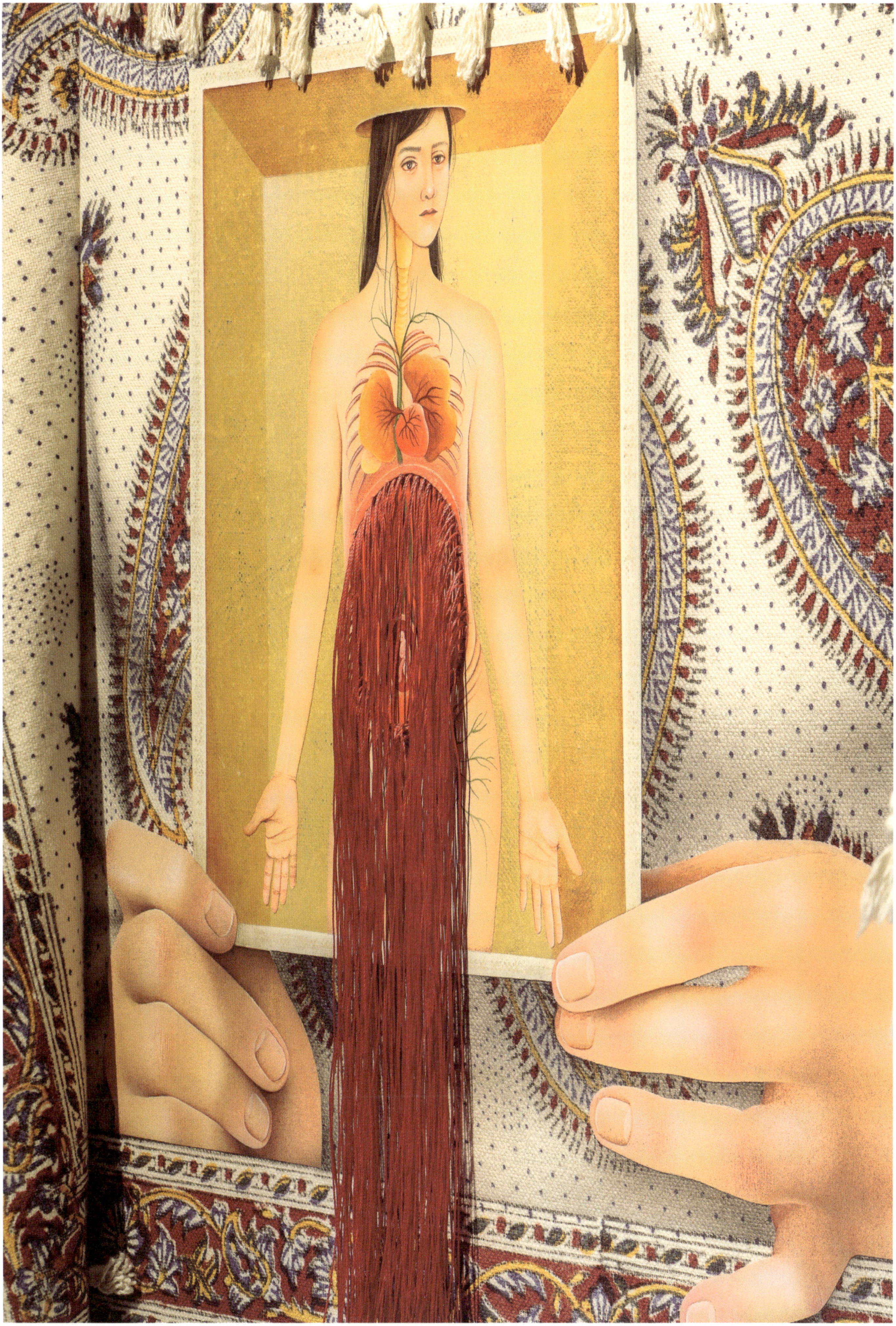

Teresa Margolles

Lives and works in Mexico City and Madrid

37, 39
Blowback / The Power, 2022
Sleeve surface inlaid with broken glass fragments from shootings, 17 October 2019, in Culiacán, Sinaloa
Haute couture dress designed by Alberto Scaal, Sinaloa
Dimensions variable
Installation views at *Uncombed, Unforeseen, Unconstrained,* Conservatorio di Musica Benedetto Marcello, Venice, 2022

38, 40
Blowback / The Power, 2022 (details)

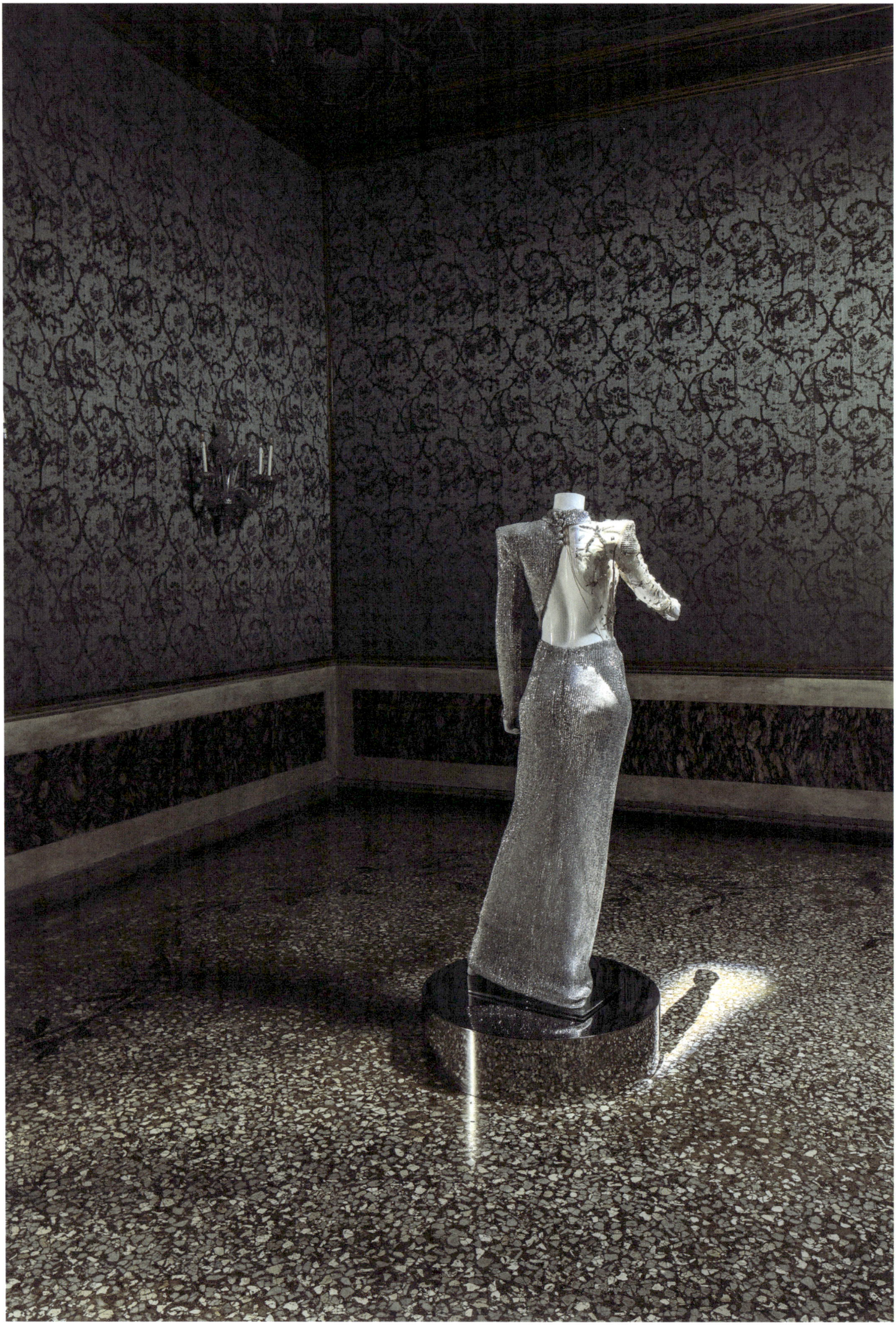

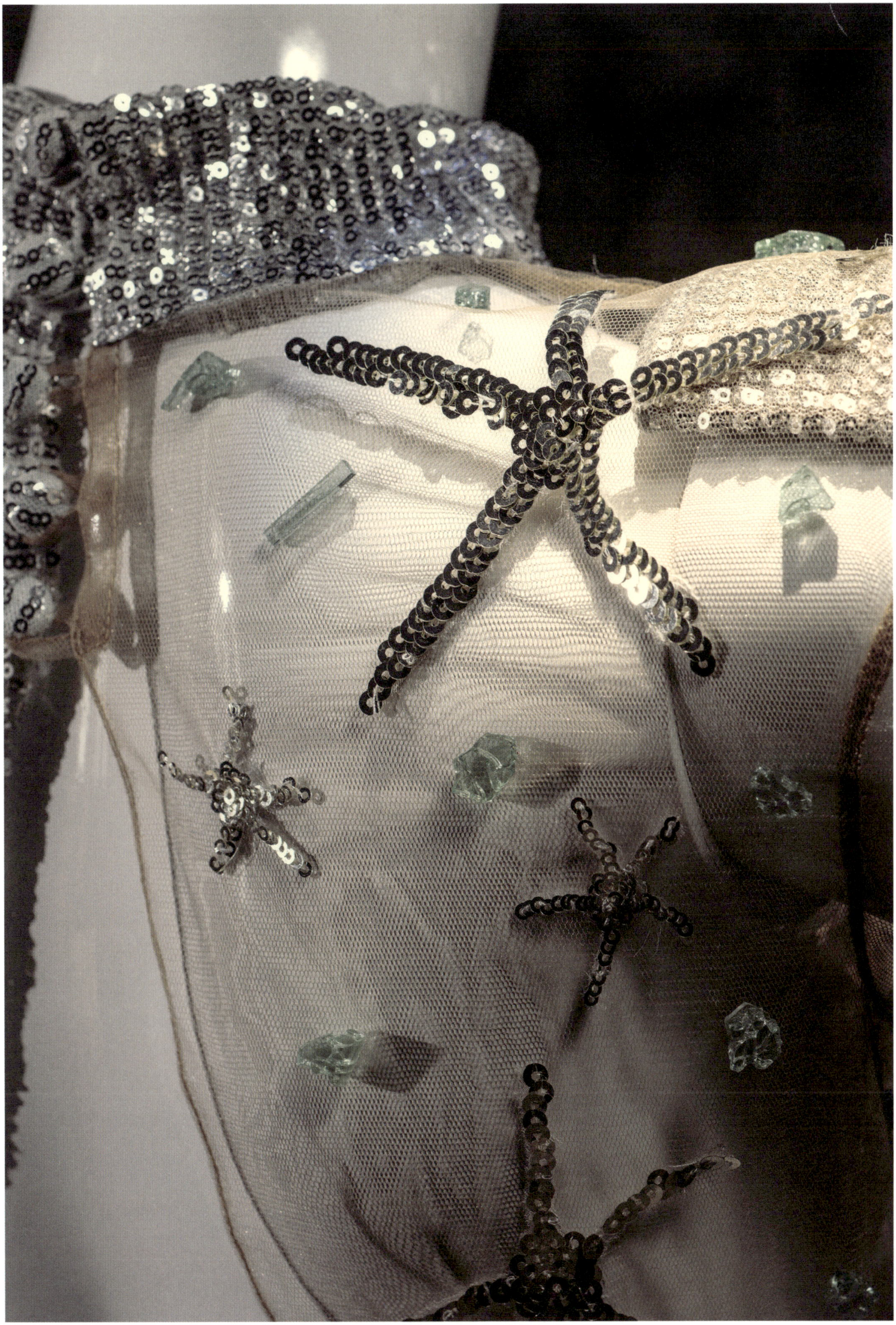

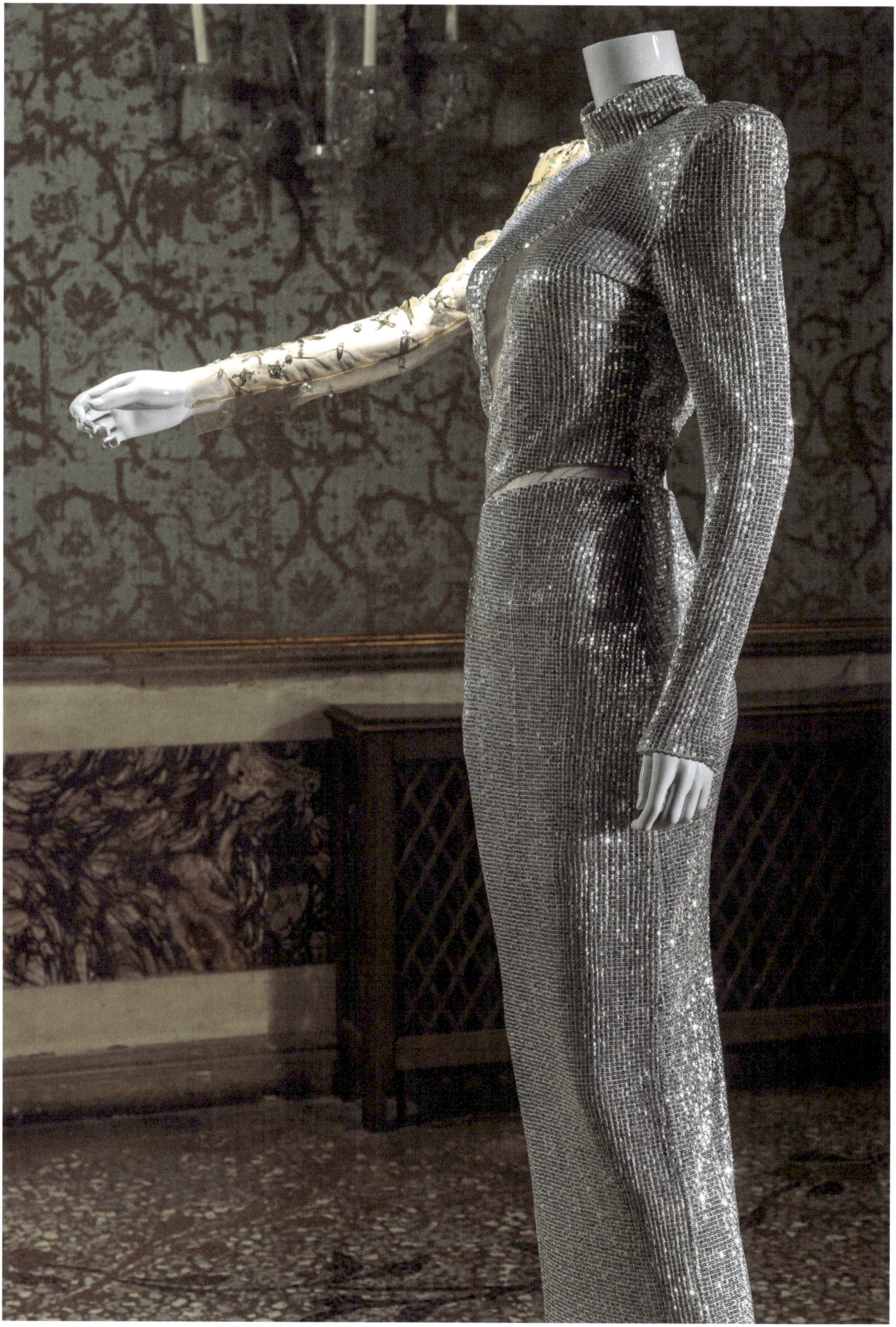

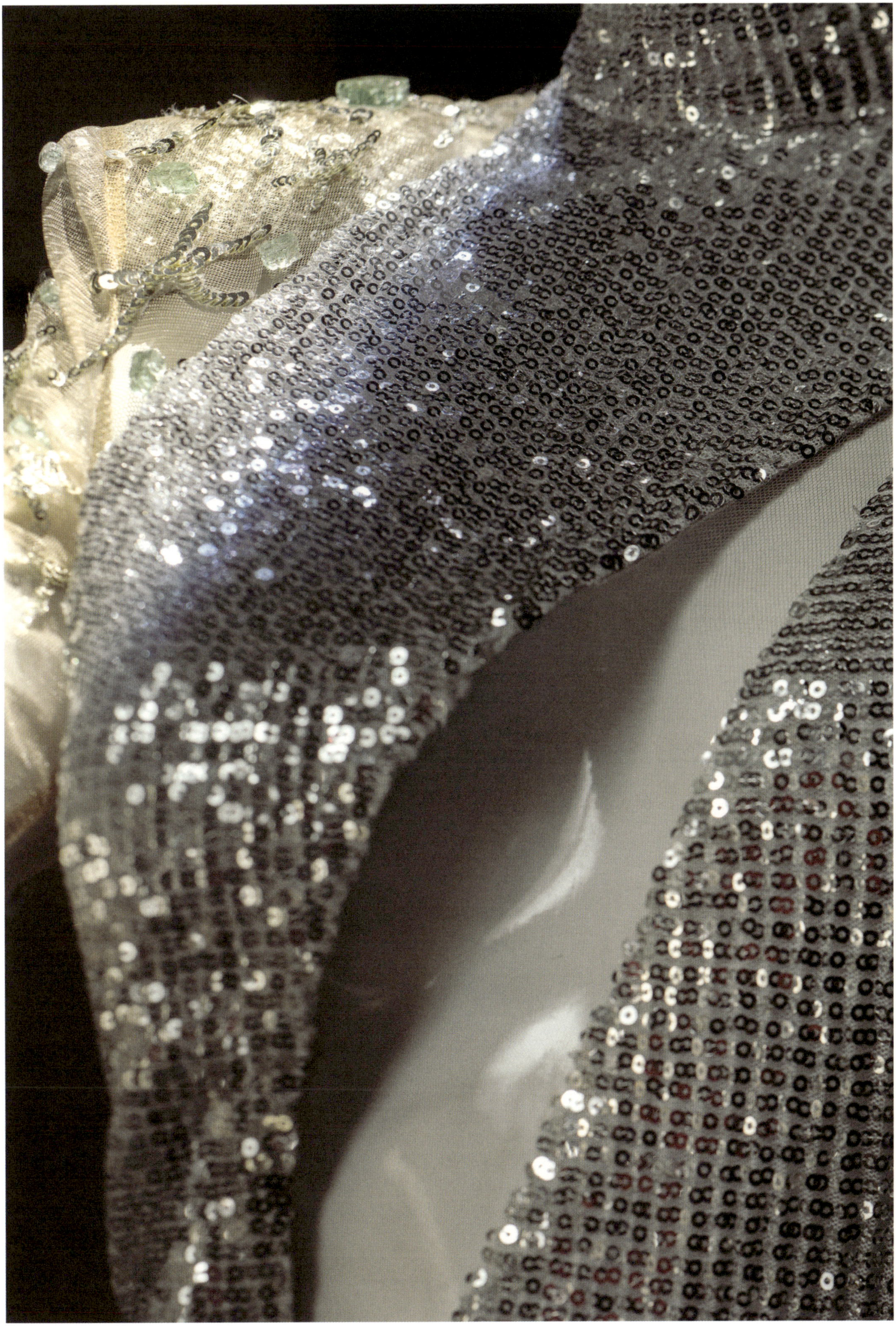

Si On

Lives and works in Krakow

41,42,45
Doomsday, 2020
Metal, wood, clothing, wooden sculptures
Dimensions variable
Overall installation approx. 9 × 8 m (354 × 315 in)
Installation views at *Uncombed, Unforeseen, Unconstrained,* Conservatorio di Musica Benedetto Marcello, Venice, 2022

43,44
Doomsday, 2020 (details)

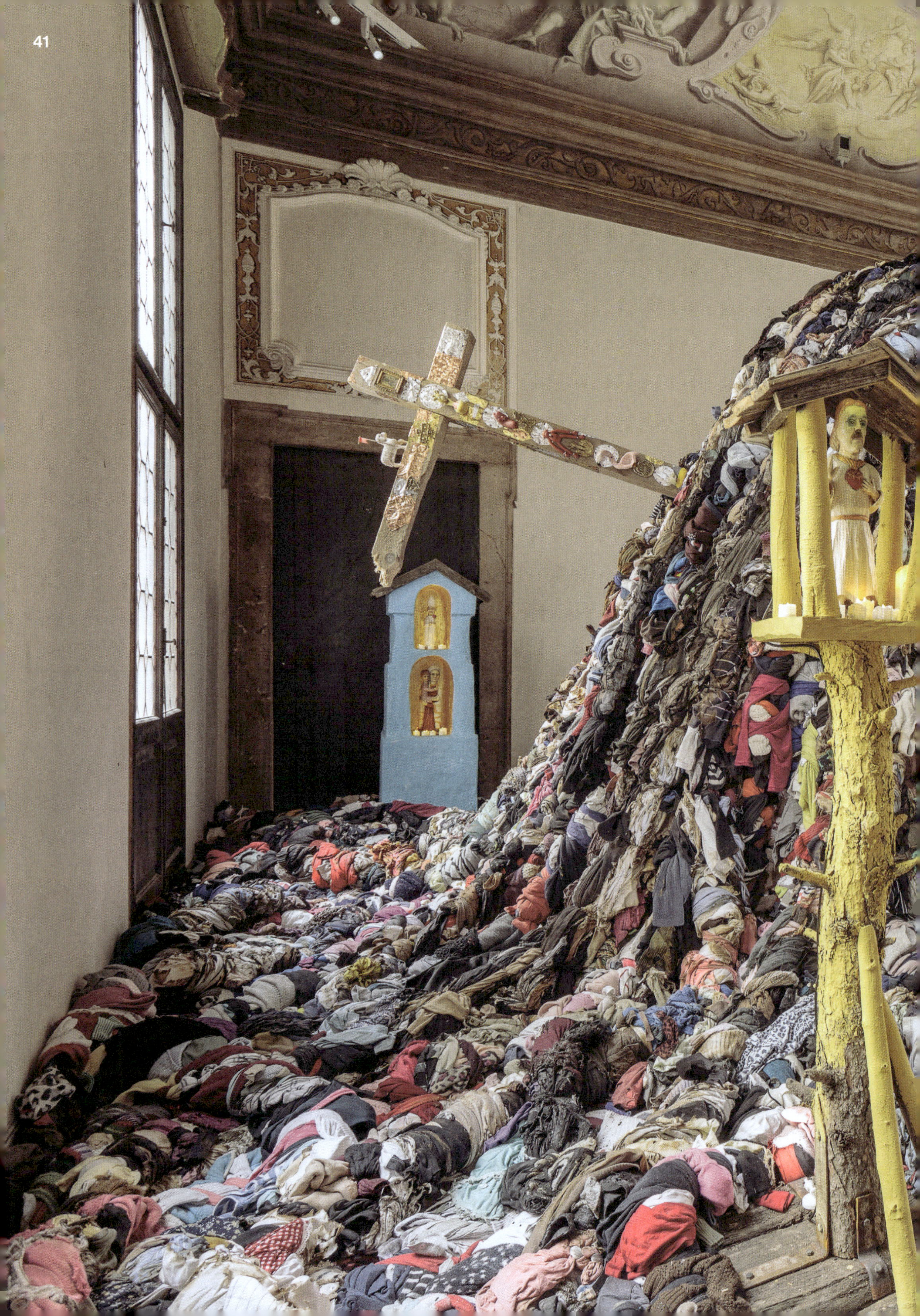

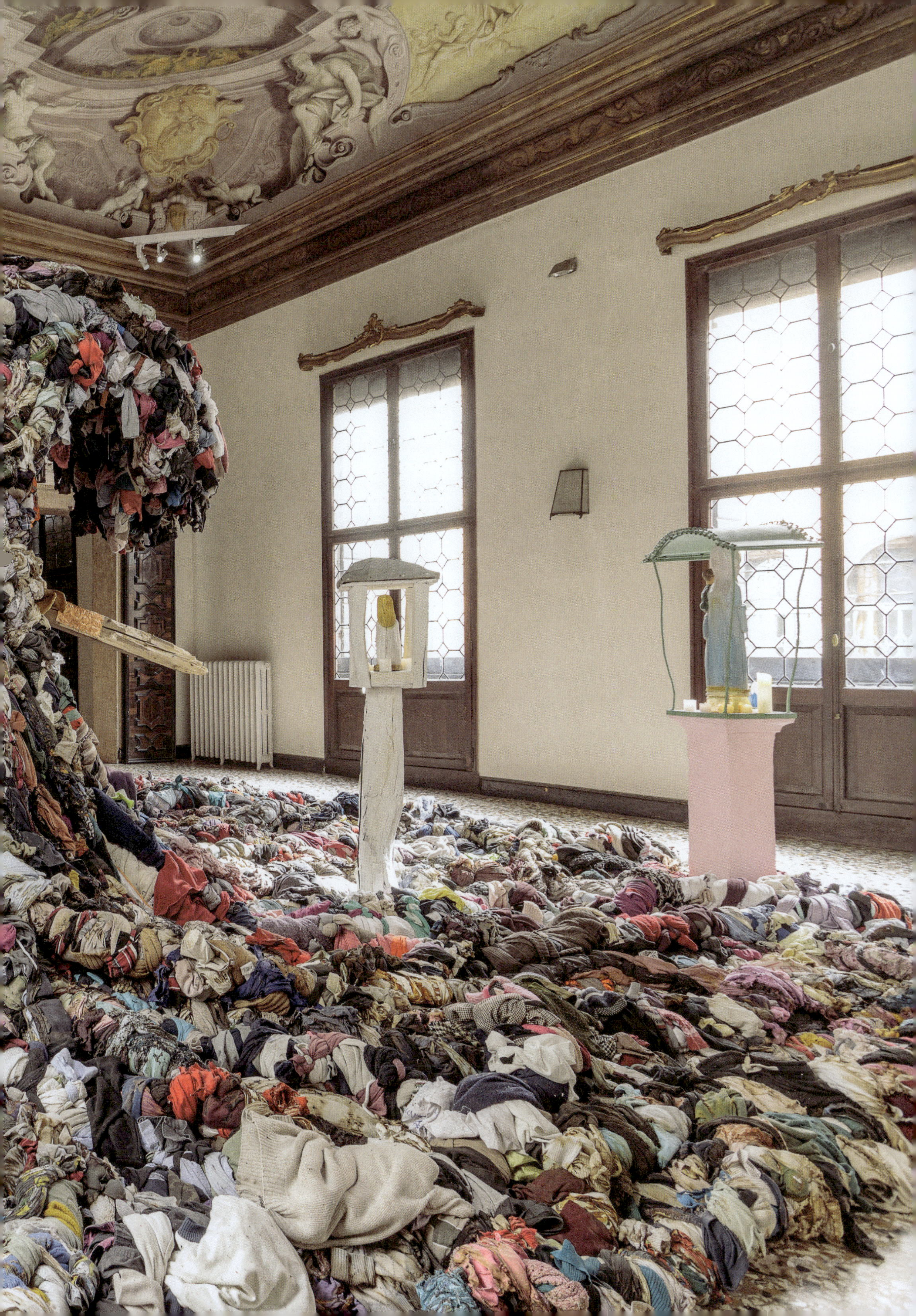

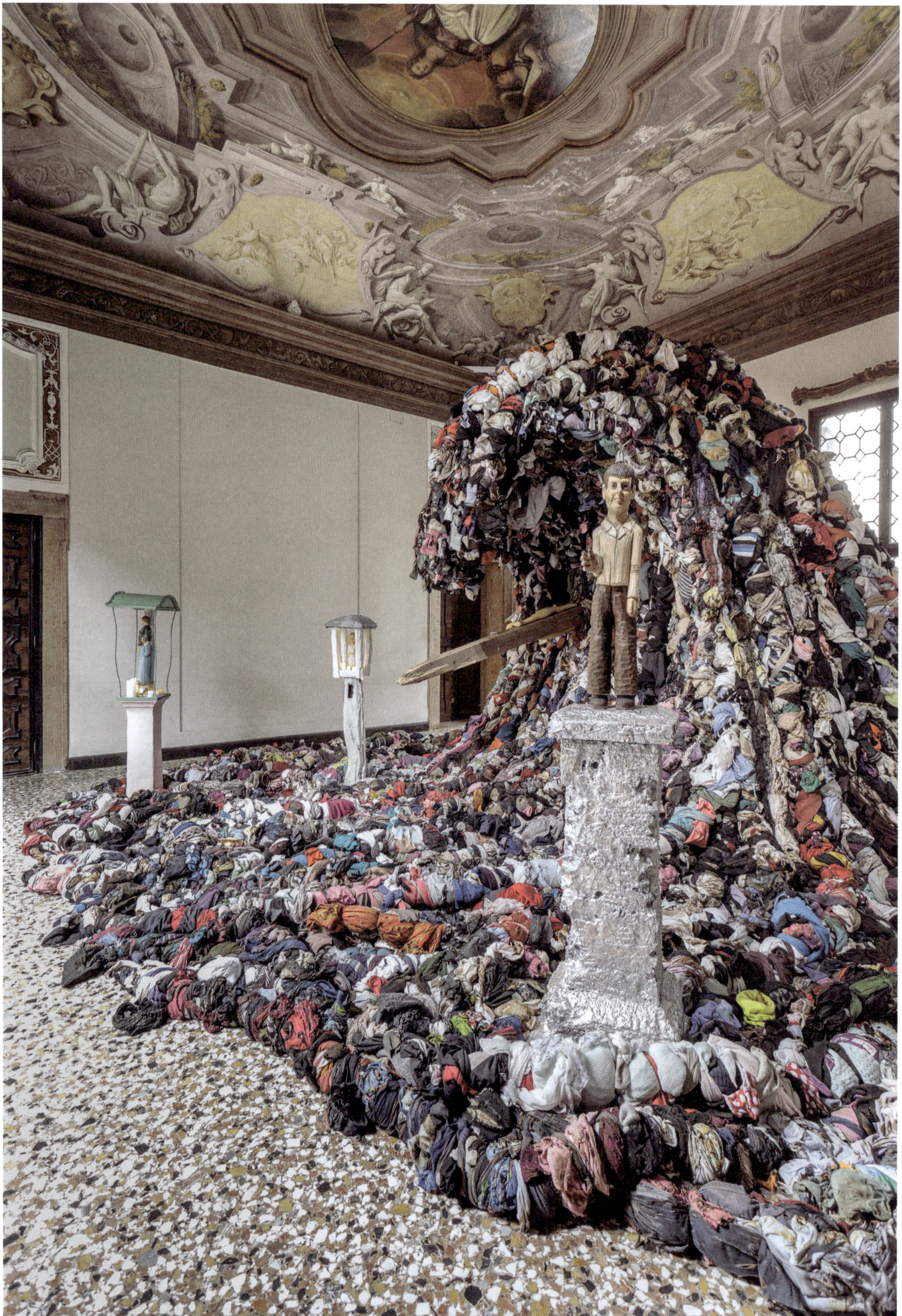

43

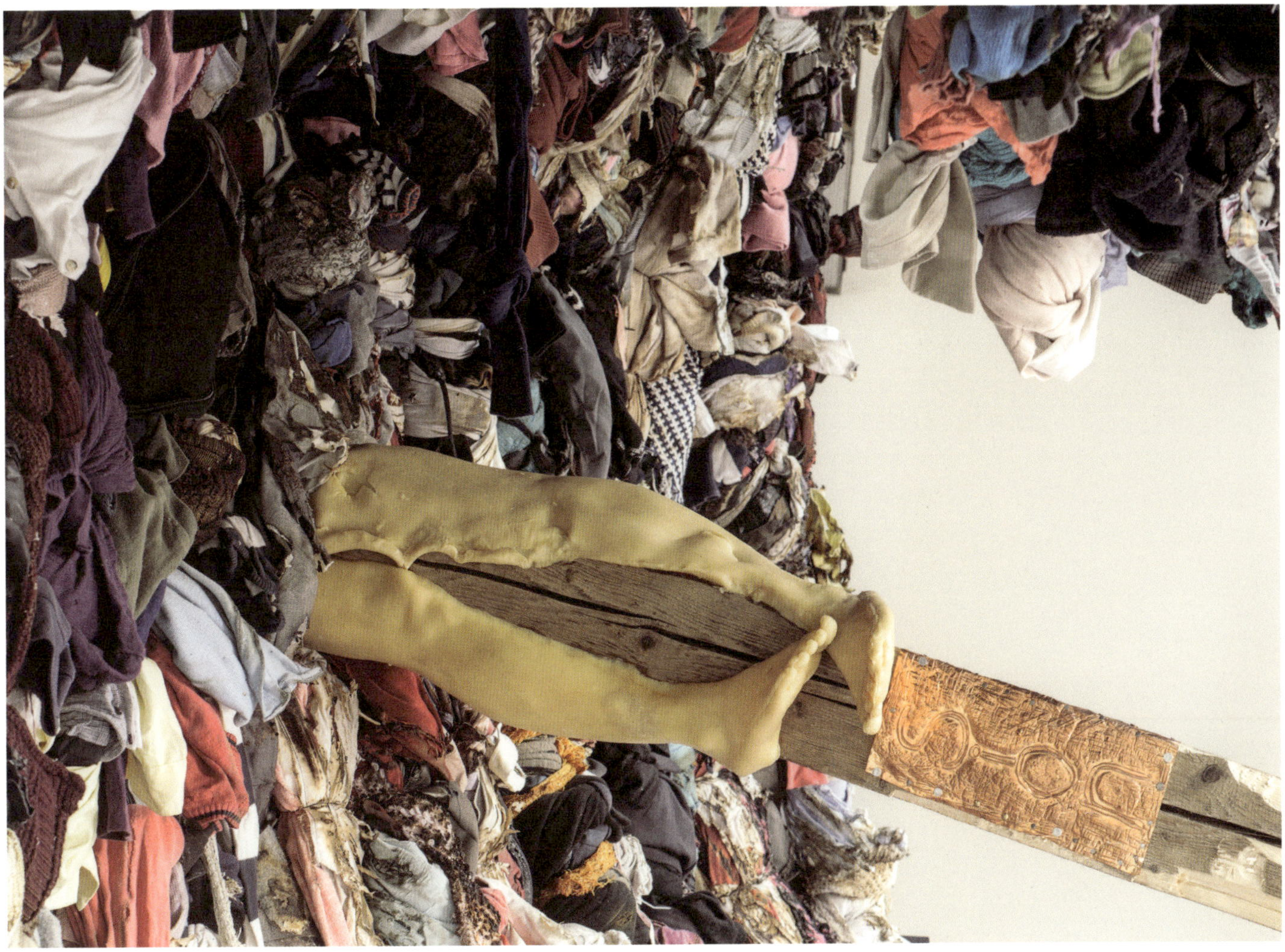

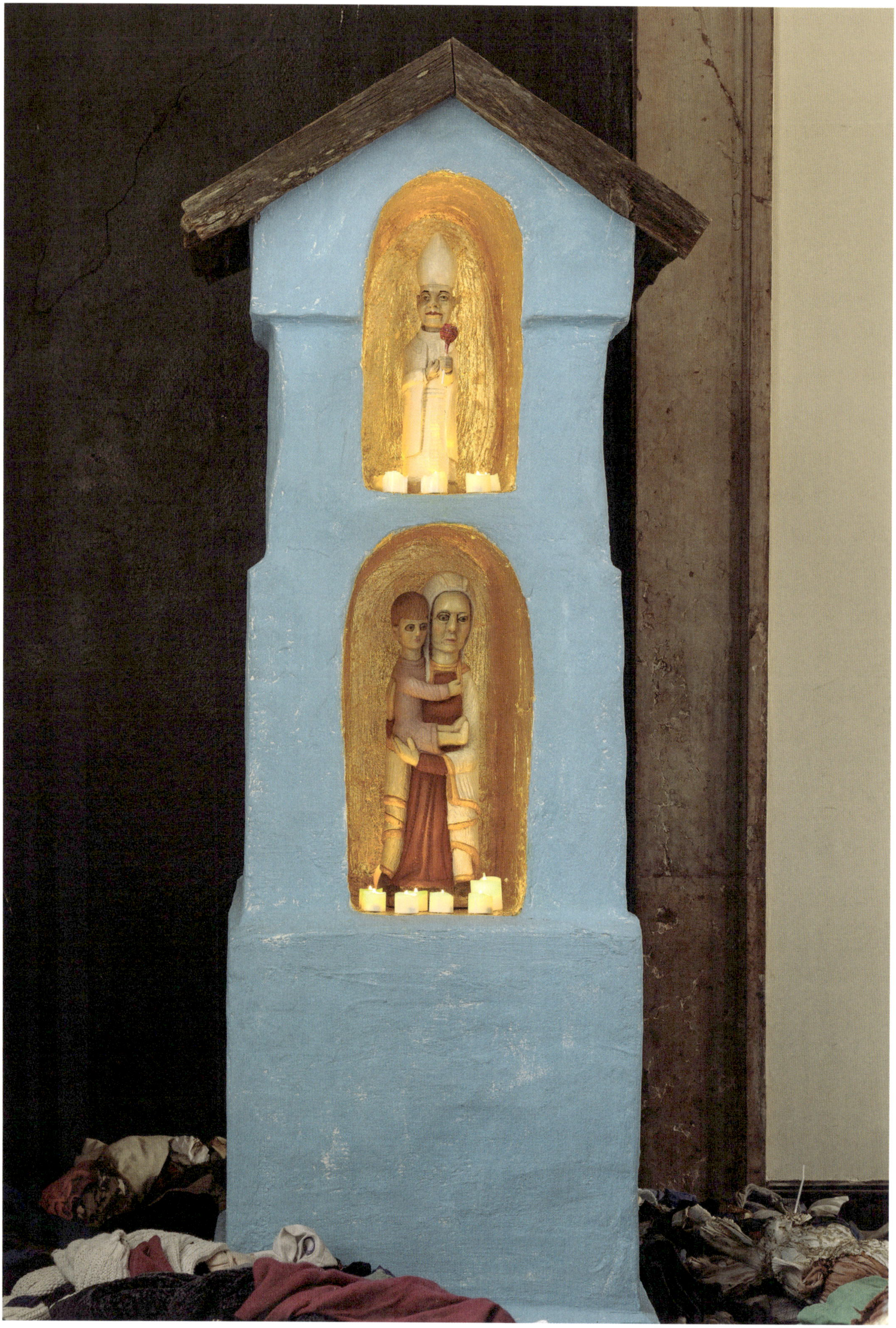

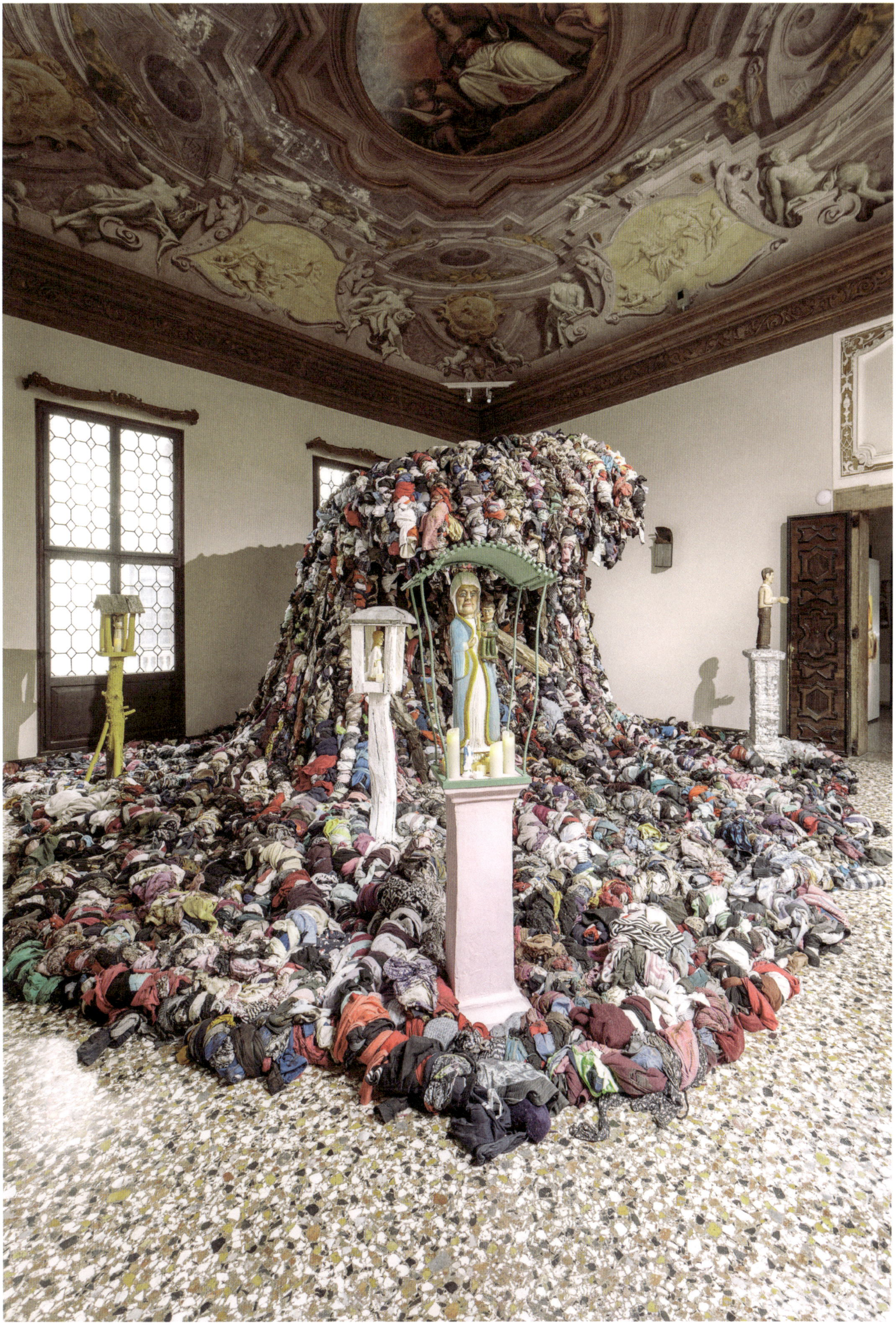

Martin Puryear

Lives and works in the Hudson Valley, NY

46, 47, 48, 49
Shackled, 2014
Iron
70 × 78 × 21.3 cm (27½ × 30⅝ × 8⅜ in)
Installation views at *Uncombed, Unforeseen, Unconstrained,* Conservatorio di Musica Benedetto Marcello, Venice, 2022

50
Shackled, 2014 (detail)

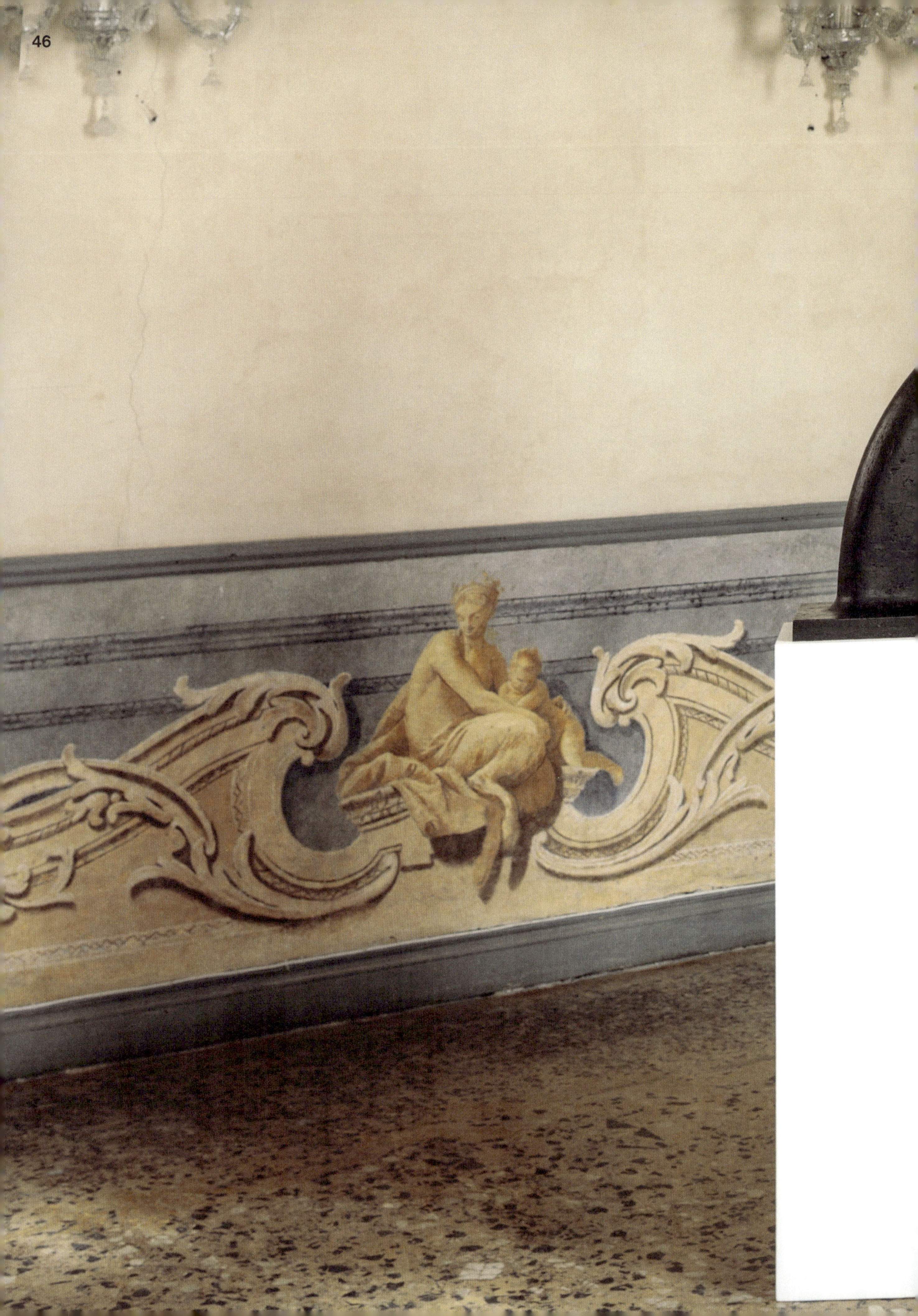

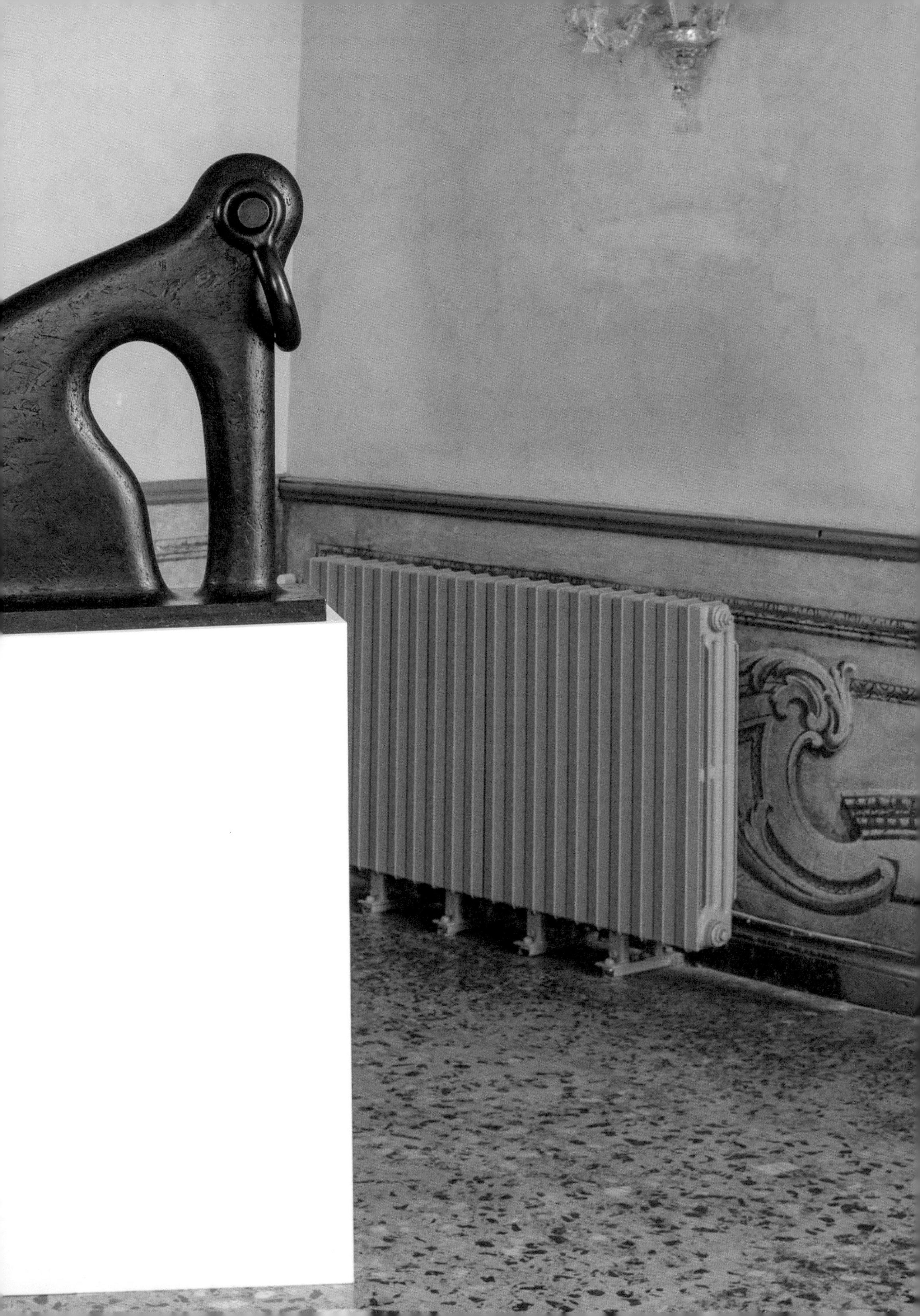

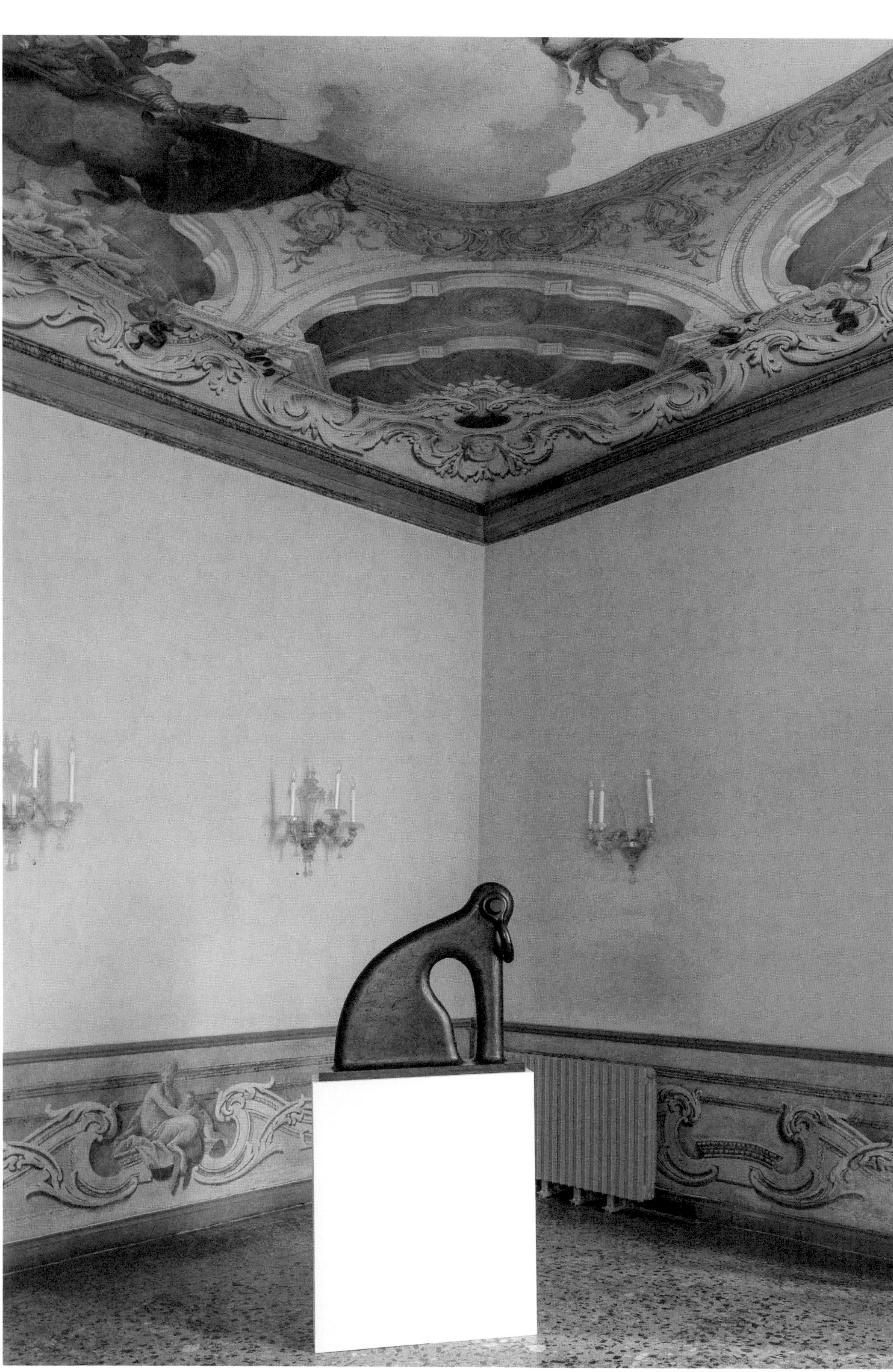

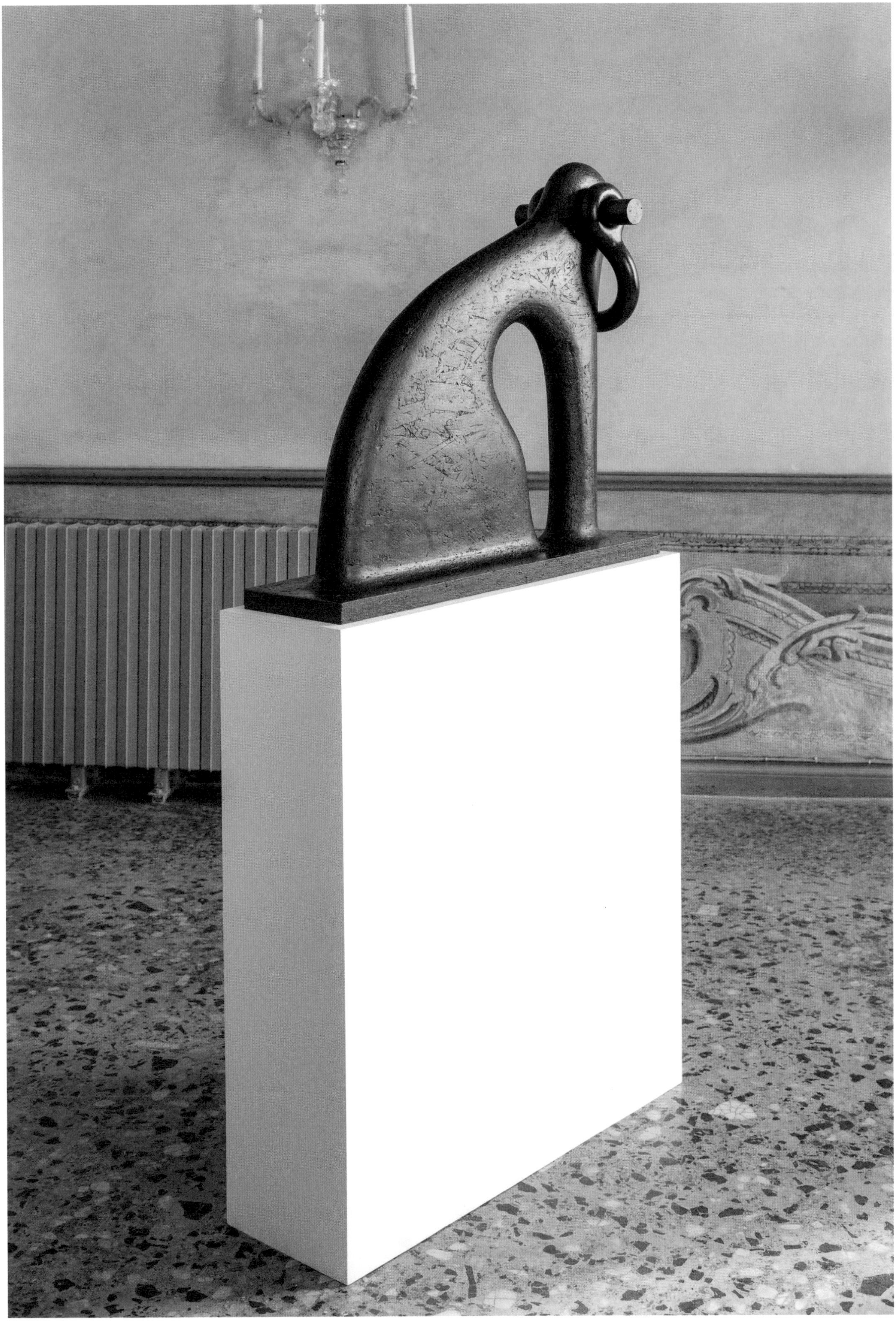

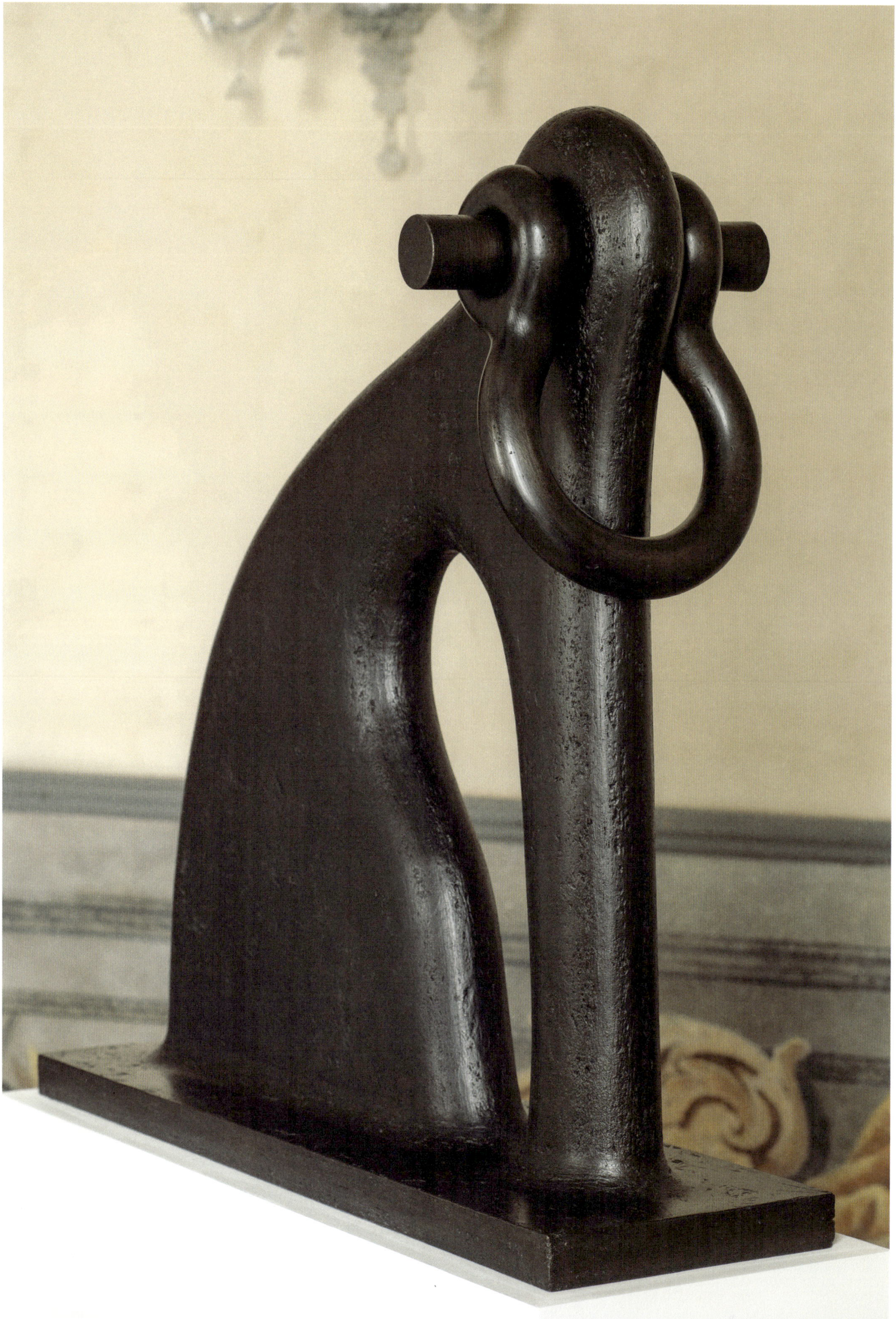

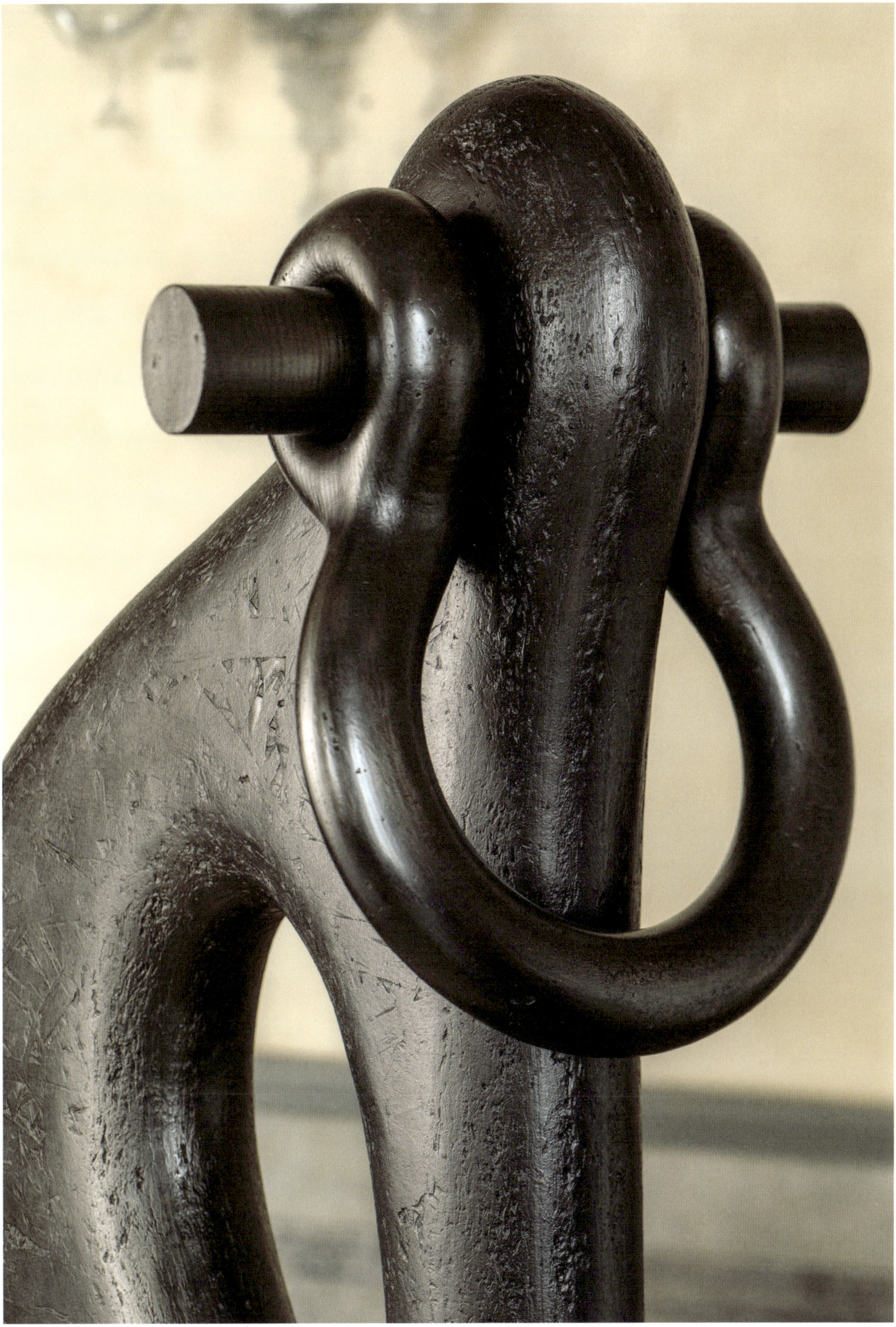

Rayyane Tabet

Lives and works in Beirut and San Francisco

51, 52
Steel Rings, 2013–
From the series *The Shortest Distance Between Two Points*, 2007–
21 of 1,213 rolled-steel rings engraved with locations along the Trans-Arabian Pipeline
Each ring: 78 × 10 × 0.6 cm (30¾ × 4 × ¼ in)
Overall dimensions variable
Installation views at *Uncombed, Unforeseen, Unconstrained,* Conservatorio di Musica Benedetto Marcello, Venice, 2022

53, 54
Steel Rings, 2013– (details)

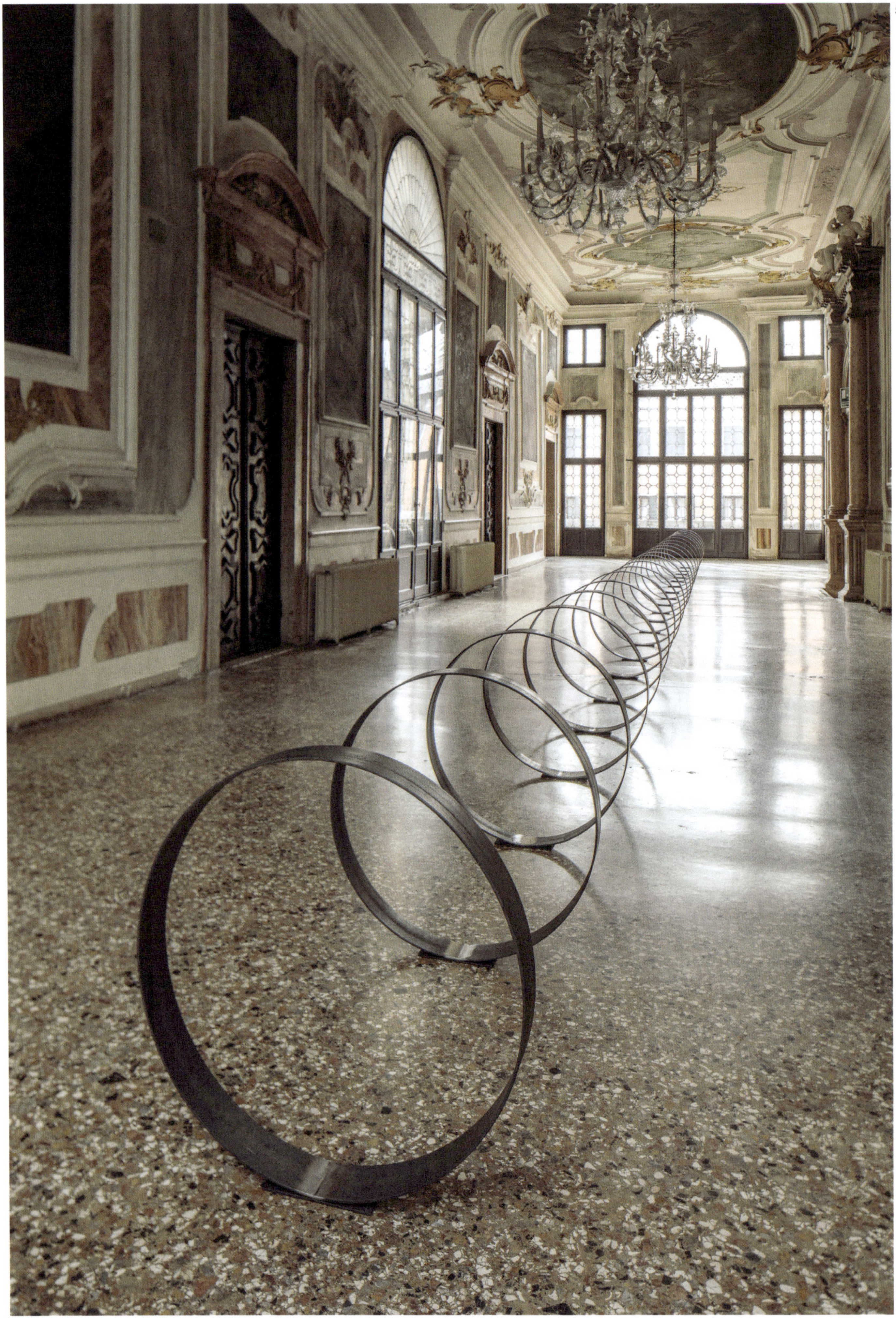

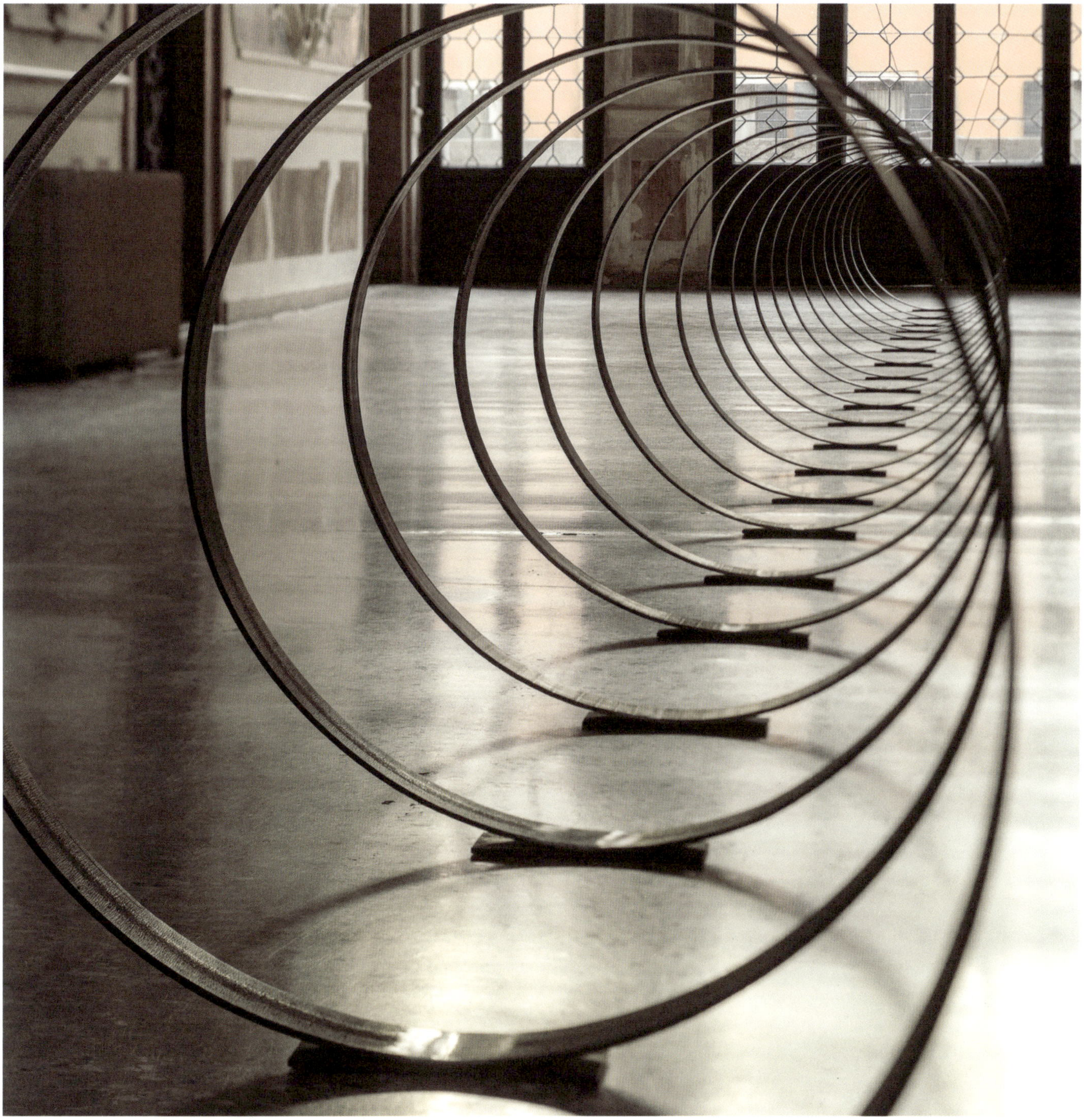

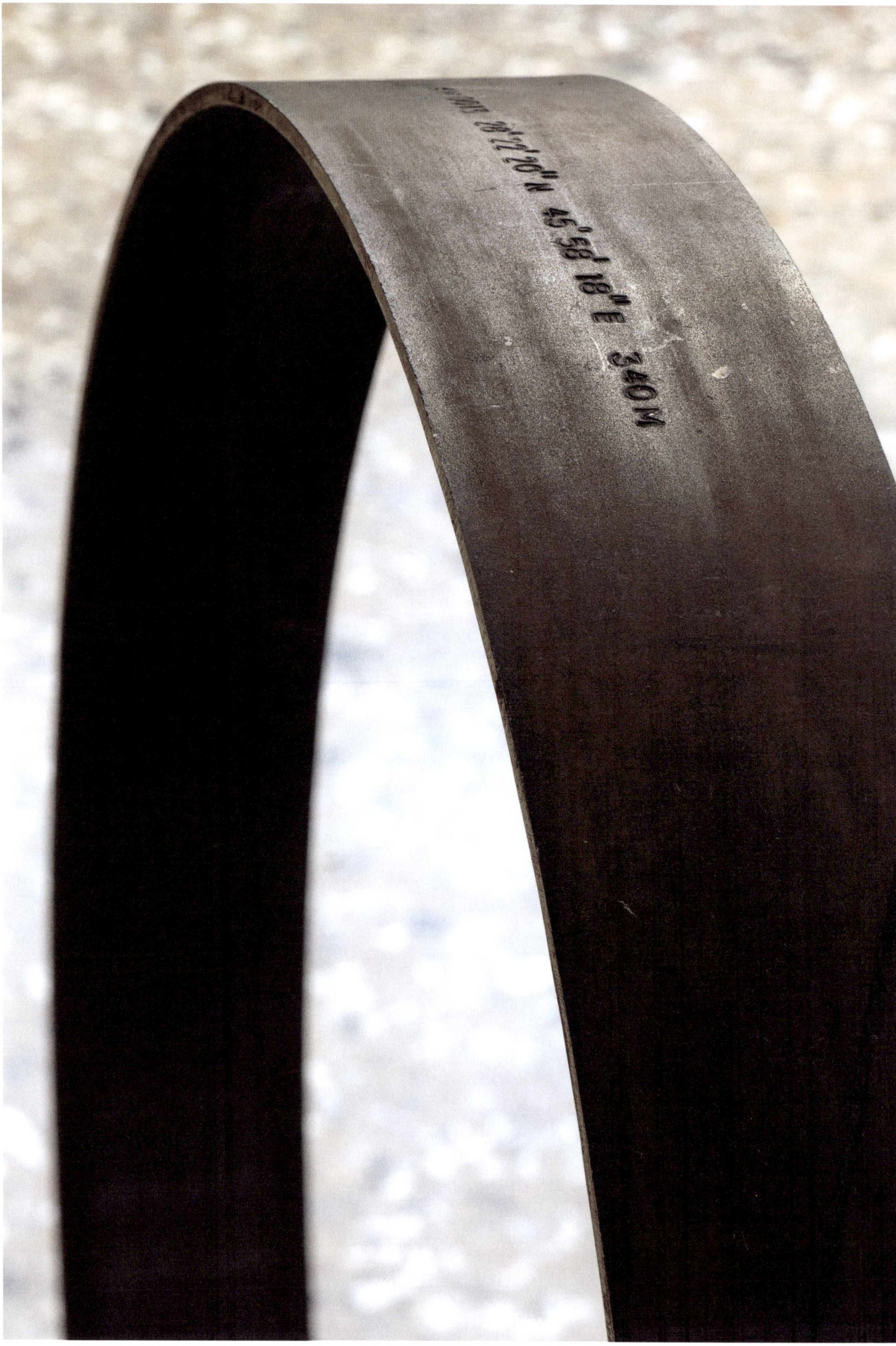

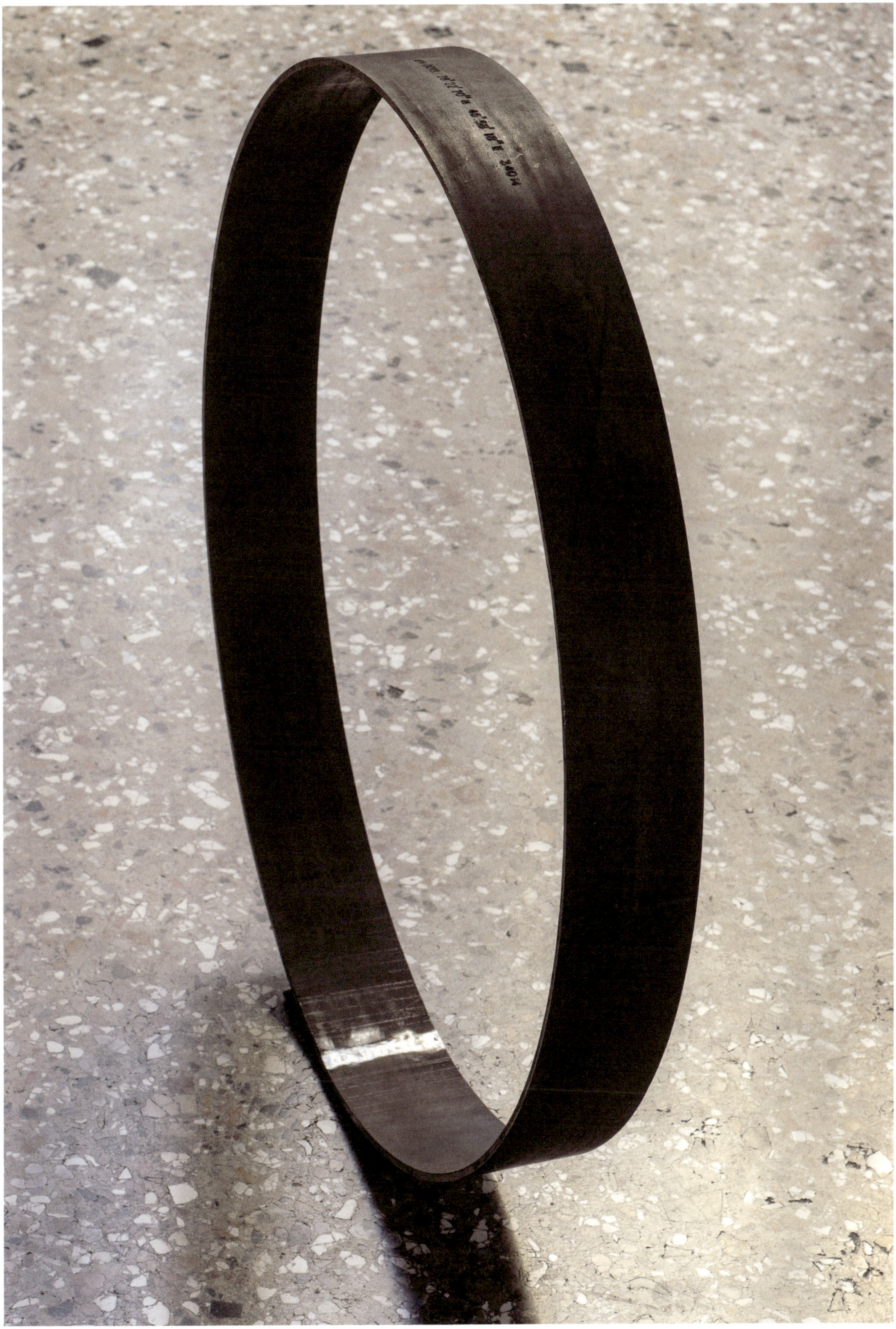

List of Works

Works in the Exhibition

Unless stated otherwise, each work is shown courtesy of and copyright to the respective artist and/or their named representative. All images, unless stated otherwise, are copyright to the individual artists.
Dimensions: height × width × depth

44–49
Darren Almond
In The Between, 2006
3-channel HD video with audio
14 min., 3 screens
Courtesy White Cube London and the artist
Installation views at *Uncombed, Unforeseen, Unconstrained*, Conservatorio di Musica Benedetto Marcello, Venice, 2022
Photography by Francesco Allegretto

52–55
Oliver Beer
Little Gods (Chamber Organ), 2022
32 vessels, 32 microphones, speakers, plinths, audio equipment
Dimensions variable
Courtesy the artist and Almine Rech Gallery
Installation views at *Uncombed, Unforeseen, Unconstrained*, Conservatorio di Musica Benedetto Marcello, Venice, 2022
Photography by Francesco Allegretto

Vessels (in order of pitch): Elephant stand, origin unknown, 20th c. (*Elephant Stand*); Greyhound lamp, by Abigail Aherne, UK, 21st c. (*Greyhound Lamp*); Pomeranian figurine, origin unknown, 20th c. (*Pink Pomeranian*); Blue and white ceramic vessel, probably Japan, date unknown (*Fish Vase Blue*); Siamese cat figurine, origin unknown, 20th c. (*Beautiful Cat*); Porcelain vase, by Capodimonte, Italy, 20th c. (*Grandma Vase*); Imari cat, China, 20th c. (*Fat Imari Cat*); Porcelain vase, probably China, 20th c. (*Pink Vase with People*); Dragon Koi teapot, China, 20th c. (*Dragon Teapot*); Brass and cloisonne vase, China, c. 1925 (*Crazy Dragon Vase*); Vase, by Panda Chinoiserie, Japan, 20th c. (*Blue Peacock Vase*); Cast iron piggy bank, origin unknown, probably 20th c. (*Heavy Pig*); Han-style funeral figure, China, date unknown (*Han dynasty tomb dog*); Ceramic vase, origin unknown, 20th c. (*Birdy Vase*); Leopard-shaped vase, by Brown and Ginger, UK, 21st c. (*Leopard Vase*); Toucan-shaped planter, UK, 21st c. (*Toucan Vase*); Stoneware pitcher, Germany, 19th c. (*Medieval Jug*); Nelson Rockefeller Collection hawk figurine, repro. by Mottahedeh (original China, 18th c.) (*Rockefeller Hawk*); Feng Shui carp figurine, probably China, date unknown (*Golden Fish*); Carved glass vase, China, 20th c. (*Orange Yellow Vase*); Ritual brass soul boat, probably Indonesia, date unknown (*Ship of the Dead*); Blue and white ceramic vase, probably Japan, date unknown (*Gazelle Vase*); Cornelius cat vase, by Walter Eris/Benaya, New Jersey, 2006 (*Sinister Cat Vase*); Dog figurine, by Hornsea Pottery, UK, 20th c. (*Pink Spaniel*); Imari lion figurine, probably Japan, date unknown (*Imari Lion*); Duck decanter, St Clement Majolica/France, 20th c. (*Duck Jug*); Glass owl pitcher, probably USA, 20th c. (*Glass Owl Vase*); Hare vase, by Quail Pottery, UK, 21st c. (*Hare Vase*); Cow jug, by F. Mendes La Caldas Da Rainha, Portugal, 20th c. (*Little Cow Jug*); British royal guard money box, by Hug Taylor, UK, 1985 (*Beefeater Money Box*); Blue and white pottery elephant teapot, probably Thailand, date unknown (*Elephant Teapot*); Bonzo Dog jug, probably Germany, 20th c. (*Bonzo Dog Jug*).

56
Oliver Beer
Cyanotype Drawing for Little Gods (Chamber Organ), 2022
Cyanotype, white ink and chalk
61 × 86 cm (24 × 34 in)
© Oliver Beer
Courtesy the artist and Almine Rech Gallery

60–63
Rana Begum in collaboration with Hyetal
No. 694 Hyetal, 2016
2 MDF panels, 46 coloured mirror Perspex, 2 vertical lights. Audio 10:10 min.
240 × 240 × 12 cm (94½ × 94½ × 4¾ in)
Installation views at *Uncombed, Unforeseen, Unconstrained*, Conservatorio di Musica Benedetto Marcello, Venice, 2022
Photography by Francesco Allegretto

67
Julian Charrière
And Beneath It All Flows Liquid Fire, 2019
UHD colour video, 16:10 aspect ratio, stereo sound
Continuous video loop
Edition of 5 + 2 AP
Courtesy the artist; Dittrich & Schlechtriem, Berlin; Galerie Tschudi, Zuoz; Sean Kelly, New York; Sies + Höke, Düsseldorf
Installation view at *Uncombed, Unforeseen, Unconstrained*, Conservatorio di Musica Benedetto Marcello, Venice, 2022
© Julian Charrière; V. G. Bild-Kunst, Bonn, Germany
Photograph by Jens Ziehe

68–73
Julian Charrière
Not All Who Wander Are Lost, 2019
Four unique pieces: glacial erratic rock, drill cores, aluminium, brass, copper, stainless steel
135 × 100 × 682 cm (53¼ × 39½ × 268½ in)
99 × 100 × 435 cm (39 × 39½ × 171¼ in)
150 × 120 × 525 cm (59 × 47¼ × 206¾ in)
120 × 100 × 738 cm (47¼ × 39½ × 290½ in)
Installation views at *Uncombed, Unforeseen, Unconstrained*, Conservatorio di Musica Benedetto Marcello, Venice, 2022
Photography by Francesco Allegretto

76–79
David Claerbout
Wildfire (Meditation on Fire), 2019–2020
Single-channel video projection, 3-D animation, stereo audio, colour, 24 min.
Collaboration with Musea Brugge
Courtesy the artist and galleries Esther Schipper, Berlin; Sean Kelly, New York; Rüdiger Schöttle, Munich; Pedro Cera, Lisbon; Annet Gelink, Amsterdam; Micheline Szwajcer, Antwerp
Installation views at *Uncombed, Unforeseen, Unconstrained*, Conservatorio di Musica Benedetto Marcello, Venice, 2022
Photography by Francesco Allegretto
Video stills [pp. 76, 79] courtesy the artist

82–87
Bharti Kher
The Intermediaries (series), 2019
Mixed media, unless otherwise noted: clay, wax, brass, copper, cement
Dimensions do not include base or plinth
Courtesy the artist and Hauser & Wirth | Courtesy the artist and Perrotin
Installation views at *Uncombed, Unforeseen, Unconstrained*, Conservatorio di Musica Benedetto Marcello, Venice, 2022
Photography by Francesco Allegretto

Adoring Audience, 2019
16.5 × 6.4 × 7.6 cm (6½ × 2½ × 3 in)
Courtesy the artist and Perrotin

All Kinds of Brothers, 2019
38 × 10 × 15.2 cm (15 × 4 × 6 in)
Courtesy the artist and Perrotin

Ardhanarishvara, 2016
36 × 11 × 12 cm (14¼ × 4¼ × 4¾ in)
Courtesy the artist and Perrotin

85 (*middle*)
As Dangerous as an Albatross, 2019
26.4 × 10.1 × 20.3 cm (10½ × 4 × 8 in)
© Bharti Kher, courtesy the artist and Hauser & Wirth

87
Bird Girl, 2018
Clay, cement, wood, paint, wax, brass
36 × 13 × 10 cm (14¼ × 5 × 4 in)
Courtesy the artist and Perrotin

Echidna, 2019
44.2 × 12.7 × 15.2 cm (17½ × 5 × 6 in)
© Bharti Kher, courtesy the artist and Hauser & Wirth

Homonym, 2019
39.4 × 12.7 × 12.7 cm (15½ × 5 × 5 in)
© Bharti Kher, courtesy the artist and Hauser & Wirth

Intermediary Family Maquette, 2018
Clay, 35 × 20 × 11 cm (13¾ × 8 × 4¼ in)
© Bharti Kher, courtesy the artist and Hauser & Wirth

Man Woman, 2019
32 × 17.8 × 18 cm (12½ × 7 × 7 in)
29.2 × 10 × 10 cm (11½ × 4 × 4 in)
Courtesy the artist and Perrotin

Matters of the Spirit, 2019
49.2 × 24.3 × 26.4 cm (19¼ × 9½ × 10½ in)
© Bharti Kher, courtesy the artist and Hauser & Wirth

Namaste Henry Moore, 2019
37 × 14 × 20 cm (14½ × 5½ × 7¾ in)
Courtesy the artist and Perrotin

Nationalist, 2019
41.1 × 10.6 × 17.7 cm (16¼ × 4¼ × 7 in)
© Bharti Kher, courtesy the artist and Hauser & Wirth

Self-Portrait, 2019
46 × 18 × 21.5 cm (18 × 7 × 8½ in)
Courtesy the artist and Perrotin

84
Ship of Fools, 2019
38 × 26.5 × 26.5 cm (15 × 10½ × 10½ in)
© Bharti Kher, courtesy the artist and Hauser & Wirth

Shit Heads, 2019
32 × 10 × 14 cm (12½ × 4 × 5½ in)
32 × 10 × 18 cm (12½ × 4 × 7 in
7.6 × 18 × 21.5 cm (3 × 7 × 8½ in)
Courtesy the artist and Perrotin

Silly Men with Problems, 2019
19 x 5 x 5 cm (7½ x 2 x 2 in)
17.8 x 9 x 12.7 cm (7 x 3½ x 5 in)
Courtesy the artist and Perrotin

85 (*top*)
Sisters, 2019
31.6 × 11.5 × 20.3 cm (12½ × 4½ × 8 in)
© Bharti Kher, courtesy the artist and Hauser & Wirth

85 (*bottom*)
Talisman for September, 2019
19 × 12.7 × 26.4 cm (7½ × 5 × 10½ in)
© Bharti Kher, courtesy the artist and Hauser & Wirth

The Fallow Maquette, 2018
Clay, 34 × 20 × 11 cm (13½ × 8 × 4¼ in)
© Bharti Kher, courtesy the artist and Hauser & Wirth

86
The Great Seat of Learning, 2019
63.5 × 15.2 × 25.4 cm (25 × 6 × 10 in)
Courtesy the artist and Perrotin

The Patriarchy of Bananas, 2019
43 × 20.3 × 20.3 cm (17 × 8 × 8 in)
Courtesy the artist and Perrotin

The Players, 2019
33.5 × 10 × 17.7 cm (13¼ × 4 × 7 in)
10.7 × 5 × 7.6 cm (4¼ × 2 × 3 in)
23 × 6.3 × 12.7 cm (9 × 2½ × 5 in)
Courtesy the artist and Perrotin

This Funny Family I Know, 2019
36.8 × 16.5 × 17.7 cm (14½ × 6½ × 7 in)
21.6 × 7.6 × 15.2 cm (8½ × 3 × 6 in)
Courtesy the artist and Perrotin

90, 91
Arghavan Khosravi
This Shall Also Pass (*The Anatomy of A Woman Series #6*), 2019
Acrylic, found textile, wooden panel, Plexiglas, thread, wooden cut-out
94 × 48 cm (37 × 19 in)
Private collection
Installation view at *Uncombed, Unforeseen, Unconstrained*, Conservatorio di Musica Benedetto Marcello, Venice, 2022
Photography by Francesco Allegretto

92
Arghavan Khosravi
Quite Determined (The Anatomy of A Woman Series #4), 2019
Acrylic, cotton canvas, found textile, wooden panels, rope
94 × 43 cm (37 × 17 in)
Private collection
Installation view at *Uncombed, Unforeseen, Unconstrained*, Conservatorio di Musica Benedetto Marcello, Venice, 2022
Photography by Francesco Allegretto

93
Arghavan Khosravi
The Anatomy of A Woman Series #5, 2019
Acrylic, cotton canvas, found textile, wooden panels, thread, mirror
96.5 × 78.8 cm (38 × 31 in)
Private collection, Europe
Installation view at *Uncombed, Unforeseen, Unconstrained*, Conservatorio di Musica Benedetto Marcello, Venice, 2022
Photography by Francesco Allegretto

94, 95
Arghavan Khosravi
The Anatomy of A Woman Series #2, 2019
Acrylic, cotton canvas, found woodblock-printed textile, wooden panels, thread
137 × 63.5 cm (54 × 25 in)
Private collection
Installation view at *Uncombed, Unforeseen, Unconstrained*, Conservatorio di Musica Benedetto Marcello, Venice, 2022
Photography by Francesco Allegretto

98–101
Teresa Margolles
Blowback / The Power, 2022
Sleeve surface inlaid with broken glass fragments from shootings, 17 October 2019, in Culiacán, Sinaloa. Haute couture dress designed by Alberto Scaal, Sinaloa.
Dimensions variable
Courtesy the artist and Galerie Peter Kilchmann, Zurich
Installation views at *Uncombed, Unforeseen, Unconstrained*, Conservatorio di Musica Benedetto Marcello, Venice, 2022
Photography by Francesco Allegretto

104–109
Si On
Doomsday, 2020
Metal, wood, clothing, wooden sculptures
Dimensions variable.
Overall installation approx. 9 × 8 m (354 × 315 in)
Installation views at *Uncombed, Unforeseen, Unconstrained*, Conservatorio di Musica Benedetto Marcello, Venice, 2022
Photography by Francesco Allegretto

112–117
Martin Puryear
Shackled, 2014
Iron
70 × 78 × 21.3 cm (27½ × 30⅝ × 8⅜ in)
© Martin Puryear, courtesy Matthew Marks Gallery
Installation views at *Uncombed, Unforeseen, Unconstrained*, Conservatorio di Musica Benedetto Marcello, Venice, 2022
Photography by Francesco Allegretto

120–123
Rayyane Tabet
Steel Rings, 2013–
From the series *The Shortest Distance Between Two Points*, 2007–
21 of 1,213 rolled-steel rings engraved with locations along the Trans-Arabian Pipeline
Each ring: 78 × 10 × 0.6 cm (30¾ × 4 × ¼ in)
Overall dimensions variable
Courtesy the artist and Sfeir-Semler Gallery Beirut/Hamburg
KM015 to KM026 Collection of the Ministry of Culture, Saudi Arabia
Installation views at *Uncombed, Unforeseen, Unconstrained*, Conservatorio di Musica Benedetto Marcello, Venice, 2022
Photography by Francesco Allegretto

Other Images

8
Caspar David Friedrich
Wanderer Above the Sea of Fog, c. 1817
Oil on canvas
94.8 × 74.8 cm (37¼ × 29½ in)
Collection Hamburger Kunsthalle
© Hamburger Kunsthalle/bpk
Photograph by Elke Walford

10
Katsushika Hokusai
Under the Wave off Kanagawa (Kanagawa oki nami ura), also known as *The Great Wave*, from the series *Thirty-six Views of Mount Fuji (Fugaku sanjūrok-kei)*, c. 1830–1832
Woodblock print; ink and colour on paper
25.7 × 37.9 cm (10 × 15 in)
Collection The Metropolitan Museum of Art, New York, H.O. Havemeyer Collection, Bequest of Mrs H.O. Havemeyer, 1929

Artist Biographies

DARREN ALMOND
Born 1971, Wigan, United Kingdom
Lives and works in London, United Kingdom

Education
1993 BA Fine Arts, Winchester School of Art, University of Southampton, UK

Selected Solo Exhibitions
2021 *Dark Light*, Galerie Max Hetzler, Paris, France
2019 *In Light of Time*, Jesus College, University of Cambridge, UK
In Temple Grounds, Galeria Alfonso Artiaco, Naples, Italy
2018 *Light of Time*, Institute for Sociology of the Arts, Tokyo, Japan
The Light Between Us, Villa Pignatelli-Casa della Fotografia, Naples, Italy
Darren Almond, White Cube, London, UK
The Light of Time, Crown Point Press, San Francisco, CA, USA
The Swerve / The Light of Time, Galerie Xippas, Geneva, Switzerland
2017 *Timescape*, Mudam, Luxembourg
2016 *Darren Almond: New Work*, NewArtCentre, Salisbury, UK
Shadow and Light, Museum Sinclair Haus, Bad Homburg, Germany
...beyond reach but within reason, Galerie Max Hetzler, Paris, France
Within The Shadow of The Sun, SCAI The Bathhouse, Tokyo, Japan
Time and Being, White Cube, Hong Kong
2015 *The Amalfi Sketchbook,* Neue Galerie, Graz, Austria
Darren Almond, Dirimart, Istanbul, Turkey
Fullmoons, Galleri K, Oslo, Norway
Present Form, Christie's Mayfair, London, UK
Works on Paper, Galerie Max Hetzler, Berlin, Germany
2014 *In the Shadow of Words*, Bloomberg Space, London, UK
Darren Almond, Matthew Marks Gallery, Los Angeles, CA, USA
Work Work Work, Galleri Bo Bjerggaard, Copenhagen, Denmark
Darren Almond, Galeria Alfonso Artiaco, Naples, Italy
To Leave A Light Impression, White Cube, London, UK
2013 *Second Thoughts*, Art Tower Mito, Japan
Darren Almond, Atmos, Sala Alcalá 31, Madrid, Spain
Hemispheres and Continents, Matthew Marks Gallery, New York, NY, USA
2012 *Fullmoon and Night + Fog*, Domaine de Chaumont-sur-Loire, France
All Things Pass, Galerie Max Hetzler, Berlin, Germany
2011 *Landscape with Path,* High Line, New York, NY, USA
Nocturne, Villa Merkel, Esslingen, Germany
... Between Here and the Surface of the Moon, FRAC Auvergne, Clermont-Ferrand; FRAC Haute-Normandie, Sotteville-lès-Rouen, France
2010 *As it is*, Alfonso Artiaco, Naples, Italy
The Principle of Moments, White Cube, London, UK
Fullmoon@Eifel, Weidingen, Eifel, Germany
Matthew Marks Gallery, New York, NY, USA
PKM Trinity Gallery, Seoul, South Korea
2009 *Sometimestill*, Galerie Max Hetzler, Berlin, Germany
2008 *Fire Under Snow*, Parasol unit foundation for contemporary art, London, UK
Nail to Nail, David Patton, Los Angeles, CA, USA
In The Between, Eye of Gyre, Omotesando, Tokyo, Japan
Substitute, Galleri K, Oslo, Norway
Moons of the lapetus Ocean, White Cube, London, UK
2007 *In The Between*, MAC | Musée d'Art Contemporain de Montréal, Canada
Day Return, Centre for Contemporary Art Ujazdowski Castle, Warsaw, Poland
Almond, SITE Santa Fe, NM, USA
Darren Almond, Galeria Alfonso Artiaco, Naples, Italy
Night + Fog, Galerie Max Hetzler, Berlin, Germany
Darren Almond, Matthew Marks Gallery, New York, NY, USA
2006 *Day Return,* Museum Folkwang, Essen, Germany
If I Had You, DA2 | Domus Artium 2002, Salamanca, Spain
2005 *Isolation*, K21 Kunstsammlung Nordrhein-Westfalen, Düsseldorf, Germany
Darren Almond, Matthew Marks Gallery, New York, NY, USA
2004 *Live Sentence,* Lentos Kunstmuseum Linz, Austria
2003 *If I Had You,* Fondazione Nicola Trussardi, Palazzo della Ragiona, Milan, Italy
Darren Almond, The Herzliya Museum of Contemporary Art, Herzliya, Israel
Darren Almond, Galleri K, Oslo, Norway
11 Miles ... from Safety, White Cube, London, UK
Nightvision, Sommer Contemporary Art, Tel-Aviv, Israel
2002 *A*, National Theatre, Fourth Wall, South Bank, London, UK
2001 *Night As Day,* Tate Britain, London, UK
Darren Almond, Kunsthalle Zürich, Switzerland
Darren Almond, De Appel Foundation Centre for Contemporary Art, Amsterdam, Netherlands
Coming Up For Air, Matthew Marks Gallery, New York, NY, USA
2000 *Traction,* Chisenhale Gallery, London, UK
Transport Medium, Matthew Marks Gallery, New York, NY, USA
Geisterbahn, The Approach, London, UK
1999 *Darren Almond,* The Renaissance Society, University of Chicago, IL, USA
Darren Almond, Galerie Max Hetzler, Berlin, Germany
1997 *Darren Almond*, ICA | Institute of Contemporary Arts, London, UK
Darren Almond, Jay Jopling / White Cube, London, UK
1995 *KN 120,* Great Western Studios, London, UK
1991 *Darren Almond,* Crawford Art College, Cork, Ireland

Selected Group Exhibitions
2022 *Uncombed, Unforeseen, Unconstrained*, Parasol unit foundation for Contemporary art. A Collateral Event of the 59th International Art Exhibition | La Biennale di Venezia, Conservatorio di Musica Benedetto Marcello di Venezia, Venice, Italy
2021 *Bienalsur 2021: Echoes. A World between the Analogue and the Virtual*, JAX District, Riyadh; Qasr Khuzam, Jeddah, Saudi Arabia
Focus China. Works from Collection Wemhöner, Mönchehaus Museum Goslar, Germany
The Expanded Landscape, J. Paul Getty Museum, Los Angeles, CA, USA
Geneva Decade. 10th Anniversary Group Show, Galerie Xippas, Geneva, Switzerland
2020 *My Cartography: The Erling Kagge Collection,* Santander Art Gallery, Madrid, Spain; Fondation Vincent van Gogh Arles, France
Slow Painting, Hayward Gallery Touring exhibition; The Edge and University Gallery, Bath; The Levinsky Gallery, Plymouth; Inverness Museum and Art Gallery; Thurso Art Gallery, UK
Time in Space: The Life Style, PKM Gallery, Seoul, South Korea
2019 *Now,* Scottish National Gallery of Modern Art, Edinburgh, UK
The Moon, Royal Museums Greenwich, London, UK
Fly Me To The Moon. The Lunar Landing, 50 Years Later, Kunsthaus Zürich, Switzerland; Museum der Moderne, Salzburg, Austria
Dojima River Biennale 2019, Osaka, Japan
Apollo's Muse: The Moon in the Age of Photography, The Metropolitan Museum of Art, New York, NY, USA
The Gifts of Tony Podesta, American University Museum, Washington, DC, USA
Daedalus' Choice, Galerie Xippas, Paris, France
2018 *Wilderness,* Schirn Kunsthalle Frankfurt, Germany
In My Shoes: Art and the Self since

the 1990s, Yorkshire Sculpture Park, Wakefield; Aberystwyth Arts Centre, UK
The Moon. From Inner Worlds to Outer Space, Louisiana Museum of Modern Art, Humlebaek, Denmark
Art Capital: Art for the Elizabeth Line, Whitechapel Gallery, London, UK
Painting the Night, Centre Pompidou-Metz, France
Møenlight Sonata. A homage to the starry sky of Møn, Kunsthal 44Møen, Møn, Denmark
Memory Palace, White Cube, London, UK
Oceans: A Worldview at the Rhythm of the Waves, Le Fresnoy – Studio national des arts contemporains, Tourcoing, France

2017 *Time as Landscape. Inquiries of Art and Science*, Cornell Fine Arts Museum, Rollins College, Winter Park, FL, USA
Visions of Nature, Kunst Haus Wien, Vienna, Austria
Tidalectics, TBA21 | Thyssen-Bornemisza Art Contemporary, Vienna, Austria
The Garden, ARoS | Aarhus Kunstmuseum, Denmark
Botánica, John Berggruen Gallery, San Francisco, CA, USA

2016 *Nightfall*, Musée Rath, Geneva, Switzerland
The End Of The World, Centro Pecci, Prato, Italy
Sublime. The Tremors of the World, Centre Pompidou-Metz, France
Fire Under Snow, Louisiana, Humlebaek, Denmark

2015 *The Nothing That Is*, RA | Royal Academy of Arts, London, UK
Photographing Monet's Gardens: Five Contemporary Views, Musée des impressionismes, Giverny, France
Harmony and Transition. Reflecting Chinese Landscapes, MARTa Herford, Germany
Momentum, CerModern, Ankara, Turkey
Landscape in Motion, Universalmuseum Joanneum, Kunsthaus Graz, Austria
Rights of Nature. Art and Ecology in the Americas, Nottingham Contemporary, Nottingham, UK
Boolean Expressions – Contemporary Art and Mathematical Data, Lewis Gluckman Gallery, Cork, Ireland
Art and Technology, a Shared Sphere, Mudam, Luxembourg
No Man Nature, Palazzo Da Mosto, Reggio Emilia, Italy

2014 *Branched. Trees in Contemporary Art*, Altana Kulturstiftung, Bad Homburg, Germany
Busan Biennale, Busan, South Korea
Cool Place. Sammlung Scharpff, Kunstmuseum Stuttgart, Germany
Man in the Mirror, Vanhaerents Art Collection, Brussels, Belgium
Playtime, Lenbachhaus, Munich, Germany
Halftone: Through the Grid, Galerie Max Hetzler, Paris, France; Berlin, Germany
Vertigo, SIM Galeria, Curitiba, Brazil
1+1=1: When Collections Collide, Montreal Museum of Fine Arts, Canada

2013 *Landmark: The Fields of Photography*, Somerset House, London, UK
Artist File 2013: The NACT. Annual Show of Contemporary Art, The National Art Center, Tokyo, Japan
Arctic, Louisiana, Humlebaek, Denmark
On Nature, Sean Kelly, New York, NY, USA
Landscapes, A Palazzo Gallery, Brescia, Italy
The future's not what it used to be, The Exchange, Cornwall; Newlyn Art Gallery; Chapter Gallery, Cardiff, UK
Theatrical Gestures, Herzliya Museum, Israel

2012 *Im Schein des Unendlichen. Romantik und Gegenwart*, Sinclair-Haus, Bad Homburg, Germany
1st Montevideo Biennial: The Great South, Montevideo, Uruguay
The Undercurrent of Boredom, Städtische Kunsthalle München, Munich, Germany
Number Three: From Home to the Factory, Virreina Centre de la Imatge, Barcelona, Spain
Static Movement. Film Installations of Darren Almond, David Claerbout and Anri Sala, Museum Folkwang, Essen, Germany
Night, Israel Museum, Jerusalem, Israel

2011 *Natur. Zeitgenössische Kunst aus der Sammlung der Altana Kulturstiftung*, Karl Ernst Osthaus Museum, Hagen, Germany
The Wilderness, Miami Art Museum, FL, USA
Mysticism, Helmhaus, Zurich, Switzerland
6th Bienal VentoSul, Curitiba, Brazil
Le réel est inadmissible d'ailleurs il n'existe pas, Hangar à Bananes, Nantes; L'Etoffe du Temps L'Institut Culturel Bernard Magrez, Bordeaux, France; National Museum of Art of Monte Carlo, Monaco

2010 *Platform Seoul 2010: Projected Image*, Artsonje Center, Seoul, South Korea
Let's Dance, MAC VAL | Musée d'art contemporain du Val-de-Marne, Vitry-sur-Seine, France
To the Highest Mountain, Galleri Christina Wilson, Copenhagen, Denmark
Nature, Gerhardsen Gerner, Berlin, Germany
Célébration, FRAC Auvergne, Clermont-Ferrand, France

2009 *Prix Pictet 2009*, Passage de Retz, Paris, France; Thessaloniki Museum of Photography, Greece; The Empty Quarter Gallery, Dubai, UAE; Eindhoven University of Technology, Netherlands
The Times of a Place, Centro de Arte y Naturaleza, Fundación Beulas, Huesca, Spain
Altermodern: Tate Triennial, Tate Britain, London, UK
Esthétique des Pôles. Le testament des glaces, FRAC Lorraine, Metz, France
Just with your eyes I will see, Fonds d'art moderne et contemporain – Espace Boris Vian, Montluçon, France

2008 *Ego Documents. Das Autobiografische in der Kunst*, Kunstmuseum Bern, Switzerland
Moving Horizons: The UBS Art Collection 1960s to the present day, National Art Museum of China, Beijing, China
Unspeakable: The Artist as Witness to the Holocaust, Imperial War Museum, London, UK
Die Weite des Eises, Albertina, Vienna, Austria
Night, Royal West of England Academy, Bristol, UK
The Cinema Effect: Illusion, Reality and the Moving Image, Hirshhorn Museum and Sculpture Garden, Washington, DC, USA
First Show, Contemporary Art, Israel Museum, Jerusalem, Israel
a.b.c. / art berlin contemporary, Alter Postbahnhof, Berlin, Germany
Implant, The Horticultural Society of New York, NY, USA
Du Jardin au Cosmos, Espace de l'art concret, Mouans-Sartoux, France
YouPrison: Reflections on the Limitation of Freedom and Space, Fondazione Sandretto Re Rebaudengo, Turin, Italy
Sammlung als Aleph – Thyssen-Bornemisza Art Contemporary, Kunsthaus Graz, Germany
God & Goods, Villa Manin, Passariano, Italy
War & Art – Terror and Simulacrum of Beauty II, Gallery Aube, Kyoto, Japan
Art is for the Spirit: Works from the UBS Art Collection, Mori Art Museum, Tokyo, Japan

2007 *Ensemble*, ICA | Institute of Contemporary Art, Philadelphia, PA, USA
Issue, CGAC | Centro Galego de Arte Contemporáneo, Santiago de Compostela, Spain
Numerica, Palazzo delle Papesse, Siena, Italy
Acceleration, Kunstart, Neuchâtel, Switzerland
Her(his)story, Museum of Cycladic Art, Athens, Greece
Going Staying: Movement, Body, Place in Contemporary Art, Kunstmuseum Bonn, Germany
Light, Winchester Cathedral, UK
Full House. Faces of a Collection, Kunsthalle Mannheim, Germany
2nd Moscow Biennale of Contemporary Art, Moscow, Russia
Closed Circuit: Video and New Media, The Metropolitan Museum of Art, New York, USA
100 Jahre Kunsthalle Mannheim, Kunsthalle Mannheim, Germany
Titled / Untitled: The Rubell and Devonshire Family Collections, Lismore Castle, Ireland
L'Œil Écran ou la Nouvelle Image, Casino Luxembourg – Forum d'art contemporain, Luxembourg

2006 *Darren Almond and Janice Kerbel: The Impossible Landscape*, Horticultural Society of New York, NY, USA
Shoot the Family, Cranbrook Art Museum, Bloomfield Hills, MI; Knoxville Museum of Art, TN; Western Gallery, Western Washington University, Bellingham, WA; Canzani Center Gallery, Columbus College of Art & Design, OH, USA
Caspar David Friedrich, Museum Folkwang, Essen; Hamburger Kunsthalle, Hamburg, Germany
Work, Rest and Play, Laing Art Gallery, Newcastle, UK
Between a Rock and a Hard Place, Kenny Schachter Rove, London, UK
Carbonic Anhydride, Galerie Max Hetzler, Berlin, Germany
The Black Show, David Patton, Los Angeles, CA, USA

2005 *Turner Prize 2005*, Tate Britain, London, UK
World Without End, ACMI | Australian Centre for the Moving Image, Melbourne, Australia
Getting Emotional, Institute of Contemporary Art, Boston, MA, USA
Universal Experience: Art, Life, and the Tourist's Eye, Hayward Gallery, London, UK; MCA | Museum of Contemporary Art Chicago, IL, USA
Bibidibobidiboo, Fondazione Sandretto Re Rebaudengo, Turin, Italy

En Attente, Casino Luxembourg – Forum d'art contemporain, Luxembourg
20:Twenty: A Timeline of Cornerhouse Exhibitions 1985–2005, Manchester, UK
Sequences, Q Arts Gallery, Derby, UK

2004 *Ein-leuchten*, Museum der Moderne, Salzburg, Austria
Witness, Museum of Contemporary Art, Sydney, Australia
Die Neue Kunsthalle III: Materiell-Immateriell, Kunsthalle Mannheim, Germany
After Images: Kunst als Soziales Gedächtnis, Neues Museum Weserburg, Bremen, Germany
Busan Biennale 2004, Busan, South Korea
Open Secrets: Something Old, Something New, Redefining the Boundaries of the Art Collection, Imperial War Museum, London, UK
Other Times: British Contemporary Art, City Art Gallery, Prague, Czech Republic
Sequences, Peterborough Digital Art, UK
Biennial of Pontevedra, Pontevedra, Italy

2003 *Heißkalt: Aktuelle Malerei aus der Sammlung Scharpff,* Staatsgalerie Stuttgart; Hamburger Kunsthalle, Hamburg, Germany
The Spirit of White, Fondation Beyeler, Basel, Switzerland
Imagination: Perception in Art, Kunsthaus Graz am Landesmuseum Joanneum, Austria
Outlook: International Art Exhibition Technopolis, Benaki Museum, Athens, Greece
Game Over, Grimm/Rosenfeld, Munich, Germany
50th International Art Exhibition | La Biennale di Venezia, Biennale Arte: Dreams and Conflicts, Venice, Italy
Edén, La Colección Jumex, Antiguo Colegio de San Ildefonso, Mexico City
Witness, The Curve, Barbican Art Gallery, London, UK
The Guest, Schwebebahn, Herzliya Museum, Israel
In Light: Video Projections by Eight Contemporary Artists, Art Gallery of Ontario, Toronto, Canada

2002 *Video Acts. Single Channel Video Works from the Collections of Pamela and Richard Kramlich and the New Art Trust*, ICA | Institute of Contemporary Arts, London, UK; MoMA PS1, New York, NY, USA
Melodrama. Lo Excesivo En La Imaginación Posmoderna, Artium Museao - Centre Museo Vasco de Arte Contemporáneo, Vitoria-Gasteiz; MARCO | Museo de Arte Contemporáneo de Vigo; Centro José Guerrero/Palacio de los Condes de Gabia, Granada, Spain
Video Zone - International Video-Art Biennial, Tel Aviv, Israel
The Hate U Give Little Infants Fucks Everyone, SMART Project Space, Amsterdam, Netherlands
Contextualize, Kunstverein Hamburg, Germany
The Rowan Collection: Contemporary British & Irish Art, IMMA | Irish Museum of Modern Art, Dublin, Ireland
In the Freud Museum, Freud Museum, London, UK
Happy Outsiders from London and Scotland, Pro Arte Institute, St Petersburg, Russia; Katowice City Gallery; Zacheta Gallery, Warsaw, Poland

2001 *Presentness is Grace. Experiencing the Suspended Moment,* Arnolfini Gallery, Bristol; Spacex Gallery, Exeter, UK
Casino 2001, S.M.A.K. | Stedelijk Museum voor Actuele Kunst Ghent, Belgium
Nature in Photography, Galerie nächst St Stephan, Vienna, Austria
Berlin Biennale, Berlin, Germany
Unreal Time Video, Fine Art Center, Korean Culture & Arts Foundation, Seoul, South Korea
Open Plan P3 – The Marathon, Alphadelta Gallery, Artio Gallery, Athens, Greece
Tracking, Kent and Vicki Logan Gallery, California College of Arts and Crafts, Oakland, CA, USA
Deliberate Living, Greene Naftali Gallery, New York, NY, USA

2000 *Apocalypse: Beauty and Horror in Contemporary Art*, RA | Royal Academy of Arts, London, UK
Making Time: Considering Time as a Material in Contemporary Video and Film, PBICA | Palm Beach Institute of Contemporary Art, FL, USA
Diary, Cornerhouse, Manchester, UK
British Short Film Festival, UCI Cinema, London, UK
Geographies, Galerie Chantal Crousel, Paris, France
Darren Almond, Mark Hosking, Kerstin Engholm Galerie, Vienna, Austria

1999 *Chronos and Kairos,* Museum Fridericianum, Kassel, Germany
Seeing Time, SFMOMA | San Francisco Museum of Modern Art, CA, USA
Common People, Fondazione Sandretto Re Rebaudengo, Turin, Italy
Sleeping Waters, Galerie Chantal Crousel, Paris, France
So Far Away, So Close, Encore...Bruxelles, Espace Méridien, Brussels, Belgium
Concrete Ashtray, Friedrich Petzel Gallery, New York, NY, USA

1998 *Hidden Desires and Images, Art Dynamics,* Tayayo Lida, Tokyo, Japan
Art Crash, ARoS | Aarhus Kunstmuseum, Denmark

1997 *Delta,* Musée d'Art Moderne de la Ville de Paris, France
Sensation: Young British Artists from the Saatchi Collection, RA | Royal Academy of Arts, London, UK; Hamburger Bahnhof, Museum für Gegenwart, Berlin, Germany

1996 *Toshiba Art & Innovation Prize*, ICA | Institute of Contemporary Arts, London, UK
A Small Shifting Sphere of Serious Culture, ICA | Institute of Contemporary Arts, London, UK

Selected Public Collections

Art Institute of Chicago, IL, USA
Cnap | Le Centre national des arts plastiques, Paris, France
Elgiz Museum of Contemporary Art, Istanbul, Turkey
Fondation Beyeler, Basel, Switzerland
Fondazione Sandretto Re Rebaudengo, Turin, Italy
FRAC Auvergne, Clermont-Ferrand, France
FRAC Haute Normandie, Sotteville-lès-Rouen, France
Government Art Collection, London, UK
The Herzliya Museum of Contemporary Art, Herzliya, Israel
Imperial War Museum, London, UK
Israel Museum, Jerusalem, Israel
Kramlich Collection, San Francisco, CA, USA
Fundación Jumex Arte Contemporàneo, Mexico City, Mexico
MAC | Musée d'art contemporain de Montréal, Canada
The Metropolitan Museum of Art, New York, NY, USA
Museum Folkwang, Essen, Germany
MCA | Museum of Contemporary Art, Chicago, IL, USA
MoMA | The Museum of Modern Art, New York, NY, USA
Museum Sinclair-Haus, Bad Homburg, Germany
National Galleries of Scotland, Edinburgh, UK
QAGOMA | Queensland Art Collection, Brisbane, Australia
Tate Gallery, London, UK
TBA21 | Thyssen-Bornemisza Art Contemporary, Vienna, Austria

OLIVER BEER
Born 1985, Pembury, Kent, United Kingdom
Lives and works in London, United Kingdom, and Paris, France

Education
2009 Ruskin School of Art, University of Oxford, UK
Sorbonne, Paris, France
2004 Academy of Contemporary Music, Guildford, UK

Selected Solo Exhibitions
2022 *Oliver Beer: Resonance Paintings (Two Notes)*, Thaddaeus Ropac, Seoul, South Korea
2021 *Composition for Mouths (Songs My Mother Taught Me)*, Opéra Garnier, Paris, France
Ghost Notes (Part I) and *Ghost Notes (Part II)*, THE CLUB, Tokyo, Japan
2020 *Oliver Beer: Oma*, Thaddaeus Ropac, London, UK
2019 *A Thousand Faces* (in collaboration with Louvre Abu Dhabi), Al Jahili Fort | Qasr al Hosn, Abu Dhabi, UAE
Oliver Beer: Vessel Orchestra, The Met Breuer, New York, NY, USA
Recomposition (Baloo Stripped Bare), Quebec City Biennial – Manif d'art 9, Quebec City, Canada
Household Gods, Thaddaeus Ropac, Paris, France
Oliver Beer: Impossible Composition, University of New South Wales Gallery, Sydney, Australia
2018 *Reanimation (Alice Falling)*, Ruya Foundation, Baghdad, Iraq
Reanimation (Snow White), George Eastman Museum, Rochester, NY, USA
2017 *Oliver Beer*, Ikon Gallery, Birmingham, UK
Oliver Beer: New Performance & Sculpture, Thaddaeus Ropac, London, UK
2015 *Life, Death and Tennis*, Daiwa Foundation Art Prize 2015 Exhibition, Aoyama Meguro, Tokyo, Japan
Making Tristan, Artist in Residence, Watermill Center, New York, NY, USA
Call to Sound, Istanbul Biennale, Kilic Ali Pasa Hamam, Istanbul, Turkey
Deconstructing Sound, Asakusa, Tokyo, Japan
2014 *Composition for a New Museum*, Fondation Louis Vuitton, Paris, France
Diabolus in Musica, Thaddaeus Ropac, Pantin, France
Rabbit Hole, MAC | Musée d'art contemporain de Lyon, France
Prospectif Cinéma 2014: Oliver Beer, Centre Pompidou, Paris, France
2013 *Outside-In*, Ikon Gallery, Birmingham, UK
The Resonance Project, Art Brussels, WIELS, Brussels, Belgium
The Resonance Project: Deep and Meaningful, Centre Pompidou, Paris, France
Composition For Hearing An Architectural Space, Thaddaeus Ropac, Pantin, France
2012 *KLANG*, Palais de Tokyo Art Club, Paris
2011 *The Resonance Project: Pay and Display*, Autumn Almanac, Ikon Gallery, Birmingham, UK
2010 *Deep and Meaningful*, murmurART, 20 Hoxton Square Project, London, UK
Training, Ikon Gallery, Birmingham, UK
2009 *Die Budgie History*, Dolphin Gallery, Oxford, UK
2008 *The Resonance Project*, Centre Pompidou, Paris, France
2007 *Oliver Beer*, La Viande Gallery, London, UK

Selected Group Exhibitions
2022 *Uncombed, Unforeseen, Unconstrained*, Parasol unit foundation for contemporary art. A Collateral Event of the 59th International Art Exhibition | La Biennale di Venezia, Conservatorio di Musica Benedetto Marcello di Venezia, Venice, Italy
2021 *Formes du Transfert*, Atelier Hermès, Seoul, South Korea; Le Forum, Tokyo, Japan; Magasins généraux, Pantin, France
British Art Show 9, Wolverhampton Art Gallery, Wolverhampton School of Art; The Box, KARST, The Levinsky Gallery, MIRROR Plymouth College of Art, Plymouth; HOME, Manchester Art Gallery, Castlefield Gallery, The Whitworth, Manchester, UK
Sables Brûlants, La Grande Place, Musée du cristal Saint-Louis, Saint-Louis-lès-Bitche, France
Polyphon, Kunstsammlung Gera and Museum für Angewandte Kunst Gera, Germany
Sound Vision: Harmonious Relationships in Art and Music, Lehman College Art Gallery, CUNY | City University of New York, NY, USA
When in Doubt, Go to a Museum, City Museum of Ljubljana, Slovenia
The Still Point, THE CLUB, Kudan House, Tokyo, Japan
Flat Work, Solid Haus, Melton, UK
Inner Space, Oliver Beer Studio, London, UK
2020 *Reverb: Sound into Art*, Hayward Gallery, London, UK
Rendez-vous, Voorlinden museum, Wassenaar, Netherlands
RIBOCA2 | Riga International Biennial of Contemporary Art: and suddenly it all blossoms, Riga, Latvia
2019 *Where We Now Stand. In Order to Map the Future*, 21st Century Museum of Contemporary Art, Kanazawa, Japan
Hidden Pulse, Vivid Live, Sydney Opera House, Australia
Syncopation: Contemporary Encounters with the Modern Masters, Pola Museum of Art, Hakone, Japan
Hypertimes, FuturDome, Milan, Italy
Rassegna di Video Arte del XXI secolo al MACRO, MACRO | Museo d'Arte Contemporanea di Roma, Italy
...Et l'Obscur, L'Abbaye du Thoronet Paris
2018 *21st Biennale of Sydney: Superposition*, Sydney, Australia
Wonderland, ACMI, Melbourne, Australia
The Myriad Forms of Visual Art: 196 Works with 19 Themes, National Museum of Art, Osaka, Japan
À Bâtons Rompus, Les Abattoirs, FRAC Occitanie, Toulouse, France
Abstract/ion, Galerie Klüser, Munich, Germany
2017 *Voyage d'Hiver*, Château de Versailles, France
Sans Réserve, MAC VAL, Vitry-sur-Seine, France
7th Socle du Monde Biennale, Herning, Denmark
2016 *Polyphonies*, Centre Pompidou, Paris, France
Nuit Blanche 2016, Paris, France
VG Award Exhibition, Annely Juda Fine Art, London, UK
Imprisoned, Jailbreak, Imprisoned, Jailbreak, Aoyama/Meguro, Tokyo, Japan
2015 *Where the Day Begins*, LaM | Lille Métropole musée d'art moderne, d'art contemporain et d'art brut, Villeneuve-d'Ascq, France
Collective Collection, Le BBB centre d'art, Toulouse, France
Sounds Like Music, D+T Project Gallery, Brussels, Belgium
2014 *Orkest!*, Netwerk Aalst | Center for Contemporary Art, Aalst, Belgium
Bright Intervals, Sunday Sessions, MoMA PS1, New York City, NY, USA
Condensation, Le Forum, Maison Hermès, Tokyo, Japan
Saint Jerome, Meessen de Clerq, Brussels, Belgium
2013 *Oliver Beer / Shingo Yoshida*, Villa Arson, Nice, France
12th Lyon Biennale of Contemporary Art: The Present is Unfinished, Lyon, France
Nouvelles Vagues, Palais de Tokyo, Paris, France
2012 *100 Curators*, Saatchi Gallery, London, UK
Nuit Blanche 2012, Paris, France
Whitstable Biennale 2012, Whitstable, UK
(Entre)Ouverture, Palais de Tokyo, Paris, France
Pavillon Neuflize OBC, Palais de Tokyo, Ménagerie de Verre, Paris, France
La Part de l'Ombre, Galerie de Roussan, Paris, France
2011 *Mindful*, Old Vic Tunnels, London, UK
2010 Sir John Soane's Museum, London, UK
Reflections, DNA Galerie, Berlin, Germany
2008 ICA | Institute of Contemporary Arts, Performance with Goodbooks, London, UK
Box Ladder, Modern Art Oxford, UK
Performance with Matmos, Beaconsfield Gallery, London, UK
Nemzetközi Művésztelepek kiállítása, Vízivárosi Galéria, Budapest, Hungary

Selected Public Collections
Arts Council Collection, UK
Centre Pompidou, Paris, France
Cnap | Le Centre national des arts plastiques, Paris, France
FRAC Bretagne, Rennes, Francia
FRAC Ile-de-France, Le Plateau, Paris, France
FRAC Occitanie, Les Abattoirs, Toulouse, France
Guggenheim Abu Dhabi, UAE
MAC | Musée d'art contemporain de Lyon, France
MONA | Museum of Old and New Art, Hobart, Australia
National Museum of Art, Osaka, Japan
Voorlinden museum, Wassenaar, Netherlands

RANA BEGUM
Born 1977, Sylhet, Bangladesh
Lives and works in London, United Kingdom

Education
2002 MFA Painting, Slade School of Fine Art, London, UK
1999 BFA Painting, Chelsea College of Art and Design, London, UK
1996 BTEC Foundation Studies in Art and Design, University of Hertfordshire, Hatfield, UK

Selected Solo Exhibitions
2022 *Rana Begum: Dappled Light*, Mead Gallery, Warwick Arts Centre, Coventry; Pitzhanger Manor & Gallery, London, UK
2021 *Infinite Geometry*, Wanås Konst, Knislinge, Sweden
Rana Begum, Kate MacGarry, London, UK
2019 *Rana Begum,* Jhaveri Contemporary, Mumbai, India
Perception and Reflection, The Third Line Gallery, Dubai, UAE
2018 *Rana Begum*, Galerie Christian Lethert, Cologne, Germany
Space Light Colour, Djanogly Gallery, University of Nottingham, UK
Conversation with Light and Colour, Gallery 10, Tate St Ives, UK
2017 *Space, Light, Colour*, Sainsbury Centre for Visual Arts, Norwich, UK
2016 *Rana Begum: The Space Between*, Parasol unit foundation for contemporary art, London, UK
2015 *Towards an Infinite Geometry*, Jhaveri Contemporary, Mumbai, India
Rana Begum, Touchstone Gallery, Rochdale, UK
Linear Abstraction, Gutstein Gallery, SCAD | Savannah College of Art and Design, GA, USA
2014 *Rana Begum*, Galeri Mana, Istanbul, Turkey
Dhaka Art Summit, Dhaka, Bangladesh
2013 *No. 10*, The Third Line, Dubai, UAE
Manifold, Galerie Christian Lethert, Cologne, Germany
2012 *Rana Begum*, Bischoff/Weiss, London, UK
2011 *The Folded Page*, Jhaveri Contemporary, Mumbai, India
2010 *Fractured Symmetry*, Bischoff/Weiss, London, UK
Rana Begum, Delfina Foundation, London, UK
2009 *The Moment of Alignment*, The Third Line, Dubai, UAE
2008 *Transient Symmetry*, Vine Space, London, UK
2007 *Colour Codes*, The Third Line, Dubai, UAE

Selected Group Exhibitions
2022 *Uncombed, Unforeseen, Unconstrained*, Parasol unit foundation for contemporary art. A Collateral Event of the 59th International Art Exhibition | La Biennale di Venezia, Conservatorio di Musica Benedetto Marcello di Venezia, Venice, Italy
2021 *Breaking the Mould*, Longside Gallery, Yorkshire Sculpture Park, Wakefield, UK
Creative Folkestone Triennial 2021, UK
2020 *Guests: Artists and Craftspeople,* Istanbul Modern, Turkey
Dhaka Art Summit: Seismic Movements, Dhaka, Bangladesh
2019 *Is This Tomorrow?*, Whitechapel Gallery, London, UK; Alserkal Arts Foundation, Dubai, UAE
2018 *Frieze Sculpture 2018*, London, UK
Heavy Metal: Women to Watch, NMWA | National Museum of Women in the Arts, Washington, DC, USA
Actions. The Image of The World Can Be Different, Kettle's Yard, Cambridge, UK
Eruption from The Surface. The Origami Principle of Art, MARTa Herford, Germany
Summer Show, RA | Royal Academy of Arts, London, UK
2017 *Heavy Metal: Women to Watch*, Philips, London, UK
Occasional Geometries, Yorkshire Sculpture Park, Wakefield, UK
31 Women, Breese Little, London, UK
The Order of Things, The Wilson, Cheltenham Art Gallery & Museum, UK
2016 *Tribute to Sol LeWitt*, Gemeentemuseum, The Hague, Netherlands
11th Gwangju Biennale, Gwangju, South Korea
Flatland/Narrative Abstractions, Mrac | Musée régional d'art contemporain Occitanie, Serignan, France
New Visions, Tensta Konsthal, Stockholm, Sweden
2015 *Triplicity*, ATHR, Jeddah, Saudi Arabia
Vienna Biennale: Future Light, MAK | Museum of Applied Arts, Vienna, Austria
Geometries of Difference, Dorsky Museum, New York, NY, USA
The Great Festival of Creativity, Long Museum, Shanghai, China
2014 *Ethereal*, Leila Heller Gallery, New York, NY, USA
2013 *The Edge of Painting*, The Piper Gallery, London, UK
Empty Line, Galerie Bertrand Grimont, Paris, France
2012 *Summer Exhibition*, RA | Royal Academy of Arts, London, UK
2011 *The Art and Math of the Fold*, Fiedler Taubert Contemporary, Berlin, Germany
The New Middle East, Willem Baars, Amsterdam, Netherlands
Common Logic, IMT | ImageMusicText, London, UK
2010 *Form & Phenomenon*, Project 88, Mumbai, India
2009 *How Nations are Made*, Cartwright Hall and Manor House, Bradford, UK
Pattern Recognition, The City Gallery, Leicester, UK
Lines of Control, Green Cardamom, London, UK
2007 *Repetition and Sequence*, Jerwood Space, London, UK
2006 *Monologue/Dialogue*, BU Gallery, Bangkok, Thailand
2005 *Art:21 Power/Memory/Structures/Play*, Art Museum of Western Virginia, Roanoke, VA, USA
Ad Infinitum: The Aesthetics of Repetition II, Haines Gallery, San Francisco, CA, USA

Selected Public Collections
Arts Council Collection, London, UK
British Council, London, UK
CoCCA | Coimbatore Centre for Contemporary Arts, India
Collection Pictet, Geneva, Switzerland
Government Art Collection, London, UK
MONA | Museum of Old and New Art, Hobart, Australia
Sainsbury Centre for Visual Arts, Norwich, UK
Taubman Museum of Art, Roanoke, VA, USA
University of the Arts, London, UK

HYETAL
Born 1982, Swindon, United Kingdom
Lives in London, United Kingdom

Education
2011 BA Music Technology, Bath Spa University, UK

Group Exhibition
2022 Artist-musician collaboration with Rana Begum, *No. 694 Hyetal*, 2016, in *Uncombed, Unforeseen, Unconstrained*, Parasol unit foundation for contemporary art. A Collateral Event of the 59th International Art Exhibition | La Biennale di Venezia, Conservatorio di Musica Benedetto Marcello di Venezia, Italy

JULIAN CHARRIÈRE
Born 1987, Morges, Switzerland
Lives and works in Berlin, Germany

Education
2013 UdK | Universität der Künste Berlin, Germany
2011 Institut für Raumexperimente / UdK | Universität der Künste Berlin, Germany
2007 UdK | Universität der Künste Berlin, Germany
2006 ECAV | Ecole cantonale d'art du Valais, Sierre, Switzerland

Selected Solo Exhibitions
2021 Concentrations 63: *Towards No Earthly Pole*, DMA | Dallas Museum of Art, TX, USA
Soothsayers, Dittrich & Schlechtriem, Berlin, Germany
2020 *Thickens, Pools, Flows, Rushes, Slows*, Sies + Höke, Düsseldorf, Germany
2019 *Towards No Earthly Pole*, MASI | Museo d'Arte della Svizzera Italiana, Lugano; Aargauer Kunsthaus, Aarau, Switzerland
All We Ever Wanted Was Everything and Everywhere, MAMbo | Museo d'Arte Moderna di Bologna, Italy
Iroojrilik. Video des Monats, Hessisches Landesmuseums Darmstadt, Germany
2018 *As We Used to Float*, GASAG Kunstpreis 2018, Berlinische Galerie, Berlin, Germany
Ever Since We Crawled Out, Galerie Tschudi, Zuoz, Switzerland
I'm Afraid I Must Ask You To Leave (with Julius von Bismarck), Kunstpalais, Erlangen, Germany
An Invitation to Disappear, Kunsthalle Mainz, Germany
2016 *For They That Sow the Wind*, Parasol unit foundation for contemporary art, London, UK
Julian Charrière, Kaiserringstipendium für Junge Kunst 2016, Mönchehaus Museum Goslar, Germany
Siempre Cuenta Cuántos Cuentos Cuentas, Despacio, San José, Costa Rica
Objects In Mirror Might Be Closer Than They Appear (with Julius von Bismarck), Villa Bernasconi, Grand-Lancy, Switzerland
2015 *Polygon*, Bugada & Cargnel, Paris, France
2014 *Future Fossil Spaces*, Musée cantonal des Beaux-Arts, Lausanne, Switzerland
Somewhere, Wilhelm-Hack-Museum, Ludwigshafen, Germany
Die Welt ist mittelgross, Kunstverein Arnsberg, Germany
Clockwork (with Julius von Bismarck), OBEN, Vienna, Austria
We Are All Astronauts, Centre Culturel Suisse, Paris, France

Selected Group Exhibitions
2022 *Uncombed, Unforeseen, Unconstrained*, Parasol unit foundation for contemporary art. A Collateral Event of the 59th International Art Exhibition | La Biennale di Venezia, Conservatorio di Musica Benedetto Marcello di Venezia, Italy
Climate of Concern: Burning Out in the Age of Fossil Expressionism, RADIUS CCA, Delft, Netherlands
Im Wald. Eine Kulturgeschichte, Schweizerisches Nationalmuseum, Landesmuseum, Zurich, Switzerland
16th Lyon Biennale of Contemporary Art: Manifesto of Fragility, Lyon, France
2021 *17th International Architecture Exhibition | La Biennale di Venezia, Biennale Architettura*, Venice, Italy
Prix Marcel Duchamp 2021, Centre Pompidou, Paris, France
Scratching the Surface, Hamburger Bahnhof, Museum für Gegenwart, Berlin, Germany
Angespannte Zustände, Staatsgalerie Stuttgart, Germany
Guangzhou Image Triennial, Guangzhou, China
Earth Beats. Naturbild im Wandel, Kunsthaus Zürich, Switzerland
Schwarzes Licht, Kunstmuseum Solothurn, Switzerland
Biocenosis. Art of Change 21, Parc Chanot, Marseille, France
Im Wald, Kunsthaus Grenchen, Switzerland
2020 *Potential Worlds 2: Eco-Fictions*, Migros Museum für Gegenwartskunst, Zurich, Switzerland
Critical Zones. Observatories for Earthly Politics, ZKM | Center for Art and Media Karlsruhe, Germany
Tiger in Space, Contemporary Art Museum of Estonia, Tallinn, Estonia
Global Media Forum 2020: Pluralism. Populism. Journalism, WordCCBonn, Germany
La Collection, Musée cantonal des Beaux-Arts, Lausanne, Switzerland
2019 *Elementarteile. 40 Jahre Kunst im Sprengel Museum*, Sprengel Museum, Hannover, Germany
Tomorrow is the Question, ARoS | Aarhus Kunstmuseum, Denmark
Nowness Experiments: The Mesh, K11 Foundation, Shanghai, China
La Fabrique du Vivant, Centre Pompidou, Paris, France
Water, QAGOMA | Queensland Art and Gallery of Modern Art, Brisbane, Australia
14 Bienal de Artes Mediales de Santiago: El Cuarto Mundo, Santiago, Chile
Toronto Biennial of Art: The Drowned World, Toronto, Canada
Modell-Naturen in der Zeitgenössischen Fotografie, Stadtgalerie Kiel; Museum Haus Ludwig, Saarlouis; Kallmann Museum, Ismaning, Germany
When Species Meet, CAC | Contemporary Arts Center, Cincinnati, OH, USA
Nature in Art, MOCAK | Museum of Contemporary Art in Krakow, Poland
Memoria del Sublime. Il Paesaggio nel Secolo XXI, Museo Villa dei Cedri, Bellinzona, Switzerland
2018 *11th Taipei Biennial: Post-Nature. A Museum as an Ecosystem*, Taipei, Taiwan
Wildnis, Schirn Kunsthalle Frankfurt, Germany
Adapt to Survive: Notes from the Future, HENI Project Space, Hayward Gallery, London, UK
Entangle. Physics and the Artistic Imagination, Bildmuseet, Umeå, Sweden
Zeitspuren. The Power of Now, Kunsthaus Pasquart, Biel, Switzerland
RIBOCA | Riga International Biennial of Contemporary Art: Everything Was Forever Until It Was No More, Riga, Latvia
Swiss Institute Presents: Objects in Mirror Might Be Closer Than They Appear, Anthology Film Archives, New York, USA
There Will Come Soft Rains, Basis, Frankfurt, Germany
Artefact expo: This Rare Earth. Stories from Below, STUK, Leuven, Belgium
Océans. Une vision du monde au rythme des vagues, Le Fresnoy, Tourcoing, France
2017 *57th International Art Exhibition | La Biennale di Venezia, Biennale Arte: Viva Arte Viva*, Venice, Italy
1st Antarctic Biennale, Antarctica
Le Rêve des Formes, Palais de Tokyo, Paris, France
Produktion. Made in Germany Drei, Sprengel Museum, Hannover, Germany
Tidalectics, TBA21 | Thyssen-Bornemisza Art Contemporary, Vienna, Austria
Apocalypse. End Without End, Naturhistorisches Museum, Bern, Switzerland
Festival of Future Nows, Hamburger Bahnhof, Berlin, Germany
Notes On Our Equilibrium, CAB Art Center, Brussels, Belgium
Metamorfosi. Uno sguardo alla scultura contemporanea, Museo d'arte, Mendrisio
2016 *Zeitgeist. Arte da Nova Berlim*, CCBB | Centro Cultural Banco do Brasil, Rio de Janeiro, Brazil
The End of the World, Centro per l'Arte Contemporanea Luigi Pecci, Prato, Italy
La Timidité des Cîmes, Le Parvis, centre d'art contemporain, Tarbes, France
+Ultra. Gestaltung Schafft Wissen, Martin-Gropius-Bau, Berlin, Germany
The Edge of the Earth, Ryerson Image Centre, Toronto, Canada
Zeit Verstreichen. Moment und Dauer in der Gegenwartskunst, Kunstmuseum Solothurn, Switzerland
5th Moscow International Biennale for Young Art: Deep Inside, Moscow, Russia
Sculptuur Bredelar 2016: Hybrid Modus, Bredelar, Netherlands
Interractions 4, Les Abattoirs, FRAC Midi-Pyrénées, Toulouse, France
2015 *The Forces Behind the Forms. Earth's History, Matter, Process in Contemporary Art*, Galerie Taxispalais, Innsbruck, Austria; Museen Haus Lange und Haus Esters, Krefeld, Germany; Kunstmuseum Thun, Switzerland
Unter 30, Junge Schweizer Kunst XI – Kiefer Hablitzel Preis 2015, Kunsthaus Glarus, Switzerland
Invento. As Revoluções Que Nos Inventaram, Oca – Parque Ibirapuera, São Paulo, Brazil
Waterbound. Vom Leben mit dem Wasser, Neue Galerie Dachau/Kallmann-Museum Ismaning, Germany
KIK 5: Fathoms, KIK | Kino International Kunst, Berlin, Germany
Playing Future, Kunsthalle zu Kiel, Germany
Destination Vienna 2015, Kunsthalle Wien, Vienna, Austria
Systémique, CEAAC | Centre européen d'actions artistiques contemporaines, Strasbourg, France
Métamorphisme II, Musée d'art du Valais, Sion, Switzerland
2014 *The Go-Between*, Museo Nazionale di Capodimonte, Milan, Italy
De Generation of Painting, Fondazione 107, Turin, Italy

Kochi-Muziris Biennale, Kochi, India
Das Numen, 3 1/2, KW Institute for Contemporary Art, Berlin, Germany
Festival of Future Nows, Neue Nationalgalerie, Berlin, Germany
Devant Derrière, Trudelhaus Baden, Aargau, Switzerland
One Place Next to Another, Winzavod Centre for Contemporary Art, Moscow, Russia
Jenseits der Ansichtskarte: Die Alpen in der Fotografie, Vorarlberg Museum, Bregenz, Austria

2013 *< 30 IX Jeune Art Suisse*, Le Commun, Bâtiment d'art contemporain, Geneva, Switzerland
Das Numen – Momentum, DAZ | Deutsches Architektur Zentrum, Berlin, Germany
Les Modules du Palais de Tokyo, 12th Lyon Biennale of Contemporary Art, France
Move, Align. Avoid. Vom Schwarm als Prinzip und Phänomen, Kunstverein Harburger Bahnhof, Hamburg, Germany
Rules of Attraction, insitu Berlin, Germany
(n)on site, km temporaer, Berlin, Germany

2012 *13th International Architecture Exhibition | La Biennale di Venezia*, *Biennale Architettura*, Venice, Italy
Heiliges Leben, UdK | Universität der Künste Berlin, Germany
Life Clock, Den Frie Centre of Contemporary Art, Copenhagen, Denmark
The World is Not Fair, Die Grosse Welt Ausstellung 2012, Tempelhof, Berlin, Germany

2011 *Transformation – Das Numen*, Haus am Lützowplatz, Berlin, Germany
Fragments of an Unknown City, Krasnoe Znamya (Red Banner Factory), St Petersburg, Russia
Berlin 2000–2011. Playing Among the Ruins, MOT | Museum of Contemporary Art Tokyo, Japan
Ideas are Motion, MaMa Multimedijalmi Institut, Zagreb, Croatia
Über Lebenskunst, HKW | Haus der Kulturen der Welt, Berlin, Germany
Das Numen Day Light, 401 Contemporary, Berlin, Germany
100° Festival, Hebbel am Ufer, Berlin, Germany
Without Destination, Reykjavik Art Museum, Iceland

2010 *Let's Start To Implement Little Errors*, Institut für Raumexperimente, Pefferbergkeller, Berlin, Germany
Théorie des Modèles, Art & Science: Trop Simple, Trop Complexe, HEAD, Geneva, Switzerland

Selected Public Collections

Berlinische Galerie, Museum of Modern Art, Berlin, Germany
Centre Pompidou, Paris, France
FRAC Alsace, Sélestat, France
FRAC Franche-Comté, Besançon, France
Kunsthaus Zürich, Switzerland
Kunstlerhaus Stuttgart, Germany
Kunstmuseum Thun, Switzerland
Kunstmuseum Solothurn, Switzerland
Kunstpalais Erlangen, Germany
Kunstverein Arnsberg, Germany
Kunstverein Göttingen, Germany
Mönchehaus Museum, Goslar, Germany
Musée cantonal des Beaux-Arts, Lausanne, Switzerland
Musée cantonal du Valais, Sion, Switzerland
Museo Civico Villa dei Cedri, Bellinzona, Switzerland
MASI | Museo d'Arte della Svizzera Italiana, Lugano, Switzerland
Sprengel Museum, Hannover, Germany
Städtische Galerie Wolfsburg, Germany
TBA21 | Thyssen Bornemisza Art Contemporary, Vienna, Austria
The Getty, Los Angeles, CA, USA

DAVID CLAERBOUT
Born 1969, Kortrijk, Belgium
Lives and works in Antwerp, Belgium, and Berlin, Germany

Education

1995 Nationaal Hoger Instituut voor Schone Kunsten, Antwerp, Belgium

Selected Solo Exhibitions

2021 *Unseen Sound*, LAB Garage Museum, Moscow, Russia
Video installations, drawings and storyboards from the collection, De Pont Museum, Tilburg, Netherlands

2020 *Laziness of Action*, Kunst Museum Winterthur, Switzerland
Olympia, Galerie Rudolfinium, Prague, Czech Republic
Olympia, Samstag Museum of Art, Adelaide, Australia

2019 *The Pure Necessity*, Parasol unit in Zuoz, San Bastiaun Chapel, Switzerland
The Bee Who Forgot the Honey, Casa Vicens Gaudi, Barcelona, Spain

2018 *David Claerbout*, Kunsthaus Bregenz, Austria
David Claerbout, Les Abattoirs, FRAC Occitanie, Toulouse, France
David Claerbout, Talbot Rice Gallery, The University of Edinburgh, UK

2017 *Kunst Kino*, Neues Museum Nürnberg, Germany
Olympia, MNAC | Museu Nacional d'Art de Catalunya, Barcelona, Spain
David Claerbout, Contemporary Art Museum, Tampa, FL, USA
King e The Pure Necessity, Pinacoteca de São Paulo, Brazil

2016 *Future,* De Pont Museum, Tilburg, Netherlands
Olympia, KINDL, Berlin, Germany
Die Reine Notwendigkeit, Städel Museum, Frankfurt am Main, Germany

2015 *David Claerbout*, FRAC Auvergne, Clermont-Ferrand, France
David Claerbout, Performed Pictures, Mamco | Musée d'art moderne et contemporain, Geneva, Switzerland

2014 *Grijs/Grey*, Nederlands Fotomuseum, Rotterdam, Netherlands

2013 *David Claerbout*, Kunsthalle Mainz, Germany

2012 *Diese Sonne Strahlt Immer*, Secession, Vienna, Austria
The Time That Remains, Parasol unit foundation for contemporary art, London, UK; Tel Aviv Museum of Art, Israel
David Claerbout, Leopold-Hoesch-Museum, Düren, Germany
David Claerbout, MART | Museo di Arte Moderna e Contemporanea di Trento e Rovereto, Italy

2011 *Le temps qui reste*, WIELS, Brussels, Belgium
David Claerbout: Architecture of Narrative, SFMOMA, San Francisco, CA, USA

2010 *Uncertain Eye*, Pinakothek der Moderne, Munich, Germany

2009 *The Shape of Time*, De Pont Museum of Contemporary Art, Tilburg, Netherlands
David Claerbout, Museo do Chiado, Lisbon, Portugal

2008 *After the Quiet*, Kunstmuseum St Gallen, Switzerland

David Claerbout, EMST | National Museum of Contemporary Art, Athens, Greece
Long Goodbye, Belkin Galleries at the University of British Columbia, Vancouver, Canada
David Claerbout, MIT List Visual Arts Center, Cambridge, MA, USA
2007 *David Claerbout*, Centre Pompidou, Paris, France
David Claerbout. 3 Works, Musées royaux des Beaux-Arts de Belgique, Brussels, Belgium
2005 *Background Time Gezeiten*, Akademie der Künste, Berlin, Germany
David Claerbout, Dundee Contemporary Arts Centre, UK
David Claerbout, Van Abbemuseum, Eindhoven, Netherlands
2004 *David Claerbout*, Kunstbau im Lehnbachhaus, Munich, Germany
2003 *David Claerbout*, CGAC | Centro Galego de Arte Contemporánea, Santiago de Compostela, Spain
David Claerbout, Museum Boijmans Van Beuningen, Rotterdam, Netherlands
2002 *David Claerbout*, Kunstverein Hannover, Germany
2000 *Present*, DIA Center for the Arts, New York, NY, USA
1999 *De Vereniging*, S.M.A.K. | Stedelijk Museum voor Actuele Kunst, Ghent, Belgium

Selected Group Exhibitions
2022 *Uncombed, Unforeseen, Unconstrained*, Parasol unit foundation for contemporary art. A Collateral Event of the 59th International Art Exhibition | La Biennale di Venezia, Conservatorio di Musica Benedetto Marcello di Venezia, Italy
AntiCamera – An exhibition of David Claerbout and Ősz Gábor, Robert Capa Contemporary Photography Center, Budapest, Hungary
David Claerbout: The Close / Christoph De Boeck: Surfaces. New video and sound art for the Concertgebouw, Concertgebouw Brugge, Belgium
XNL Piacenza Contemporanea, Piacenza, Italy
New Works in the Collection. From Abramovic to Warhol, Louisiana Museum of Modern Art, Humlebaek, Denmark
Collection, FRAC Grand Large - Hauts-de-France, Dunkerque, France
Mythos Wald. Das Flüstern der Blätter, Kunsthalle Emden, Germany
Les Fabriques du Cœur, MACS | Musée des Arts Contemporains, Grand Hornu, Belgium
Traverser la nuit, MAAT | Museum of Art, Architecture and Technology, Lisbon, Portugal
Extended Present, Ludwig Muzeum, Budapest, Hungary
Nadir, Laarne Castle, Belgium
Mix & Match. Rediscover The Collection, Pinakothek der Moderne, Munich, Germany
2021 *Media Art in Focus. Part II: David Claerbout and Paul Pfeiffer,* Pinakothek der Moderne, Munich, Germany
Fragments of Sphere, Project Space on the Inside, Amsterdam, Netherlands
We Are Animals, Kunsthal Rotterdam, Netherlands
The Nature of Art, Busan Museum of Art, South Korea
The World Reglitterized, Haus der Kunst, Munich, Germany
Kinderbiennale – Embracing Nature, Japanese Pavilion, Dresden, Germany
2020 *Memling Now: Hans Memling in contemporary art*, Sint-Janshospitaal, Brugge, Belgium
Continuously Contemporary, Kunstmuseum Basel, Switzerland
Wild at Heart. Schweizer Romantik von Füssli bis Böcklin, Kunsthaus Zürich, Switzerland
Inspire, ISELP, Brussels, Belgium
The Sound of Disney, DFF | Deutsches Filminstitut & Filmmuseum, Frankfurt, Germany
De Nacht, De Warande, Turnhout, Belgium
2. Biennale für Aktuelle Fotografie, Mannheim, Germany
Museum for All, Museum for Dogs, MMCA | National Museum of Modern and Contemporary Art, Seoul, South Korea
Win-Win. Synergies in Art, Kunstsammlung, Frankfurt am Main, Germany
2019 *3rd Biennial of Coimbra: The Third Bank*, Coimbra, Portugal
Fiction and Fabrication. Photography of Architecture after the Digital Turn, MAAT, Lisbon, Portugal
Trois Fois Rien. The Centre National des Arts Plastiques au CDN, CND | Centre National de la Danse, Paris, France
Animalesque/Art Across Species and Beings, Bildmuseet, Umea, Sweden
Technosphere, MAST Foundation, Bologna, Italy
2018 *Small Histories of Photography*, Sprengel Museum, Hannover, Germany
Beyond the Body, Kunstcentret, Silkeborg, Denmark
The Archeology of the Screen, Kumu Art Museum, Tallinn, Estonia
2017 *Dimensões Variáveis*, MAAT, Lisbon, Portugal
Warten. Zwischen Macht und Möglichtkeit, Hamburger Kunsthalle, Hamburg, Germany
The Sky is the Limit. Vlaamse landschapsschilderkunst in de 16e en 17e eeuw, Museum Rockoxhuis, Antwerp, Belgium
Biotopia, Kunsthalle Mainz, Germany
Ways of Seeing, ARTER, Istanbul, Turkey
The Still Point of the Turning World, FOMU fotomuseum, Antwerp, Belgium
The Image of War, Bonniers Konsthall, Stockholm, Sweden
La Vie Simple, Simplement la Vie, Fondation Vincent van Gogh, Arles, France
2016 *Magical Surfaces: The Uncanny in Contemporary Photography*, Parasol unit foundation for contemporary art, London, UK
Little Lies, Yarat Contemporary Art Space, Baku, Azerbaijan
EchtZEIT / RealTIME, Kunstmuseum Bonn, Germany
Zeit Verstreichen. Moment und Dauer in der Gegenwartskunst, Kunstmuseum Solothurn, Switzerland
The Power of the Avant-Garde, Bozar, Brussels, Belgium
Paradise on Earth. Landscapes from Bruegel to Rubens, Kunsthalle im Lipsiusbau, Dresden, Germany
Rebel Rebel. Art + Rock, MACS | Museum of Contemporary Arts Grand Hornu, Belgium
2015 *The Collection of the Emanuel Hoffmann Foundation*, Schaulager, Münchenstein, Switzerland
A Few Free Years: Von Absalon bis Zobernig. Schenkungen von Friedrich Christian Flick und die Nationalgalerie, Hamburger Bahnhof, Berlin, Germany
The Importance of Being..., Museo Nacional de Bellas Artes, Havana, Cuba; MACBA | Museo de Arte Contemporáneo, Buenos Aires, Argentina; Museu de Arte Moderna, Rio de Janeiro, Brazil
2014 *Variation of the Moon*, Nam June Paik Art Center, Giheung-gu, Yongin-si, South Korea
19th Biennale of Sydney: You Imagine What You Desire, Sydney, Australia
L'Illusion des Lumières, Palazzo Grassi, Venice, Italy
Bad Thoughts. Collectie Martijn en Jeannette Sanders, Stedelijk Museum Amsterdam, Netherlands
Days of Endless Time, Hirshhorn Museum and Sculpture Garden, Washington, DC, USA
2013 *SLOW: Marking Time in Recent Photography and Film*, Museum of Contemporary Art Jacksonville, FL, USA
Sharjah Biennial 11: Re:emerge, Towards a New Cultural Cartography, Sharjah, UAE
Constable, Delacroix, Friedrich und Goya, Staatliche Gemäldegalerie Dresden, Germany
The Red Queen, MONA | Museum of Old and New Art, Hobart, Australia
Performing Still Images: Matthew Buckingham and David Claerbout, University of Michigan Museum of Art, Ann Arbor, MI, USA
5th Moscow Biennale of Contemporary Art: More Light, Moscow, Russia
2012 *Disappearances*, MacKenzie Art Gallery, Regina, Canada
Found Footage: Cinema Exposed, Eye Film Instituut Nederland, Amsterdam, Netherlands
7th Seoul International Media Art Biennale (Media City Seoul 2012): Spell On You, Seoul, South Korea
Static Movement, Museum Folkwang, Essen, Germany
2011 *Yebisu International Festival for Art & Alternative Visions 2011*, Tokyo, Japan
Jeff Wall: The Crooked Path, Bozar, Brussels; CGAC | Galician Centre for Contemporary Art, Santiago de Compostela, Spain
The World Belongs to You, Palazzo Grassi, Venice, Italy
2010 *29th São Paulo Biennial: There is always a cup of sea to sail in*, São Paulo, Brazil
Panoramic Views, The Herzliya Museum of Contemporary Art, Israel
Venedig, Von Canaletto und Turner bis Monet, Fondation Beyeler, Basel, Switzerland
2007 *Mois de la Photo: Explorations Narratives*, Montreal Museum of Fine Arts, Canada
2006 *Slow Motion*, Museum Boijmans Van Beuningen, Rotterdam, Netherlands
2005 *Monopolis*, Witte de With Center for Contemporary Art, Rotterdam, Netherlands
What's New, Pussycat?, MMK | Museum für Moderne Kunst, Frankfurt, Germany
2004 *Taipei Biennial: Do You Believe in*

Reality?, Taipei, Taiwan
Non-Sect Radical: Contemporary Photography III, Yokohama Museum of Art, Japan

2003 *War (What is it Good For?)*, MCA | Museum of Contemporary Art, Chicago, IL, USA
Attack! Kunst und Krieg in den Zeiten der Medien, Kunsthalle Wien, Vienna, Austria

2002 *Malerei Ohne Malerei*, Museum der bildenden Künste, Leipzig, Germany

2001 *Winter Exhibition: Tiong Ang, Serhiy Bratkov, David Claerbout, José Antonio Hernandez-Diez*, INOVA | Institute of Visual Arts, University of Wisconsin, Milwaukee, WI, USA

1999 *Trouble Spot Painting*, MuHKA | Museum of Contemporary Art, Antwerp, Belgium

1998 *I never promised you a rose garden*, Beelden Buiten, Tielt, Belgium

1997 *Prix de la Jeune Peinture Belge*, Palais des Beaux-Arts, Brussels, Belgium

Selected Public Collections

Art Gallery of Ontario, Toronto, Canada
MAM/ARC | Musée d'Art Moderne de la Ville de Paris, France
Boijmans van Beuningen, Rotterdam, Netherlands
Centre Pompidou, Paris, France
De Pont Museum voor Hedendaagse
Galerie Neue Meister, Dresden, Germany
GAM | Galleria d'Arte Moderna et Contemporanea, Turin, Italy
Guggenheim Museum, New York, NY, USA
Hirshhorn Museum and Sculpture Garden, Washington, DC, USA
Israel Museum, Jerusalem, Israel
Kunst, Tilburg, Netherlands
Lenbachhaus, Munich, Germany
MOCA | The Museum of Contemporary Art, Los Angeles, CA, USA
Museum Brandhorst, Munich, Germany
MMK | Museum für Moderne Kunst, Frankfurt am Main, Germany
Mudam, Luxembourg
M HKA | Museum van Hedendaagse Kunst, Antwerp, Belgium
Pinakothek der Moderne, Munich, Germany
Sammlung Goetz, Munich, Germany
S.M.A.K. | Stedelijk Museum voor Actuele Kunst, Ghent, Belgium
Städel Museum, Frankfurt am Main, Germany
Walker Art Center, Minneapolis, MN, USA

BHARTI KHER
Born 1969, London, United Kingdom
Lives and works in New Delhi, India

Education

1991 BA Fine Art, Painting, Newcastle Polytechnic, Newcastle, UK

1988 Foundation Art and Design, Middlesex Polytechnic, London, UK

Selected Solo Exhibitions

2022 *Bharti Kher*, Arnolfini, Bristol, UK
Ancestor, Public Art Fund, Doris C. Freedman Plaza, Central Park, New York, NY, USA

2021 *Strange Attractors*, Nature Morte, New Delhi, India

2020 *A Consummate Joy*, IMMA | Irish Museum of Modern Art, Dublin, Ireland
The Unexpected Freedom of Chaos, Galerie Perrotin, New York, NY, USA

2019 *A Wonderful Anarchy*, Hauser & Wirth, Somerset, UK

2018 *Djinns, Things, Places*, Galerie Perrotin, Tokyo, Japan
Points de Départ, Points qui Lient, DHC/ART | Foundation for contemporary art, Montreal, Canada
Messengers, Grunwald Gallery of Art, Indiana University, Bloomington, IN, USA
Chimeras, Kunsthaus Pasquart, Biel, Switzerland

2017 *Dark Matter (MM)*, Museum Frieder Burda/ Salon Berlin, Germany
Sketchbooks and Diaries, Isabella Stewart Gardner Museum, Boston, MA, USA

2016 *This Breathing House*, Freud Museum, London, UK
The Laws of Reversed Effort, Galerie Perrotin, Paris, France
Matter, Vancouver Art Gallery, Vancouver, Canada

2014 *Three Decimal Points. Of a minute of a second of a degree*, Hauser & Wirth, Zurich, Switzerland
Misdemeanours, Rockbund Art Museum, Shanghai, China

2013 *Anomalies*, Kukje Gallery, Seoul, South Korea
Bind the Dream State to your Waking Life, Nature Morte, New Delhi, India

2012 *Bharti Kher*, Parasol unit foundation for contemporary art, London, UK
The Hot Winds That Blow From The West, Hauser & Wirth New York, NY, USA
Many, (Too) Many, More Than Before, Galerie Emmanuel Perrotin, Hong Kong
Reveal The Secrets That You Seek, SCAD | Savannah College for Art and Design, Savannah, GA, USA

2011 *Leave Your Smell*, Galerie Emmanuel Perrotin, Paris, France

2008 *Virus*, BALTIC Centre for Contemporary Art, Gateshead, UK

2007 *An Absence of Assignable Cause*, Jack Shainman Gallery, New York, NY, USA

2006 *Do not Meddle in the Affairs of Dragons, Because You Are Crunchy and Taste Good with Ketchup*, Gallery 88 and Gallery Ske, Mumbai, India

2004 *Quasi-, mim-, ne-, near-, semi-, -ish, -like*, Gallery Ske, Bangalore, India
Hungry Dogs Eat Dirty Pudding, Nature Morte, New Delhi, India

2001 *The Private Softness of Skin*, Gallery Chemould, Mumbai, India

2000 *The Private Softness of Skin*, Bose Pacia Gallery, New York, NY, USA

1999 *Telling Tails*, Galerie FIA, Amsterdam, Netherlands

1995 Art Heritage, New Delhi, India

1993 AIFACS, New Delhi, India

Selected Group Exhibitions

2022 *Uncombed, Unforeseen, Unconstrained*, Parasol unit foundation for contemporary art. A Collateral Event of the 59th International Art Exhibition | La Biennale di Venezia, Conservatorio di Musica Benedetto Marcello di Venezia, Italy

2021 *Sculpture at Firstsite*, Colchester, UK

2020 *Relations (Diaspora and Painting)*, Phi Foundation, Montreal, Canada
Résonance, Fondation Opale, Lens, Switzerland
Animals in Art, Arken Museum of Modern Art, Ishøj, Denmark
Dhaka Art Summit (DAS 2020): Seismic Movements, Dhaka, Bangladesh
Contemporary Female Identities in the Global South, JCAF | Joburg Contemporary Art Foundation, Johannesburg, South Africa
Tantra. Enlightenment to Revolution, The British Museum, London, UK
Visions from India. 21st Century Art from the Pizzuti Collection, The Columbia Museum of Arts, SC, USA

2019 *In the Company of Artists, 25 Years of Artists-In-Residence*, Isabella Stewart Gardner Museum, Boston, MA, USA
Vision Exchange: Perspectives from India to Canada, University of Toronto Art Centre; Art Gallery of Alberta, Canada

2018 *Thailand Biennale: Edge of the Wonderland*, Krabi, Thailand
Frieze Sculpture 2018, London, UK
Facing India, Kunstmuseum Wolfsburg, Germany
Life: Sculpture, Color, and the Body (1300–Now), The MET Breuer, New York, NY, USA
My Monster: The Human Animal Hybrid, RMIT Art Gallery, Melbourne, Australia
Bronze Age c. 3500 BC–AD 2018, Firstsite, Colchester, UK
Surface Work, Victoria Miro, London, UK

2017 *Versus Rodin: Bodies Across Space and Time*, Art Gallery of South Australia, Adelaide, Australia

2016 *I Prefer Life*, Weserburg Museum of Modern Art, Bremen, Germany
20th Biennale of Sydney: The Future Is Already Here. It's Just Not Evenly Distributed, Sydney, Australia

2015 *Go East. The Gene & Brian Sherman Contemporary Asian Art Collection*, Art Gallery of NSW, Sydney, Australia

2014 *Kochi-Muziris Biennale*, Kochi, India
Seeing Through Light, Guggenheim Abu Dhabi, UAE

2013 *We are Ours: A Collection of Manifestos for the Instant*, Khoj International Artists' Association, New Delhi, India

2012 *Dot. Systems From Pointillism to Pixelation*, Wilhelm-Hack-Museum, Ludwigshafen am Rhein, Germany
1st International Biennale of Contemporary Art: The Best of Times, The Worst of Times. Rebirth and Apocalypse in Contemporary Art, Kiev, Ukraine

India: Art Now, Arken Museum of Modern Art, Denmark
Massive/Intensive: Contemporary Art from India, Tel Aviv Museum of Art, Israel
Misled by Nature: Contemporary Art and the Baroque, Art Gallery of Alberta, Edmonton; MOCA | Museum of Contemporary Canadian Art, Toronto, Canada
Domination, Hegemony and The Panopticon, Traffic, Dubai, UAE
2011 *Paris-Delhi-Bombay*, Centre Pompidou, Paris, France
Festival der Tiere, Essl Museum, Klosterneuburg, Austria
Time Unfolded, Kiran Nadar Museum of Art, New Delhi, India
Indian Highway IV, Musée d'Art Contemporain, Lyon, France
2010 *Gothenburg Culture Festival*, Gothenburg, Sweden
Tokyo Art Meeting. Transformation, MOT | Museum of Contemporary Art Tokyo, Japan
Signs of Life – Ancient Knowledge in Contemporary Art, Kunstmuseum Luzern, Switzerland
Susan Hefuna, Bharti Kher, Fred Tomaselli: Between the Worlds, Kunstmuseum Thun, Switzerland
Pattern ID, Akron Art Museum, OH; Kemper Museum of Contemporary Art, Kansas City, MO, USA
21st Century: Art in the first Decade, QAGOMA | Queensland Art Gallery of Modern Art, Brisbane, Australia
2009 *Marvellous Reality*, Lalit Kala Academy, New Delhi, India
Shifting Shapes, Unstable Signs, Yale University School of Art, New Haven, CT, USA
Nature Nation, Museum on the Seam, Jerusalem, Israel
2008 *Re-imagining Asia. A Thousand Years of Separation*, HKW | Haus der Kulturen der Welt, Berlin, Germany; The New Art Gallery Walsall, UK
Chalo! India: A New Era of Indian Art, Mori Art Museum, Tokyo, Japan; National Museum of Contemporary Art, Seoul, South Korea
Still Moving Image, Devi Art Foundation, New Delhi, India
Busan Biennale: Expenditure, Busan, South Korea
Ours, Chat, Cochon & Cie, Musée cantonal des Beaux-Arts, Lausanne, Switzerland
Indian Highway, Serpentine Gallery, London, UK; Astrup Fearnley Museum, Oslo, Norway; Herning Kunstmuseum, Denmark; MAXXI | Museo Nazionale delle Arti del XXI Secolo, Rome, Italy
Where in the World, Devi Art Foundation, New Delhi, India
India Moderna, IVAM | Institut Valencià d'Art Modern, Spain
2007 *Hungry God*, Art Gallery of Ontario, Toronto, Canada
Urban Manners: 15 Contemporary Artists from India, Hangar Bicocca, Milan, Italy
2006 *5th Asia-Pacific Triennial of Contemporary Art*, Brisbane, Australia
Le Troisième Œil, Lille3000, Lille, France
2005 *Zeitsprünge, Raumfolgen*, ifa-Galerie, Berlin, Germany
Indian Summer, École des Beaux Arts, Paris, France
Het offer / An intimate I: Droom en Werkelijkheid, De Beverd Museum voor Grafische Werkelijkheid, Breda, Netherlands
2004 *The Sneeze 80 × 80*, The Gazon Rouge Gallery, Athens, Greece; The South African National Gallery, Cape Town; Durban Art Gallery, Cape Town, South Africa
2003 *The Tree from the Seed: Contemporary Art from India*, Henie Onstad Kunstsenter, Hovikodden, Norway
2002 *Under Construction*, Tokyo Opera City Art Gallery, Japan
Cutting Edge Contemporary, NGMA | National Gallery of Modern Art, Mumbai, India
Silence Violence, NSA Gallery (a Pulse Project), Durban, South Africa
Sorry for the Inconvenience, Project 304, Bangkok, Thailand
Sidewinder, CIMA | Centre of International Modern Art, Kolkata, India; Habitat Centre, New Delhi, India; Coomaraswamy Hall - The Prince of Wales Museum of Western India, Mumbai, India
2001 *Kitch kitch Hota Hai*, India Habitat Center, New Delhi, India
Art on the Move, Sahmat Project, New Delhi, India
2000 *Open Circle Exhibition*, Lakeeren Art Gallery, Mumbai, India
1999 *Icons of the Millennium*, Nehru Centre, Mumbai, India
Hed end aagse Kunst uit India, Central Bureau Van de Hogeschool, Amsterdam, Netherlands
1998 *Edge of the Century*, British Council, New Delhi, India
1996 *Royal Overseas League Open Exhibition*, Edinburgh College of Art, UK
1995 *6th Bharat Bhawan Biennial of Contemporary Indian Arts*, Bhopal, India
1993 *Trends in Contemporary Indian Art*, Art Heritage, New Delhi, India

Selected Public Collections
The British Museum, London, UK
Devi Art Foundation, New Delhi, India
Guggenheim Abu Dhabi, UAE
Ishara Art Foundation, Dubai, UAE
Kiran Nadar Museum of Art, New Delhi, India
Leeum, Samsung Museum of Art, Seoul, South Korea
Museum Frieder Burda, Baden-Baden, Germany
National Museum of Canada, Ottawa, Canada
NCMA | North Carolina Museum of Art, Raleigh, NC, USA
QAGOMA | Queensland Art Gallery of Modern Art, Australia
Tate Modern, London, UK
Vancouver Art Gallery, Canada
WAM | Worcester Art Museum, MA, USA
Walker Art Center, Minneapolis, MN, USA

ARGHAVAN KHOSRAVI
Born 1984, Shahr-e-kord, Iran
Lives and works in New York, NY, USA

Education
2018 MFA Painting, Rhode Island School of Design, Providence, RI, USA
2016 Post-Baccalaureate Studio-Art, Brandeis University, Waltham, MA, USA
2009 MFA Illustration, University of Tehran, Iran
2006 BFA Graphic Design, Islamic Azad University, Tehran, Iran

Selected Solo Exhibitions
2022 *Arghavan Khosravi*, Currier Museum of Art, Manchester, NH, USA
The Witness, Kavi Gupta Gallery, Chicago, IL, USA
Truth Be Told, König Galerie, Berlin, Germany
2021 *In Search of Possibilities of Hope*, Carl Kostyal, London, UK
In Between Places, Rachel Uffner Gallery, New York, NY, USA
2020 *Presence of Others*, M+B Gallery, Los Angeles, CA, USA
This Shall Also Pass, Stems Gallery, Brussels, Belgium
2019 *Tightrope Walking The Red Lines*, Lyles & King Gallery, New York, NY, USA
Hudson D. Walker Gallery, Provincetown, MA, USA
2016 *Last Reminiscent of Heaven*, Homa Art Gallery, Tehran, Iran
2015 *Passing the Blues of Days*, Atbin Gallery, Tehran, Iran

Selected Group Exhibitions
2022 *Uncombed, Unforeseen, Unconstrained*, Parasol unit foundation for contemporary art. A Collateral Event of the 59th International Art Exhibition | La Biennale di Venezia, Conservatorio di Musica Benedetto Marcello di Venezia, Italy
2021 *Woman Element*, Montclair State University Museum, NJ, USA
A Boundless Drop to a Boundless Ocean, Orlando Museum of Art, FL, USA
2020 *Works on Paper*, Newport Art Museum, RI, USA
The Memories, Tales and Folk Songs, High Line Gallery, New York, NY, USA
2019 *Artifacts of Place*, Stand4 Gallery, Brooklyn, New York, NY, USA
Beyond the Canvas, Jamestown Art Center, RI, USA
New American Painting 25th Anniversary Summer Show, Steven Zevitas Gallery, Boston, MA, USA
Zeit-geist-zeit, Gaa Gallery, Provincetown, MA, USA
Silent Narrative, Yinchuan MOCA | Museum of Contemporary Art, China
New Visionaries, Annarumma Gallery, Naples, Italy
FOUR, Yossi Milo Gallery, New York, NY, USA
Provincetown Art Association and Museum, MA, USA
2018 *Red*, CUSP Gallery, Provincetown, MA, USA
Lifeline as Medium, 532 Gallery Thomas Jaeckel, New York, NY, USA
The Shapes of Birds: Contemporary Art of the Middle East and North Africa, Newport Art Museum, RI, USA
Strange Beach, Fridman Gallery, New York, NY, USA

Counter Narratives: Geographies of the Unfamiliar, Asya Geisberg Gallery, New York, NY, USA
I'm Yer Virgil, Super Dutchess Gallery, New York, NY, USA
Where's Your Privilege, R(ace) I(dentity)?, Hera Gallery, South Kingstown, RI, USA
2017 *Un/Settled*, Rhode Island School of Design Museum, Providence, RI, USA
Pure as the Seagull's Belly, Gelman Gallery, Providence, RI, USA
Dismantled, Sol Kaufler Gallery, Providence, RI, USA
RISD MFA Painting Group Exhibition, Morgan Lehman Gallery, New York, NY, USA
4th Biennial Best of the Northeast Masters of Fine Arts, Helen Day Art Center, Stowe, VT, USA
Painting Graduate Biennial, Sol Kaufler Gallery, Providence, RI, USA
2016 *Group Painting Exhibition*, Woods Gerry Gallery, Providence, RI, USA
Group Painting Exhibition, Dreitzer Gallery, Brandeis University, Waltham, MA, USA
2014 *Like Breeze on Trees*, Hena Gallery, Tehran, Iran
Some Screens of Heaven, Atbin Gallery, Tehran, Iran
2009 *Fajrafarinan Fine Arts Festival*, Saba Art and Culture Institute, Tehran, Iran
Iranian Children's Illustrators, Children's Book Council, Tehran, Iran

Selected Public Collections
Newport Art Museum, RI, USA
Recharge Foundation, New York, NY, USA
Rhode Island School of Design Museum, Providence, RI, USA
The Rose Art Museum, Waltham, MA, USA

TERESA MARGOLLES
Born 1963, Culiacán, Sinaloa, Mexico
Lives and works in Mexico City, Mexico, and Madrid, Spain

Education
Diploma Communication Sciences, Universidad Nacional Autónoma de México, Mexico City
Diploma Forensic Medicine

Selected Solo Exhibitions
2022 *Periferia dell'Agonia*, Mattatoio, Rome, Italy
2020 *Teresa Margolles. The Stone*, Es Baluard, Palma de Mallorca, Spain
2019 *En la Herida*, Kunsthalle Krems, Austria
Tu t'alignes ou on t'aligne, BPS22, Charleroi, Belgium
La Carne Muerta Nunca Se Abriga, MSSA | Museo de la Solidaridad Salvador Allende, Santiago, Chile
Estorbo, Nadie Nunca Nada No, Madrid, Spain
Estorbo, MAMBO | Museo de Arte Moderno de Bogotá, Colombia
2018 *Sutura*, DAAD, Berlin, Germany
A New Work by Teresa Margolles, Witte de With Center for Contemporary Art, Rotterdam, Netherlands
Ya Basta Hijos de Puta, PAC | Padiglione d'Arte Contemporanea, Milan, Italy
Sutura, Francuski Paviljon, Zagreb, Croatia
Sobre la Sangre, Tenuta dello Scompiglio, Lucca, Italy
Mundos, MAC | Musée d'Art Contemporain de Montréal, Canada
2016 *Teresa Margolles. 45 Cuerpos*, Museo de la Ciudad, Queretaro, Mexico
2015 *We Have a Common Thread*, Neuberger Museum of Art, Purchase Collage, CUNY | City University of New York, NY; Colby Museum of Art, Waterville, ME; Rubin Center, University of Texas at El Paso, USA
2014 *Enquanto for Necessário (As long as it is needed)*, Fundação Joaquim Nabuco, Recife, Brazil
La Búsqueda, Migros Museum für Gegenwartskunst, Zurich, Switzerland
El Testigo, CA2M | Centro de Arte Dos de Mayo, Madrid, Spain
2012 *Teresa Margolles: Carnal*, Prince Claus Fund, Amsterdam, Netherlands
La Promesa, MUAC | Museo Universitario de Arte Contemporáneo, Mexico City, Mexico
Teresa Margolles, Glasgow Sculpture Studios, UK
2011 *A Través...*, Museo de Arte Moderno, Mexico City, Mexico
Frontera, Museion, Bolzano, Italy
Irrigación, Museo de la Ciudad, Querétaro, Mexico
2010 *Frontera*, Kunsthalle Fridericianum, Kassel, Germany
Teresa Margolles, LACMA | Los Angeles County Museum of Art, Los Angeles, USA
2009 *Los Sonidos de la Muerte*, Centro Cultural Montehermoso Kulturenea, Vitoria-Gasteiz, Spain
What Else Could We Talk About?, 53rd International Art Exhibition | La Biennale di Venezia, Biennale Arte: *Making Worlds*, Mexican Pavilion, Venice, Italy
2008 *En Lugar de los Hechos*, Factory, Kunsthalle Krems, Austria
2007 *Decálogo*, Museo Experimental, El Eco, Mexico City, Mexico
Herida, Proyecto para Ecatepec, Museo Jumex, Mexico City, Mexico
2006 *127 Cuerpos*, Kunstverein für die Rheinlande und Westfalen, Düsseldorf, Germany
Tres Minutos, Casa Taller José Clemente Orozco, Guadalajara, Mexico
2005 *Involution*, CAC | Centre d'Art Contemporain, Brétigny, France
Caída Libre, FRAC Lorraine, Metz, France
2004 *Muerte Sin Fin*, MMK | Museum für Moderne Kunst, Frankfurt am Main, Germany
2003 *Das Leichentuch*, Kunsthalle Wien, Vienna, Austria
2000 *Lienzo*, Espacio Contexto, Guatemala City, Guatemala
Bondaje, Kunsthaus Santa Fe - San Miguel de Allende, Guanajuato, Mexico
1999 *Tarjetas Para Cortar Cocaína*, Galería Caja Dos, Mexico City, Mexico
Andén, Cali, Colombia
1997 *Cadáveres*, El Getho, Madrid, Spain

Selected Group Exhibitions
2022 *Uncombed, Unforeseen, Unconstrained*, Parasol unit foundation for contemporary art. A Collateral Event of the 59th International Art Exhibition | La Biennale di Venezia, Conservatorio di Musica Benedetto Marcello di Venezia, Italy
Resist, Again, Musée cantonal des Beaux-Arts, Lausanne, Switzerland
2021 *Alegorías del Mal Gobierno*, Museo de Arte Carillo Gil, Mexico City, Mexico
Connecting Currents, Museum of Fine Arts, Houston, TX, USA
Witch Hunt, Hammer Museum, Los Angeles, CA, USA
Thessaloniki PhotoBiennale 2021: The Real and the Record, Thessaloniki, Greece
The Wonderfulness of Memory, Gallery Cukrarna, Ljubljana, Slovenia
El Tiempo en las Cosas. Colección de Arte Contemporáneo, Museo Amparo, Puebla, Mexico
The Rise of a Social Consciousness in the Arts of Mexico since the Revolution, Neuberger Museum of Art, Purchase College, New York, NY, USA
Sound and Silence, Kunstmuseum Bonn, Germany
Fourth Plinth Shortlist Exhibition, National Gallery, London, UK
Tense Conditions, Staatsgalerie Stuttgart, Germany
2020 *In Aller Munde. Von Pieter Bruegel bis Cindy Sherman,* Kunstmuseum Wolfsburg, Germany
Infinie Liberté, FRAC Nouvelle-Aquitaine MÉCA, Bordeaux, France
We Are The Revolution. Contemporary Italian Collecting, Galleria d'Arte Moderna Ricci Oddi, Piacenza, Italy
Global(e) Resistance, Centre Pompidou, Paris, France
Nirin Naaram, Australian Centre for Contemporary Art, Sydney, Australia
Time Present, Palais Populaire, Deutsche Bank, Berlin, Germany
22nd Biennale of Sydney: NIRIN, Sydney, Australia
50 Mujeres, 50 Obras, 50 Años, Museo de la Ciudad de Mexico, Mexico
2019 *Ultrasanity*, SAVVY Contemporary, Berlin, Germany

21ª Bienal de Arte Contemporanea SESC Videobrasil: Comunidades imaginadas, São Paulo, Brazil
Bienalsur: Machinations, Contemporary Dialogues, Cuenca, Ecuador
Territorios de la Memoria, Museo de Arte Moderno, Mexico City, Mexico
58th International Art Exhibition | La Biennale di Venezia, Biennale Arte: May You Live in Interesting Times, Venice, Italy
Lille3000: Eldorama, Le Tri Postal, Lille, France
Je suis né étranger, Les Abattoirs, FRAC Occitanie, Toulouse, France
Latin America in the CA2M and Fundación ARCO Collections, Sala Alcalá 31, Madrid, Spain
Heart of Darkness, Castello di Rivoli, Turin, Italy

2018 *Destination: Latin America,* South Bend Museum of Art, IN, USA
Der Wert der Freiheit, Belvedere 21, Vienna, Austria
What Absence is Made Of, Hirshhorn Museum, Washington, DC, USA
Another Kind of Life, Barbican Art Gallery, London, UK
The Sight of Death in Contemporary Art, Stadtgalerie Saarbrücken, Germany
Unfixed: Redefining the Latin American Photograph, Cantor Arts Centre, Stanford University, CA, USA

2017 *Point/Counterpoint*, MOPA | Museum of Photographic Arts, San Diego, CA, USA
Bienalsur: Juntos Aparte, Cucutá, Colombia
La Cara Oculta de la Luna, CentroCentro, Madrid, Spain
Histórias de Sexualidad, MASP | Museo de Arte São Paulo, Brazil
I'm a Problem, Museum MMK | Für Moderne Kunst, Frankfurt am Main, Germany
The US-Mexico Border: Place, Imagination, Possibility, Pacific Standard Time: LA/LA, Craft & Folk Art Museum, Los Angeles, CA, USA
Frestas Trienal de Artes: Entre Pós-Verdades e Acontecimentos, SESC Sorocaba, Brazil
Lecturas de un Territorio Fracturado, Museo Amparo, Puebla, Mexico
Beyond The Pleasure Principles, Zacheta National Gallery, Warsaw, Poland
Alchemy: Transformations in Gold, Des Moines Art Center, IA, USA
Feminicidio en México: ¡Ya Basta!, Museo Memoria y Tolerancia, Mexico City, Mexico

2016 *Ein Knacks im Leben*, Vögele Kultur Zentrum, Pfäffikon, Switzerland
Historycode. Scarcity and Supply, Nanjing International Festival, Nanjing, China
Bienal de Arte SIART: Ver con los Odios, La Paz, Bolivia
Phantom Bodies: The Human Aura in Art, John and Mable Ringling Museum of Art, Sarasota, FL, USA
Manifesta 11: What People Do For Money, Zurich, Switzerland
Without Restraint, Kunstmuseum Bern, Switzerland
Basta!, Anya and Shiva Gallery at John Jay College of Criminal Justice, New York, USA
Woman Biennial: Silencio Vivo. Artists from Latin America, Ferrara, Italy
Depois do Futuro, Parque Lage Visual Arts School, Rio de Janeiro, Brazil

2015 *IV Trienal Poli/Gráfica*, San Juan, Puerto Rico
Feiert das Leben, Kunsthistorisches Museum Wien, Vienna, Austria
Strange Currencies. Art & Action in Mexico City 1990–2000, The Galleries at Moore, Philadelphia, PA, USA
Daros Latinamerica, Fundación Proa, Buenos Aires, Argentina
Lecciones de Historia, CAAM | Centro Atlántico de Arte Moderno, Las Palmas de Gran Canaria, Spain
Hidden Histories, Phoenix Art Museum, AZ, USA
Forensics: The Anatomy of Crime, Wellcome Collection, London, UK

2014 *Blockhouse*, La Conservera, Murcia, Spain
Horror en el Trópico, Museo Universitario del Chopo, Mexico City, Mexico
Made by... Feito por Brasileiros, Cidade Matarazzo, São Paulo, Brazil
Crime was almost perfect, PAC | Padiglione d'Arte Contemporanea, Milan, Italy
Crime in Art, MOCAK | Museum of Contemporary Art in Krakow, Poland
Death is Your Body, Frankfurter Kunstverein, Frankfurt am Main, Germany
Where The Streets Have No Name, Deviance Credits, CCS Bard Galleries, Hessel Museum of Art, Bard College, Annandale-on-Hudson, NY, USA
IX Biennial of Visual Arts of Nicaragua: Recycling Memory, Recapturing the Lost City, Managua, Nicaragua
DIRGE: Reflections on [Life and] Death, MoCA Cleveland, OH, USA
Sinful Saints and Saintly Sinners at the Margins of the Americas, Fowler Museum at UCLA, Los Angeles, CA, USA
El Hombre al Desnudo. Dimensiones de la Masculinidad a partir de 1800, Museo Nacional de Arte, Mexico City, Mexico
Ibi Et Nunc: Sobre Paradojas Democráticas, LOOP Festival 2014, Fabra i Coats, Barcelona, Spain

2013 *America Latina 1960–2013. Photographs,* Fondation Cartier pour l'art contemporain, Paris, France
I look to you and I see nothing, Sharjah Art Foundation, UAE
Power to the Powerless, Kunsthalle Baden-Baden, Germany
Remember Them, Victoria Gallery & Museum, Liverpool, UK
Beautiful Minds, Kleine Humboldt Galerie, Berlin, Germany
México: Inside Out, Modern Art Museum of Fort Worth, TX, US
Sakahàn: 1st International Quinquennial of New Indigenous Art, National Gallery of Canada, Ottawa, Canada
Dark Ages to Enlightenment, Tower of London, UK
Hay Más Rutas Que La Nuestra, Museo Tamayo, Mexico City, Mexico; Donaufestival, Krems, Austria
1ª Bienal del Sur en Panamá: Emplazando Muros, Panama
In The Heart of the Country, Museum of Modern Art in Warsaw, Poland
The Blood on my Hands, Kunstverein Ludwigsburg, Germany
Former West, HKW | Haus der Kulturen der Welt, Berlin, Germany
The Fragmented Body: Dust below the carpet, LiMAC en Madrid, Spain
Die Liebe ist kälter als das Kapital, Kunsthaus Bregenz, Austria

2012 *Touch*, Futura-Center for Contemporary Art, Prague, Czech Republic
Habeas Corpus, Centre d'Art Contemporani de Tarragona, Spain
An Oasis of Horror in a Desert of Boredom, Visual Centre for Contemporary Art Carlow, Ireland
Artes Mundi, Wales International Visual Art Exhibition and Prize, National Museum Cardiff, UK
Poznan Biennale: The Unknown, Poznan, Poland
Invisible: Art about the Unseen, 1957–2012, Hayward Gallery, London, UK
XVIII Bienal de Arte Paiz, Guatemala
Track, S.M.A.K., Ghent, Belgium
Residue of Memory, Aspen Art Museum, Aspen, CO, USA
Posada bis Alÿs, Kunsthaus Zürich, Switzerland
No Lone Zone, Tate Modern, London, UK
Copa América: Videoarte latino-americana contemporánea, Paço das Artes, São Paulo, Brazil
Chronicles of a Disappearance, DHC/ART | Foundation for contemporary art, Montreal, Canada

2011 *Memoria y Olvido*, AGN | Archivo General de la Nación, Mexico City, Mexico
The Walls That Divide Us, Apexart, New York, NY, USA
Ljubliana Biennial, Ljubljana, Slovenia
Terrible Beauty. Art, Crisis, Change & The Office of Non-Compliance, Dublin Contemporary 2011, Dublin, Ireland
México: Politica y Poetica, Nordic Watercolor Museum, Skärhamm, Sweden
Tenebrae, la Oscuridad, CEAC, Santiago, Chile; San Francisco State University, USA
El Grito, MUSAC | Museo de Arte Contemporaneo de Castilla y León, Spain
Tracing The Unseen Border, LaMaMa La Galleria, New York, NY, USA
Crisisss. Art and Confrontation in Latin America. 1910–2010, Palacio de Bellas Artes & Ex Teresa Arte Actual, Mexico City
Disponible, Walter + McBean Galleries, SFAI | San Francisco Art Institute, CA, USA
Double Take Triple Give, Contemporary Art Museum, Bat Yam, Israel

2010 *Arte no es Vida: Actions by Artists of the Americas, 1960–2000*, Museo de Arte del Banco de la República Biblioteca Luis Angel Arango, Bogota, Colombia
Epílogo, Museo de Arte de Zapopan, Guadalajara, Mexico
What Next For The Body, Inbetween Time Festival, Arnolfini, Bristol, UK
20 Sites 62 Artists 13 Weeks 7 Neighborhoods 20 Countries, Prospect 2, New Orleans, LA, USA
Beyond Borders, Museum of Sketches, Lund, Sweden
Critical Fetishes, CA2M, Madrid, Spain
El Horizonte del Topo, Bozar, Brussels, Belgium
Changing the Focus. Latin American Photography (1990–2005), MOLAA | Museum of Latin American Art, Long Beach, CA, USA
Visceral Bodies, Vancouver Art Gallery, Canada
The Living Currency, Berlin Biennial,

Berlin, Germany; Museum of Modern Art in Warsaw, Poland
2009 *Vi-Deum*, Netherlands Media Art Institute, Amsterdam, Netherlands
For You / Para Usted, Daros Exhibitions, Zurich, Switzerland
MAN SON 1969. Vom Schrecken der Situation, Galerie der Gegenwart, Hamburg, Germany
Plot/09: This World and Nearer Ones, Governor's Island, New York, NY, USA
2008 *Political/Minimal*, KW Institute for Contemporary Art, Berlin, Germany
7 + 1 Project Rooms, Marco, Vigo, Spain
Endless Sphere, Center for Contemporary Art, Kiev, Ukraine
Manifesta 7: The Rest of Now, Bolzano, Italy
Die Lucky Bush, MuHKA | Museum van Hedendaagse Kunst, Antwerp, Belgium
Contemporáneo 21. Autopsia de lo Invisible, MALBA | Museo de Arte Latinoamericano de Buenos Aires, Argentina
Arte ≠ Vida. Actions by Artists of the Americas, El Museo del Barrio, New York, NY, USA; Museo de Arte Garrillo Gil, Mexico City; Museo Amparo, Puebla, Mexico; Blaffer Gallery, University of Texas, Houston, TX, USA
2007 *¡Viva la Muerte!*, Kunsthalle Wien, Vienna, Austria; CAAM, Las Palmas de Gran Canaria, Spain
Grey Water, IMA | Institute of Modern Art, Brisbane, Australia
Theater of Cruelty, White Box, New York, USA
7. Internationale Foto-Triennale, Villa Merkel, Esslingen, Germany
Rites and Rituals, The Herzliya Museum of Contemporary Art, Israel
The Art of Failure, Kunsthaus Baselland, Muttenz, Switzerland
Into Me / Out of Me, MACRO Future, Rome, Italy
Bienal de Valencia: Otras Contemporaneidades, Valencia, Spain
Phantasmagoria: Specters of Absence, Museo de Arte del Banco de la República, Bogota, Colombia; The Contemporary Museum, Honolulu, HI; McColl Center for Visual Art, Charlotte, NC; The John and Mable Ringing Museum of Art, Sarasota, FL; Salina Art Center, KS; USC Fisher Gallery, Los Angeles, CA, USA
2006 *Fumus Fugiens,* Smart Project Space, Amsterdam, Netherlands
Six Feet Under, Kunstmuseum Bern, Switzerland
Liverpool Biennial 2006, International 06, Liverpool, UK
Pasión/Provocación, Centro de la Imagen, Mexico City, Mexico
Global Feminisms, Brooklyn Museum, New York, NY, USA
Encounters, Morris and Helen Belkin Art Gallery, University of British Columbia, Vancouver, Canada
Las Implicaciones de la Imagen, MASIN | Museo de Arte de Sinaloa, Culiacán, Mexico; Museo Unversitario de Ciencias y Artes, Mexico City, Mexico
EXCESS, Z33, Hasselt, Belgium
2005 *Un Nuevo y Bravo Mundo*, Sala de Alcalá, Madrid, Spain
9th Baltic Triennial of International Art, CAC | Contemporary Art Centre, Vilnius, Lithuania
Detonantes, Espacio OPA, Guadalajara, Mexico
Prague Biennale 2, Prague, Czech Republic
Eco: Arte Contemporáneo Mexicano, Museo Nacional Centro de Arte Reina Sofía, Madrid, Spain
2004 *Triennale Poligráfica San Juan*, San Juan, Puerto Rico
Casas en Acción, Casa de América, Madrid, Spain
Gwangju Biennale: A Grain of Dust a Drop of Water, Gwangju, South Korea
I need you, Kunsthaus Pasquart, Biel, Switzerland
Made in Mexico, Hammer Museum, Los Angeles, CA, USA
Excéntrico, Museo Provincial de Lugo, Spain
2nd Auckland Triennial: Public/Private, Auckland, New Zealand
Made in Mexico, Institute of Contemporary Art, Boston, MA, USA
2003 *IV Bienal de Mercosur*, Porto Alegre, Brazil
In Faccia al Mondo. Esperienze del ritratto fotografico contemporaneo, Museo d'Arte Contemporanea di Villa Croce, Genova, Italy
Stretch, The Power Plant, Toronto, Canada
2nd International Biennial for Contemporary Art: Against All Evens, Göteborg, Sweden
Bankett, ZKM | Center for Art and Media Karlsruhe, Germany
Mexico Attacks, Prometeo Associazione Culturale per l'Arte Contemporanea, Lucca, Italy; MADC | Museo de Arte y Diseno Contemporaneo, San José, Costa Rica
2002 *Otredad y Mismidad*, Galería de Arte Contemporáneo, Puebla, Mexico
Entre Lineas, Casa Encendida, Madrid, Spain
Mexiko-Stadt: Eine Ausstellung über den Tauschwert von Körpern und Werten, Kunst-Werke, Berlin, Germany
Mexico City, MoMA PS1, New York, NY, USA
20 Million Mexicans Can't Be Wrong, South London Gallery; John Hansard Gallery, Southampton, UK
Zebra Crossing, HKW | Haus der Kulturen der Welt, Berlin, Germany
VII Bienal de Pintura de Cuenca, Cuenca, Ecuador
2001 *Escultura Mexicana*, Museo del Palacio de Bellas Artes, Mexico City, Mexico
Hábitat Global, Guanajuato University, Mexico
25 x 25, Galeria de Arte Mexicano, Mexico City
2000 *Bienal de La Habana: Extramuros,* Havana, Cuba
Cinco Continentes y una Ciudad, Museo de la Ciudad de México, Mexico
IV Bienale de Lyon: Partage d'Exotismes, Lyon, France
1999 *Baño María,* Cineteca Nacional, Mexico City, Mexico
Bienal de Fotografía, Centro de la Imagen, Mexico City, Mexico
1998 *Bienal Bidimensional,* Mexico City, Mexico *Foto Construcciones,* Museo de Arte Contemporáneo de Morelia, Mexico
1996 *XVII Salón de la plastica Sinaloense*, Culiacán, Mexico
Muestra Latinoamericana de Fotografía, toured Latin America

Selected Public Collections

Castello di Rivoli Museo d'Arte Contemporanea, Turin, Italy
CGAC | Centro Galego de Arte Contemporánea, Santiago de Compostela, Spain
Cnap | Centre national des arts plastiques, Paris, France
CA2M | Colección Centro de Arte Dos de Mayo, Mostoles, Spain
FRAC Lorraine, Metz, France
FRAC Nord Pas-de-Calais, Dunkerque, France
FRAC des Pays de la Loire, Carquefou, France
Hirshhorn Museum and Sculpture Garden, Washington, DC, USA
Kunsthaus Zürich, Switzerland
Fundatiòn Jumex Arte Contemporàneo, Mexico City, Mexico
MACBA | Museu d'Art Contemporani de Barcelona, Spain
Maison Européenne de la Photographie, Paris, France
Migros Museum für Gegenwartskunst, Zurich, Switzerland
Modern Art Museum of Fort Worth, TX, USA
Museo Amparo, Puebla, Mexico
Museo del Banco de la Republica, Bogota, Colombia
Museo Tamayo Arte Contemporáneo, Mexico City, Mexico
MUAC | Museo Universitario Arte Contemporáneo, Mexico City, Mexico
MMK | Museum für Moderne Kunst, Frankfurt am Main, Germany
The Museum of Fine Arts, Houston, TX, USA
Museum of Modern Art in Warsaw, Poland
National Gallery of Canada, Ottawa, Canada
Neuberger Museum of Art, Purchase College, CUNY | City University of New York, NY, USA
Perez Art Museum, Miami, FL, USA
Phoenix Art Museum, AZ, USA
Tate Modern, London, UK

SI ON
Born 1979, Dangjin, South Korea
Lives and works in Krakow, Poland

Education
2011 PhD Painting, Kyoto City University of Arts, Kyoto, Japan
2008 MA Painting, Kyoto City University of Arts, Kyoto, Japan
2002 BA Western Painting, Mokwon University, Daejeon, South Korea

Selected Solo Exhibitions
2021 *Burial and Sowing*, T293 Gallery, Rome, Italy
2020 *Shaman Woman*, HOS Gallery, Warsaw Gallery Weekend, Poland
MAM Project 028, Mori Art Museum, Tokyo, Japan
Female Creature, Hunt Kastner, Prague, Czech Republic
2019 *Hyon Gyon*, Parasol unit foundation for contemporary art, London, UK
2017 *Cruel World*, Ben Brown Fine Arts, Hong Kong
2016 *She's A Riot*, Shin Gallery, New York, NY, USA
Emotional Drought, Shin Gallery, New York, NY, USA
2015 *Hyon Gyon and the Factory*, Chashama, New York, NY, USA
No-Mad Nomad, Pioneer Works, New York, NY, USA
2013 *All Night Haps*, HAPS, Kyoto, Japan
2012 *The Incarnation of The World*, Gallery Golmok, Seoul, South Korea
2011 *New Incubation 3: On a Knife Edge*, Kyoto Art Center, Japan
2010 *Giragira*, g3 gallery, Tokyo, Japan
Tamahuri, g3 gallery, Tokyo, Japan
2009 *Iyoiyo*, Gallery EXIT, Hong Kong
2008 *Iyoiyo*, Magical ArtRoom, Tokyo, Japan
TWS-Emerging 099, Awesome Wonder Site Hongo, Tokyo, Japan
Tokyo Wonder Wall, Tokyo Metropolitan Government, Japan

Selected Group Exhibitions
2022 *Uncombed, Unforeseen, Unconstrained*, Parasol unit foundation for contemporary art. A Collateral Event of the 59th International Art Exhibition | La Biennale di Venezia, Conservatorio di Musica Benedetto Marcello di Venezia, Italy
2021 *Tranchée Racine I*, Halle Saint-Pierre, Paris, France
2020 *Ode to a Nightingale*, Anima Mundi Gallery, St Ives, UK
2019 *Elements of Transcendence,* Ben Brown Fine Arts, Hong Kong
Paint, Also Known As Blood. Woman, Affect, and Desire in Contemporary Painting, Museum of Modern Art in Warsaw, Poland
Trip (with Jakub Julian Ziółkowski), BWA Wrocław Galleries of Contemporary Art, Wroclaw, Poland
2018 *Great Nobles of the Country / Wielcy sarmaci tego kraju...*, BWA Tarnów, Poland
Holy Nothing (with Jakub Julian Ziółkowski), Ujazdowski Castle Centre for Contemporary Art, Warsaw, Poland
Sue Coe, Eliza Douglas, Joseph Geagan, Hyon Gyon, James Fuentes Gallery, New York, NY, USA
2017 *Culture City of East Asia 2017*, Kyoto, Japan
The World is a Stage, but the Play is Badly Cast, Batu Museum, New York, NY, USA
Naturalia, Paul Kasmin, New York, NY, USA
2016 *Art for Art's Sake: Selections from the Frederick R. Weisman Art Foundation*, Carnegie Art Museum, Oxnard, CA, USA
Beyond Secretary, Mark Borghi Gallery, New York, NY, USA
I Wanna Be Me, Shin Gallery, New York, NY, USA
2015 *The Brooklyn Artists Ball*, Brooklyn Museum, New York, USA
Veni, Vidi, Vici, Shin Gallery, New York, NY, USA
2013 *Kawaii CAMP!*, Contemporary Art Meeting Point, Athens, Greece
Kyoto Artist Meeting 2013, Antenna Media, Kyoto, Japan
Kyoto Studio, @KCUA, Kyoto, Japan
2012 *Phantoms of Asia: Contemporary Awakens the Past*, Asian Art Museum, San Francisco, CA, USA
Transmit Program #3 Metis, @KCUA, Kyoto, Japan
2011 *Tokyo Frontline*, 3331 Arts Chiyoda, Tokyo, Japan
2010 *Tokyo Wonder Wall,* 10th Anniversary, MOT | Museum of Contemporary Art Tokyo, Japan
Part2 (girl): Neonoe Girls Open Iwato Personally / Takahashi Collection, Tokyo, Japan
2009 *Waku waku Joban-Kashiwa Project*, TSCA Kashiwa, Chiba, Japan
Pica3, Art Court Galler Osaka, Japan
2008 *New Beginning: The Show Must Go On!,* Magical Art Room, Tokyo, Japan
2007 *Worm Hole Episode 7,* Magical Art Room, Tokyo, Japan
Tokyo Wonder Wall, MOT | Museum of Contemporary Art Tokyo, Japan
Hello, Chelsea, PS35 gallery, New York, NY, USA
Brilliant Works, Art Zone, Kyoto, Japan
2006 *Art Jam,* The Museum of Kyoto, Japan

Selected Public Collections
Brooklyn Museum, New York, NY, USA
Frederick R. Weisman Art Foundation, Los Angeles, CA, USA
High Museum of Art, Atlanta, GA, USA
Kyoto Municipal Museum of Art, Japan
Kyoto City University of Arts, Japan
Kyoto Bank, Japan
Takahashi Collection, Tokyo, Japan

MARTIN PURYEAR
Born 1941, Washington, DC, USA
Lives and works in the Hudson Valley, NY, USA

Education
1971 MFA Sculpture, Yale University, New Haven, CT, USA
1966 Royal Swedish Academy of Arts, Stockholm, Sweden
1963 BA, Catholic University of America, Washington, DC, USA

Selected Solo Exhibitions
2020 *Martin Puryear*, Matthew Marks Gallery, New York, NY, USA
2019 *Liberty/Libertà*, 58th International Art Exhibition | La Biennale di Venezia, Biennale Arte: *Making Worlds*, United States Pavilion, Venice, Italy
2018 *Martin Puryear*, Voorlinden museum, Wassenaar, Netherlands
Martin Puryear, Glenstone, Potomac, USA
2017 *Martin Puryear*, Parasol unit foundation for contemporary art, London, UK
Prints 1962–2016, The Print Center, Philadelphia, PA, USA
2015 *Martin Puryear: Multiple Dimensions*, Morgan Library & Museum, New York, NY; The Art Institute of Chicago, IL; SAAM | Smithsonian American Art Museum, Washington, DC, USA
2014 *Martin Puryear*, Matthew Marks Gallery, New York, NY, USA
2012 *Martin Puryear: New Sculpture*, McKee Gallery, New York, NY, USA
Martin Puryear: Vessel, 'T' Space, Rhinebeck, NY, USA
2010 *Martin Puryear: Prints*, Cincinnati Art Museum, OH, USA
2009 Kleinert/James Arts Center, Woodstock Byrdcliffe Guild, Woodstock, NY, USA
2008 *Prints*, de Young Museum, San Francisco, CA, USA
2007 *Martin Puryear*, MoMA | Museum of Modern Art, New York, NY; Modern Art Museum of Fort Worth, TX; National Gallery of Art, Washington, DC; SFMOMA | San Francisco Museum of Modern Art, USA
2003 *New Work*, BALTIC Centre for Contemporary Art, Gateshead, UK; IMMA | Irish Museum of Modern Art, Dublin, Ireland
2002 *Martin Puryear: Sculpture of the 1990s*, Virginia Museum of Fine Arts, Richmond, VA; Miami Art Museum, FL; BAMPFA | Berkeley Art Museum and Pacific Film Archive, University of California, CA; Des Moines Art Center, IA, USA
2000 *The Cane Project*, The Studio Museum Harlem, New York, NY, USA
1999 *Drawing into Sculpture*, Contemporary Arts Center, Cincinnati, OH, USA
1997 *Martin Puryear*, Fundación La Caixa, Madrid, Spain
1993 *Martin Puryear*, Cleveland Center for Contemporary Art, OH, USA
1991 *Martin Puryear*, Art Institute of Chicago, IL; Hirshhorn Museum and Sculpture Garden; Washington, DC; MOCA | The Museum of Contemporary Art, Los Angeles, CA; Philadelphia Museum of Art, PA, USA
1990 *Connections*, Museum of Fine Arts, Boston, MA, USA
1989 Represented the USA at 20th International São Paulo Biennal, São Paulo, Brazil

1988 *Grand Lobby Installation*, Brooklyn Museum, New York, NY, USA
1987 *Public and Personal*, The Chicago Public Library Cultural Center, IL, USA
Sculpture/Drawings, Carnegie Mellon University Art Gallery, Pittsburgh, PA, USA
1985 *Matrix 86: Martin Puryear*, Berkeley Art Museum, University of California, CA, USA
1984 *Ten-Year Survey*, University Gallery, University of Massachusetts, Amherst, MA; The Berkshire Museum, Pittsfield, MA; The Museum of the National Center of Afro-American Artists, Boston, MA; New Museum, New York, NY; MCASD | Museum of Contemporary Art San Diego, La Jolla, CA, USA
1980 *Options 2*, MCA | Museum of Contemporary Art, Chicago, IL, USA
I–80 Series, Joslyn Art Museum, Omaha, NE, USA

Commissions and Special Projects
2018 *Connecting*, FAPE | Federation for Art and Preservation in Embassies, Beijing, China
2016 *Big Bling*, Madison Square Park, Madison Square Park Conservancy, New York, NY; Schuylkill River Park, Association for Public Art, Philadelphia, PA; MASS MoCA | Massachusetts Museum of Contemporary Art, North Adams, MA, USA
2014 *Slavery Memorial, Brown University*, Providence, RI, USA
One Handed Stool, New Museum, New York, NY, USA
Bench designs, Glenstone Foundation, Potomac, MD, USA
2003 *Guardian Stone*, TV Asahi, Tokyo, Japan
1999 *That Profile*, J. Paul Getty Museum, Los Angeles, CA, USA
This Mortal Coil, Festival d'Automne, Paris, France
1998 *Bearing Witness*, Reagan Building, Washington, DC, USA
1997 Courtyard, the New School for Social Research, New York, NY, USA
Everything That Rises, University of Washington, Seattle, WA, USA
1996 *Meditation in a Beech Wood*, Wanås Foundation, Knislinge, Sweden
1995 *North Cove Pylons*, Battery Park City, NY, USA
1994 *Camera Obscura*, Denver Civic Center, CO, USA
Untitled, Oliver Ranch, Geyserville, CA, USA
Pavilion in the Trees, Fairmount Park, Philadelphia, PA, USA
1991 *Griot New York*, Brooklyn Academy of Music, NY, USA
1988 *Ampersand*, Walker Art Center, Minneapolis, MN, USA
1987 *Ark*, York College, CUNY | City University of New York, Jamaica, NY, USA
1985 *River Road Ring*, Chicago O'Hare Transit Line, IL, USA
1983 *Knoll for NOAA*, Western Regional Center, Seattle, WA, USA
1982 *Bodark Arc*, Nathan Manilow Sculpture Park, University Park, IL, USA
Sentinel, Gettysburg College, PA, USA
1979 *Equivalents*, Wave Hill, New York, NY, USA
1977 *Box and Pole*, Artpark, Lewiston, NY, USA

Selected Group Exhibitions
2022 *Uncombed, Unforeseen, Unconstrained*, Parasol unit foundation for contemporary art. A Collateral Event of the 59th International Art Exhibition | La Biennale di Venezia, Conservatorio di Musica Benedetto Marcello di Venezia, Italy
2021 *Nasher Mixtape*, Nasher Sculpture Center, Dallas, TX, USA
Recent Acquisitions: Modern and Contemporary Drawings and Prints, The Morgan Library & Museum, New York, NY, USA
2020 *James Prosek: Art, Artifact, Artifice*, Yale University Art Gallery, New Haven, CT, USA
Riffs and Relations: African American Artists and the European Modernist Tradition, Phillips Collection, Washington, DC, USA
Making Community: Prints from Brandywine Workshop and Archives, Brodsky Center at PAFA, and Paulson Fontaine Press, Pennsylvania Academy of the Fine Arts, Philadelphia, PA, USA
Presence: African American Artists from the Museum's Collection, The Honolulu Museum of Art, HI, USA
PICTURE ID: Contemporary African American Works on Paper, Toledo Museum of Art, OH, USA
2019 *Five Ways In: Themes from the Collection*, Walker Art Center, Minneapolis, MN, USA
Front Room: The Mary and Paul Roberts Collection, BMA | Baltimore Museum of Art, MD, USA
Generations: A History of Black Abstract Art, BMA, Baltimore, MD, USA
Afrocosmologies: American Reflections, Wadsworth Atheneum Museum of Art, Hartford, CT, USA
Contemporary Art: Five Propositions, Museum of Fine Arts, Boston, MA, USA
Detroit Collects: Selections of African American Art from Private Collections, DIA | Detroit Institute of Arts, MI, USA
Making Knowing: Craft in Art, 1950–2019, Whitney Museum of American Art, New York, NY, USA
Bound to the Earth: Art, Materiality, and the Natural World, MCASD | Museum of Contemporary Art, San Diego, CA, USA
2018 *Modern and Contemporary Art: Selected Works from the Permanent Art Collection*, University Archives Gallery, The University of the South, Sewanee, TN, USA
Contemporary Highlights, Colby College Museum of Art, Waterville, ME, USA
Personal to Political: Celebrating the African American Artists of Paulson Fontaine Press, Bedford Gallery at the Lesher Center for the Arts, Walnut Creek, CA, USA
Studio Visit: Selected Gifts from Agnes Gund, MoMA, New York, NY, USA
Almanach 18, Le Consortium, Dijon, France
Art in Dialogue: Robert Indiana and Martin Puryear, Patricia & Phillip Frost Art Museum at Florida International University, Miami, FL, USA
Beyond Borders: Global Africa, University of Michigan Museum of Art, Ann Arbor, MI, USA
Second Look, Twice: Selections from the Collections of Jordan D. Schnitzer and his Family Foundation, Museum of the African Diaspora, San Francisco, CA, USA
Crossroads: Carnegie Museum of Art's Collection, 1945 to Now, Carnegie Museum of Art, Pittsburgh, PA, USA
Recent Acquisitions: Paintings, Ceramics, and Works on Paper, Museum of Fine Arts, St. Petersburg, FL, USA
2017 *Soul of a Nation: Art in the Age of Black Power*, Tate Modern, London, UK; Crystal Bridges Museum of American Art, Bentonville, AR; Brooklyn Museum, NY; The Broad, Los Angeles, CA, USA
One of Many: Recent Acquisitions of Prints and Portfolios, Ackland Art Museum, University of North Carolina at Chapel Hill, NC, USA
Seeking Stillness, Museum of Fine Arts, Boston, MA, USA
The Long Run, MoMA, NY, USA
2016 *Approaching American Abstraction: The Fisher Collection*, SFMOMA, San Francisco, CA, USA
Abstracting Nature, Newark Museum of Art, NJ, USA
Dimensions of Black: A Collaboration with the San Diego African American Museum of Fine Art, MCASD, San Diego, CA, USA
2015 *Black Fire: A Constant State of Revolution*, Sheldon Museum of Art, University of Nebraska, Lincoln, NE, USA
Recent Acquisitions of Prints and Drawings Spanning 500 Years, Portland Art Museum, OR, USA
River Crossings, Thomas Cole National Historic Site and Olana State Historic Site, Catskill and Hudson, NY, USA
Another Look at the Permanent Collection, Anderson Collection at Stanford University, CA, USA
2014 *Represent: 200 Years in African-American Art*, Philadelphia Museum of Art, PA, USA
Conversations: African and African American Art in Dialogue, Smithsonian National Museum of African Art, Washington, DC, USA
2013 *Against the Grain: Wood in Contemporary Art, Craft and Design,* The Museum of Arts and Design, New York, NY, USA
Legacy: The Emily Fisher Landau Collection, Asheville Art Museum, NC, USA
Multiplicity: Contemporary Prints from the Smithsonian Art Museum, Akron Art Museum, OH, USA
2012 *African American Art Since 1950: Perspectives from the David C. Driskell Center*, University of Maryland, College Park, MD, USA
2010 *A Force of Change: African American Art and the Julius Rosenwald Fund*, Montclair Art Museum, NJ, USA
2009 *The Sculptor's Hand*, Tasende Gallery, La Jolla, CA, USA
A Matter of Form, John Berggruen Gallery, San Francisco, CA, USA
The Endless Renaissance, Bass Museum of Art, Miami Beach, FL, USA
Die Gegenwart der Linie, Die Pinakothek der Moderne, Staatlich Graphische Sammlung München, Munich, Germany
Art at Colby: Celebrating the Fiftieth Anniversary of the Colby College Museum of Art, Waterville, ME, USA
New Prints 2009/Autumn, International Print Center, New York, NY, USA
2008 *Origins*, Hudson Valley Center for Contemporary Art, Peeskill, NY, USA
Art for Yale: Collecting for a new century, Yale University Art Gallery, New Haven, CT, USA
2006 *Against the Grain: Contemporary Art from the Edward R. Broida Collection*, MoMA,

New York, NY, USA
Selections from the Collection of Edward R. Broida, National Gallery of Art, Washington, DC, USA
2005 *Africa in America*, SAM | Seattle Art Museum, WA, USA
2004 *Love/Hate: From Magritte to Cattelan: Masterpieces from the Collection of the Museum of Contemporary Art, Chicago*, Villa Manin, Passariano, Italy
Gyroscope Series: Martin Puryear, Hirshhorn Museum and Sculpture Garden, Washington, DC, USA
2003 *Breathless*, Neuberger Museum of Art, Purchase College, City University of New York, USA
2002 *110 Years: The Permanent Collection of the Modern Art Museum of Fort Worth*, TX, USA
Gifts in Honor of the 125th Anniversary of the Philadelphia Museum of Art, Philadelphia Museum of Art, PA, USA
In the Spirit of Martin: The Living Legacy of Dr. Martin Luther King, Jr., Charles H. Wright Museum of African American History, Detroit, MI; Bass Museum, Miami Beach, FL; Frederick R. Weisman Art Museum, Minneapolis, MN; Brooklyn Museum, NY; Memphis Brooks Museum of Art, TN; MMFA | Montgomery Museum of Fine Arts, AL, USA
To Be Looked At: Painting and Sculpture from the Collection, MoMA, New York, USA
Material Differences: Contemporary Viewpoints, Museum for African Art, New York, NY, USA
2001 *New to the Modern: Recent Acquisitions from the Department of Drawings*, MoMA, New York, NY, USA
The Draughtsman's Colors: Fourteen New Acquisitions from Johns to Chong, Whitney Museum of American Art, New York, NY, USA
Yale University School of Art Alumni Choice Exhibition, Yale University Art Gallery, New Haven, CT, USA
New Land Marks: Public Art, Community, and the Meaning of Place, Pennsylvania Academy of Fine Arts, Philadelphia, PA, USA
2000 *Celebrating Modern Art: Highlights of the Anderson Collection*, SFMOMA, San Francisco, CA, USA
Strength and Diversity: A Celebration of African American Artists, Carpenter Center, Harvard University, Cambridge, MA, USA
Making Choices, MoMA, New York, NY, USA
1999 *The American Century: Art & Culture, 1950–2000*, Whitney Museum of American Art, New York, NY, USA
Weaving the World: Contemporary Art of Linear Construction, Yokohama Museum of Art, Japan
1998 *Narratives of African American Art of the 20th Century: The David C. Driskell Collection*, The Art Gallery of the University of Maryland, College Park, MD, USA
The African-American Odyssey: A Quest for Full Citizenship, The Library of Congress, Washington, DC, USA
1997 *Forma Lignea*, American Academy in Rome, Italy
American Stories: Amidst Displacement and Transformation, Setagaya Art Museum, Tokyo; Chiba City Museum of Art; Fukui Fine Arts Museum; Kurashiki City Art Museum; Akita Prefectural Integrated Life Cultural Hall, Japan
Envisioning the Contemporary: Selections from the Permanent Collection, MCA | Museum of Contemporary Art, Chicago, IL, USA
Selections from the Permanent Collection: Identity/Identidad, MCASD, La Jolla, CA, USA
1996 *Masterworks of Modern Sculpture: The Nasher Collection*, Fine Arts Museums of San Francisco, Legion of Honor, CA; Solomon R. Guggenheim Museum, New York, NY, USA
Abstraction in the Twentieth Century: Total Risk, Freedom, Discipline, Solomon R. Guggenheim Museum, New York, NY, USA
Wanås 1996, Wanås Foundation, Knislinge, Sweden
Art in Chicago, 1945–1955, MCA | Museum of Contemporary Art, Chicago, IL, USA
Faret Tachikawa: City and Art Today, National Technical Museum, Prague, Czech Republic
1995 *The Material Imagination*, Guggenheim Museum SoHo, New York, NY, USA
1994 *Western Artists/African Art*, Museum for African Art, New York, NY, USA
Visions of America: Landscape as Metaphor in the Late Twentieth Century, Denver Art Museum, CO, USA
Putting Things Together: Recent Sculpture from the Anderson Collection, The Art Museum of Santa Cruz County, CA, USA
1993 *Visual Arts Encounter: African Americans and Europe*, Palais du Luxembourg, Paris, France
Yale Collects Yale, Yale University Art Gallery, New Haven, CT, USA
American Art in the 20th Century: Painting and Sculpture 1913–1993, Martin Gropius Bau, Berlin, Germany; RA | Royal Academy of Arts, London; Saatchi Gallery, London, UK
Drawing the Line Against AIDS, Peggy Guggenheim Collection, Venice, Italy; Guggenheim Museum SoHo, New York, NY, USA
1992 *Allegories of Modernism: Contemporary Drawing*, MoMA, New York, NY, USA
Process to Presence: Issues in Sculpture, 1960 to 1990, Locks Gallery, Philadelphia, PA, USA
Documenta 9, Kassel, Germany
1991 *Devil on the Stairs: Looking Back at the Eighties*, Institute of Contemporary Art, Philadelphia, PA; Newport Harbor Art Museum, Newport Beach, CA, USA
Reprise: The Vera G. List Collection, David Winton Bell Gallery, List Art Center, Brown University, Providence, RI, USA
Small Scale Sculpture, Sewell Art Gallery, Rice University, Houston, TX, USA
1990 *Black USA*, Museum Overholland, Amsterdam, Netherlands
The Decade Show: Frameworks of Identity in the 1980s, New Museum, New York, NY, USA
Objects of Potential: Five American Sculptors from the Anderson Collection, Wiegand Gallery, College of Notre Dame, Belmont, CA, USA
1989 *Art in Place: 15 Years of Acquisitions*, Whitney Museum of American Art, New York, NY, USA
Traditions and Transformation: Contemporary Afro-American Sculpture, The Bronx Museum of the Arts, New York, NY, USA
Whitney Biennial, Whitney Museum of American Art, New York, NY, USA
Introspective: Contemporary American Art by Americans and Brazilians of African Descent, California Afro-American Museum, Los Angeles, CA, USA
1988 *7th Biennale of Sydney: From the Southern Cross: A View of World Art c. 1940–1988*, Sydney, Australia
The World of Art Today, Milwaukee Art Museum, WI, USA
Innovations in Sculpture, Aldrich Museum of Contemporary Art, Ridgefield, CT, USA
Skulptur: Material + Abstraktion: 2 x 5 Positionen, Aargauer Kunsthaus, Aarau; Musée cantonal des Beaux-Arts, Lausanne, Switzerland; Swiss Institute, New York, NY, USA
Sculpture Inside Outside, Walker Art Center, Minneapolis, MN; Museum of Fine Arts, Houston, TX, USA
1987 *Structure to Resemblance: Work by Eight American Sculptors*, Albright-Knox Art Gallery, Buffalo, NY, USA
Fifty Years of Collecting: An Anniversary Selection of Sculpture of the Modern Era, Solomon R. Guggenheim Museum, New York, NY, USA
Emerging Artists: 1978–1986: Selection from the Exxon Series, Solomon R. Guggenheim Museum, New York, NY, USA
1986 *Sculpture on Stetson: 1986*, Two Illinois Center, Chicago, IL, USA
Natural Forms and Forces: Abstract Images in American Sculpture, Hayden Gallery, List Visual Arts Center, MIT | Massachusetts Institute of Technology, Cambridge, MA, USA
Individuals: A Selected History of Contemporary Art, 1945–1986, MOCA | Museum of Contemporary Art, Los Angeles, CA, USA
Personal References, Kansas City Art Institute, MO, USA
1985 *Chicago Sculpture International/Mile 4*, State Street Mall, Chicago, IL, USA
Sculpture Overview 1985, Evanston Art Center, IL, USA
Choosing: An Exhibit of Changing Perspectives in Modern Art and Art Criticism by Black Americans 1925–1985, Museum of Science and Industry, Chicago, IL; Chicago State University; Portsmouth Museum, VA; Howard University, Washington, DC, USA
The Artist as Social Designer: Aspects of Public Urban Art Today, LACMA | Los Angeles County Museum of Art, CA, USA
Black Creativity, Generations in Transition: 80 Years of Black American Expression, Museum of Science and Industry, Chicago, IL, USA
Anniottanta, Invitational, Galleria Comunale d'Arte Moderna, Bologna, Italy
Transformations in Sculpture: Four Decades in American and European Art, Solomon R. Guggenheim Museum, New York, NY, USA
Artist and Architects, Challenges in Collaboration, Cleveland Center for Contemporary Art, OH, USA
Inaugural Exhibition, Tyler Gallery, Temple

University, Philadelphia, PA, USA
1984 *An International Survey of Recent Painting and Sculpture*, MoMA, New York, NY, USA
"Primitivism" in 20th Century Art: Affinity of the Tribal and Modern, MoMA, New York, NY, USA
1983 *Beyond the Monument, Documentation of Public Art Projects and Proposals*, Hayden Corridor Gallery, MIT | Massachusetts Inst. of Technology, Cambridge, MA, USA
1982 *Afro-American Abstraction*, MoMA PS1, New York, NY; Los Angeles Municipal Art Gallery, CA; Oakland Museum, CA; Memphis Brooks Museum of Art, TN; The Art Center, South Bend, IN; The Toledo Museum of Art, OH; Bellevue Art Museum, WA; Laguna Gloria Museum, Austin, TX; Everson Gallery, Syracuse, NY, USA
The 74th American Exhibition, The Art Institute of Chicago, IL, USA
American Abstraction Now, Richmond Institute of Contemporary Art, Virginia Commonwealth University, Richmond, VA, USA
Mayor Byrne's Mile of Sculpture, International Art Exposition, Chicago, IL, USA
1981 *The New Spiritualism: Transcendent Images in Painting and Sculpture*, Oscarsson Hood Gallery, New York, NY; Jorgensen Gallery, University of Connecticut, Storrs, CT; Robert Hull Fleming Museum, University of Vermont, Burlington, VT, USA
Whitney Biennial, Whitney Museum of American Art, New York, NY, USA
City Sculpture, Chicago Public Library Cultural Center, IL, USA
Instruction Drawings, Cranbrook Academy of Art Museum, Bloomfield Hills, MI, USA
Artists' Parks and Gardens, MCA | Museum of Contemporary Art, Chicago, IL, USA
Sculptural Density, Visual Arts Museum, School of Visual Arts, New York, NY, USA
1980 *Chicago, Chicago*, Contemporary Arts Center, Cincinnati, OH, USA
1979 *Whitney Biennial*, Whitney Museum of American Art, New York, NY, USA
Wave Hill: The Artist's View, Wave Hill, New York, NY, USA
1978 *Young American Artists: 1978 Exxon National Exhibition*, Solomon R. Guggenheim Museum, New York, NY, USA
The Presence of Nature, Whitney Museum of American Art, New York, NY, USA
1977 *The Material Dominant*, Pennsylvania State University Museum of Art, University Park, PA, USA
1974 National Collection of Fine Arts, Washington, DC, USA
New Talent at Maryland, Art Gallery at University of Maryland, College Park, MD, USA
1971 *Prints and Paintings by Black Artists*, Union South Gallery, University of Wisconsin, Madison, WI, USA
1968 *Annual Exhibition*, Royal Swedish Academy of Arts, Stockholm, Sweden
1965 *Group Show*, U.S.I.S. Gallery, Freetown, Sierra Leone
Annual Exhibition, Royal Swedish Academy of Arts, Stockholm, Sweden
Stockholm Biennial Exhibition, Liljevalchs Konsthall, Sweden
1962 *Annual Exhibition*, Baltimore Museum of Art, MD, USA

Selected Public Collections
Art Institute of Chicago, IL, USA
BAMPFA | Berkeley Art Museum and Pacific Film Archive, University of California, CA, USA
Colby College Museum of Art, Waterville, ME, USA
Cnap | Centre national des arts plastiques, France
DMA | Dallas Museum of Art, TX, USA
Five Colleges and Historic Deerfield Museum Consortium, MA, USA
Hirshhorn Museum and Sculpture Garden, Washington, DC, USA
Joslyn Art Museum, Omaha, NE, USA
MCA | Museum of Contemporary Art, Chicago, IL, USA
The Metropolitan Museum of Art, New York, NY, USA
MCASD | Museum of Contemporary Art San Diego, CA, USA
Milwaukee Art Museum, WI, USA
Modern Art Museum of Fort Worth, TX, USA
MoMA | The Museum of Modern Art, New York, NY, USA
National Gallery of Art, Washington, DC, USA
Philadelphia Museum of Art, PA, USA
SAM | Seattle Art Museum, WA, USA
Sheldon Museum of Art, University of Nebraska, Lincoln, NE, USA
SAAM | Smithsonian American Art Museum, Washington, DC, USA
Solomon R. Guggenheim Museum, New York, NY, USA
Studio Museum in Harlem, New York, NY, USA
The Cleveland Museum of Art, OH, USA
The Nelson-Atkins Museum of Art, Kansas City, MO, USA
Tokyo International Forum, Japan
Walker Art Center, Minneapolis, MN, USA
Whitney Museum of American Art, New York, NY, USA

RAYYANE TABET
Born 1983, Ashqout, Lebanon
Lives and works in Beirut, Lebanon, and San Francisco, CA, USA

Education
2012 MFA, University of California in San Diego, CA, USA
2008 BA Architecture, The Cooper Union, New York, NY, USA

Selected Solo Exhibitions
2021 *Exquisite Corpse*, Sharjah Art Foundation, UAE
Arabeske, Sfeir-Semler Gallery, Hamburg, Germany
Deep Blues, Walker Art Center, Minneapolis, MN, USA
2020 *Arabesque*, Storefront for Art and Architecture, New York, NY, USA
2019 *Encounters*, Parasol unit foundation for contemporary art, London, UK
Fragments, Carré d'Art - Musée d'art contemporain, Nîmes, France
Alien Property, The Metropolitan Museum of Art, New York, NY, USA
2018 *Fault Line*, Fondazione Antonio Dalle Nogare, Bolzano, Italy
Fragments, Sfeir-Semler Gallery, Beirut, Lebanon
Hidden in Plain Sight, Galleria Franco Noero, Turin, Italy
2017 *Bruchstücke / Fragments*, Kunstverein Hamburg, Germany
Kopf Hoch! Mut Hoch! Und Humor Hoch!, daadgalerie, Berlin, Germany
Ah, My Beautiful Venus!, Witte de With Center for Contemporary Art, Rotterdam, Netherlands
2016 *La Mano De Dios*, Museo Marino Marini, Florence, Italy
2015 *Only Gods Never Die*, Sfeir-Semler Gallery, Hamburg, Germany
2014 *Here Today Gone Tomorrow*, Trouw, Amsterdam, Netherlands
2013 *The Shortest Distance Between Two Points*, Sfeir-Semler Gallery, Beirut, Lebanon

Selected Group Exhibitions
2022 *Uncombed, Unforeseen, Unconstrained*, Parasol unit foundation for contemporary art. A Collateral Event of the 59th International Art Exhibition | La Biennale di Venezia, Conservatorio di Musica Benedetto Marcello di Venezia, Italy
Whitney Biennial, Whitney Museum of American Art, New York, NY, USA
Futura. Measuring Time, Hamburger Kunsthalle, Hamburg, Germany
2021 *Hiding in Plain Sight*, Pace Gallery, New York, NY, USA
2020 *A Sun Yellow with Anger*, Sfeir-Semler Gallery, Hamburg, Germany
Yokohama Triennale 2020: Afterglow, Yokohama, Japan
Desert X AlUla, AlUla, Saudi Arabia
Lahore Biennale 02: Between the Sun and the Moon, Lahore, Pakistan
2019 *Phantom Limb*, Jameel Arts Centre, Dubai, UAE
When the Present is History, Depo, Istanbul, Turkey
Royaumes Oubliés, Musée du Louvre, Paris, France
No Habrá Nunca una Puerta. Estas

Adentro, Fundación Banco Santander, Madrid, Spain
2018 *Inhabiting the Mediterranean*, IVAM | Institut Valencià d'Art Modern, Spain
Crude, Jameel Art Center, Dubai, UAE
Rashid Karami International Fair: Cycles of Collapsing Progress, Tripoli, Lebanon
21st Biennale of Sydney: Superposition, Sydney, Australia
Fast Forward Festival Five, Onassis Cultural Centre, Athens, Greece
Manifesta 12: The Planetary Garden, Palermo, Italy
Truth Is Black, Write Over It With A Mirage's Light, Darat al Funun, Amman, Jordan
2017 *15th Istanbul Biennial: Good Neighbour*, Istanbul, Turkey
4.543 Billion, The Matter of Matter, CAPC | musée d'art contemporain de Bordeaux, France
The Restless Earth, Trussardi Foundation at the Triennale di Milano, Milan, Italy
Waiting: Between Power and Possibility, Kunsthalle Hamburg, Germany
The Upset Bucket, Whitechapel Gallery, London, UK
2016 *32nd São Paulo Biennial: Incerteza Viva*, São Paulo, Brazil
... und eine Welt noch, Kunsthaus Hamburg, Germany
Wunderlust, High Line Art, New York, NY, USA
Marrakech Biennale 6: Not New Now, Marrakech, Morocco
2015 *New Skin*, Aïshti Foundation, Beirut, Lebanon
Sharjah Biennial 12: The Past, The Present, The Possible, Sharjah, UAE
Heartland, Beirut Exhibition Center, Lebanon
Presque Rien, Marian Goodman Gallery, Paris, France
2014 *This is the Time. This is the Record of the Time*, Stedelijk Museum Bureau Amsterdam, Netherlands
Un Nouveau Festival, Centre Pompidou, Paris, France
2013 *The Abraaj Group Art Prize 2013: Extra / Ordinary*, Dubai, UAE
Durub Al Tawaya, Abu Dhabi, UAE
2012 *Future Generation Art Prize*, Pinchuk Art Center, Kiev, Ukraine
2nd New Museum Triennial: The Ungovernables, New York, NY, USA
2011 *Sharjah Biennial 10: Plot for a Biennial*, Sharjah, UAE
2010 *Noise*, Sfeir-Semler Gallery, Beirut, Lebanon
2008 *Art Now in Lebanon*, Darat Al Funun, Amman, Jordan
2006 *Moving Homes*, Sfeir-Semler Gallery, Beirut, Lebanon

Selected Public Collections
MoMA | Metropolitan Museum of Art, New York, NY, USA
Ministry of Culture, Saudi Arabia

This book is published on the occasion of the Parasol unit foundation for contemporary art exhibition

Uncombed, Unforeseen, Unconstrained
23 April – 27 November 2022
Conservatorio di Musica Benedetto Marcello.
A Collateral Event of the 59th International Art Exhibition | La Biennale di Venezia

Edited by
Ziba Ardalan, Parasol unit foundation for contemporary art, London

Texts by
Ziba Ardalan, Julien Bismuth, Tom Morton

Publishing Editor
Ilaria Bombelli, Mousse

Editorial Coordination
Agnese Cantelmi, Mousse
Sophie Moiroux, Parasol unit

Copy Editor
Helen Wire

Graphic Design
Mousse

Published and Distributed by
Mousse Publishing –
Contrappunto s.r.l.,
via Pier Candido Decembrio 28, 20137,
Milan–Italy

First edition 2022

Printed in Italy by
Grafiche Veneziane, Venice

ISBN
978-88-6749-545-0

€ 35 / $ 40 / £ 30

Available through
Mousse Publishing, Milan
moussemagazine.it
DAP | Distributed Art Publishers, New York
artbook.com
Les presses du réel, Dijon
lespressesdureel.com
Antenne Books, London
antennebooks.com
Idea Books, Amsterdam
ideabooks.nl

Parasol unit
foundation for contemporary art

Cover Image
Julian Charrière, *And Beneath It All Flows Liquid Fire*, 2019. (video still)

Image Credits
Unless otherwise stated, all images are reproduced courtesy of the individual artists and respectively of: Almine Rech Gallery, pp. 52–55, 56; Annet Gelink Gallery, Amsterdam, pp. 76–79; Dittrich & Schlechtriem, Berlin, front cover, p. 67; Esther Schipper, Berlin, pp. 76–79; Hamburger Kunsthalle, © Hamburger Kunsthalle|bpk, p.8; Hauser & Wirth, pp. 82–83, 84, 85 [x3]; Matthew Marks Gallery, pp. 112–117; Metropolitan Museum of Art, New York, H.O. Havemeyer Collection, Bequest of Mrs H.O. Havemeyer, 1929, p. 10; Micheline Szwajcer, Antwerp, pp. 76–79; Ministry of Culture, Saudi Arabia, pp. 120–123; Musea Brugge, pp. 76–79; Pedro Cera, Lisbon, pp. 76–79; Perrotin, pp. 82–83, 86, 87; Galerie Peter Kilchmann, Zurich, pp. 98–101; Galerie Rüdiger Schöttle, Munich, pp. 76–79; Sean Kelly, New York, front cover, p. 67, pp. 76–79; Sfeir-Semler Gallery, Beirut|Hamburg, pp. 120–123; Sies + Höke, Düsseldorf, front cover, p. 67; Galerie Tschudi, Zuoz, front cover, p. 67; V.G. Bild-Kunst, p. 67; White Cube, London, pp. 44–49; and others who chose to remain anonymous.

Photography
Francesco Allegretto, pp. 44–49, 52–55, 60–63, 68–73, 77–78, 82–87, 90–95, 98–101, 104–109, 112–117, 120–123; Elke Walford, p.8; Jens Ziehe, p. 67.

Acknowledgements
The *Uncombed, Unforeseen, Unconstrained* exhibition has been generously supported by: Pro Helvetia, Bareva Foundation, G+B Schwyzer Foundation, Almine Rech, Esther Schipper, Galerie Peter Kilchmann, Hauser & Wirth, Perrotin, Sean Kelly Gallery, White Cube, Akris, Atelier d'architectes Charrière-Partenaires, Central Street Foundation, Key Capital, Trinity Street Asset Management, Venice Art Factory, Conservatorio di Musica Benedetto Marcello, Richard and Claire Bruce, Laura Colnaghi Calissoni, Christian and Kristine de Juniac, Conor and Mary Killeen, Bernard and Genevieve Mensah, Lukas and Dorothea Mühlemann, Benjamin Nieto, Iman and Jacques de Saussure, Marwan and Tania Shakarchi, Claudia and Christian Norgren Steinfels, Berna and Tolga Tuğlular, Ruth Whaley, Yvonne and Pierre Winkler. Further support was provided by private individuals and organisations from around the world.

Parasol unit
foundation for contemporary art
32 Fitzroy Square, London W1T 6EX
www.parasol-unit.org
T +44 (0)207 380 4537
E info@parasol-unit.org

swiss arts council
prohelvetia
BAREVA FOUNDATION
GEORG UND BERTHA SCHWYZER-WINIKER STIFTUNG